"A man's man is a godly man, and a godly man reflects the heart of his Father in who he is and what he does. With the conviction of a man who knows the Word of God, the courage of a leader, and the compassion of a shepherd, Stu addresses the core issues of how to become a man after God's own heart in ways that ordinary guys like you and me can understand and apply. You will be nourished by its sound Biblical teaching, refreshed by its clarity, and encouraged by its practicality."

GARY J. OLIVER, PH.D. PSYCHOLOGIST, SEMINARY PROFESSOR,
AND AUTHOR OF *REAL MEN HAVE FEELINGS TOO* AND
HOW TO GET IT RIGHT AFTER YOU'VE GOTTEN IT WRONG
LITTLETON, COLORADO

"Stu Weber has done it again, in providing a vital, urgent message to men and couples who desire an impacting, fruitful, and joyful life following the Lord. In *Four Pillars of a Man's Heart,* Stu uses riveting life stories, underpinned with God's Word to illuminate critical aspects of living the successful Christian life. I highly recommend this book to men and couples who want to make their lives count for Christ."

PHIL DOWNER
CHRISTIAN BUSINESS MEN'S COMMITTEE OF USA
CHATTANOOGA, TENNESSEE

"Stu Weber speaks a man's language. This book, like the best-selling *Tender Warrior* before it, will help a man look up from the fog of everyday circumstances and catch a glimpse of the sun shining on distant mountain peaks. And then he inspires us and energizes us to stay on the trail and reach for God's very best. Lots of books talk about what a man should *do.* This book shows us what a man can *be.*"

GARY SMALLEY
PRESIDENT, TODAY'S FAMILY
BRANSON, MISSOURI

"Want a breathtaking, eye-popping tour of real manhood? There's no better tour guide anywhere than Stu Weber. Insightful, inspirational, practical, and passionate. *Four Pillars of a Man's Heart* offers you the masculine ride of your life!"

ROBERT LEWIS

PASTOR, FELLOWSHIP BIBLE CHURCH

LITTLE ROCK, ARKANSAS

"Stu tells us that you never really love someone until you sacrifice for that person. That's one truth I'm committed to driving deep into my heart. If you're looking for a blueprint for building leadership and love in your home, then read *Four Pillars of a Man's Heart.*"

RON MEHL

AUTHOR, *MEETING GOD AT A DEAD END*

PASTOR, BEAVERTON FOURSQUARE CHURCH

BEAVERTON, OREGON

"Stu Weber has a knack for getting to the nub of what we men need to become manly without becoming 'manish.' The former is the Creator's target—the latter ultimately everything but true manhood. "

JACK HAYFORD

PASTOR, THE CHURCH ON THE WAY

VAN NUYS, CALIFORNIA

Stu Weber

KING | WARRIOR | MENTOR | FRIEND

Four Pillars

of a Man's Heart

BRINGING STRENGTH INTO BALANCE

MULTNOMAH

SISTERS, OREGON

FOUR PILLARS OF A MAN'S HEART
published by Multnomah Books
a part of the Questar publishing family

© 1997 by Stu Weber

International Standard Book Number: 1-57673-102-2

Cover design by David Carlson

Printed in the United States of America

Most Scripture quotations are from:
New American Standard Bible (NASB) © 1960, 1977 by the Lockman Foundation

Also quoted:
The Holy Bible, New International Version (NIV) © 1973, 1984 by International Bible
Society, used by permission of Zondervan Publishing House

Scripture quotations marked (NLT) are taken from the Holy Bible, New Living
Translation, copyright © 1996. Used by permission of Tyndale House Publishers,
Inc., Wheaton, Illinois 60189. All rights reserved.

The New English Bible (NEB) © 1970 by Oxford University Press
and Cambridge University Press

Library of Congress Cataloging-in-Publication Data
Weber, Stu.
    The four pillars of a man's heart: bringing strength into balance
by Stu Weber.
        p. cm.
    Includes bibliographical references.
    ISBN 1-57673-102-2 (alk. paper)
    1. Men--Religious life. 2. Men (Christian theology) I. Title.
BV4528.2.W42 1997
248.8'42--dc21   97-7168
                                                                CIP

97 98 99 00 01 02 03 04 — 10 9 8 7 6 5 4 3 2

To all those good men
determined to become
the Tender Warriors
God intended them to be
when He made them men

ACKNOWLEDGMENTS

No man is an island. And no ministry is a solo. I am fortunate to be surrounded by some of the most competent people in the world, both in my family and my church. Like climbers roped together, we are constantly adjusting to one another—providing a little slack when needed, carrying additional weight when necessary.

I'm particularly grateful to my wife, Linda, and to the ministry and support staffs at Good Shepherd Community Church. Kathy Norquist, Theda Hlavka, and Joan Petersen have been especially helpful.

And the same goes for the great team at Questar. But Larry Libby, you excel them all.

AUTHOR'S NOTE

Rick Taylor and I have been brothers for a long time.

More than twenty-five years ago we married sisters. My Linda and his Judy are the wives of our youth, and the mothers of our children—three sons in my case, three sons and a daughter in his. But our commitment to each other as brothers goes far beyond the fact that we are "in-laws." We don't even like that term. But we do like each other. A lot. And over the years we have consulted each other on everything from parenting to duck hunting to ministry.

Rick and I have both served as pastors for most of our adult lives: I've pastored in Oregon; Rick has served in the Midwest and, most recently, in Oregon. He is the senior pastor of Grace Community Fellowship in Eugene, Oregon. No book is the product of a single individual. This one less so than many. Rick has been with me every step of the way on this project. We work well together. I tend to bring the passion and the big picture. Rick is the more analytical thinker, and more practically minded. Not to mention more patient. (And gracious.) He has been my collaborator on the thinking, outlining, writing, and editing. This book would not have been done without Rick. He is one of those treasures that every man needs—a brother...and a friend for life.

Rick graduated from the University of Texas (at Arlington), finished his graduate training in counseling at Emporia State University in Kansas, and received his Th.M. and Doctor of Ministry degrees from Dallas Seminary. He's enjoyed many years of kingdom-impacting, people-growing ministry.

Thanks, Rick.

CONTENTS

PROLOGUE

I'm one of those fortunate souls who gets to live in country he loves. Number me among those Oregonians who can't stop bragging about their state. To be sure, the climate isn't always fun. *Neither* climate—the meteorological nor the political one. Yes, there is the rain in the western valleys—more than even the moss-backed natives can bear some years. And yes, there are the predictable liberal politics—gray and hopeless as the leaden skies in December.

But the country. Oh, the country!

I could show you some places. Mountains that stretch to and beyond the blue sky. Rivers that run clear and free. Wildlife that still spooks at the sight of a human. And canyons that stop you in your tracks and force you to take a breath. You come up over a rise and look down into a perfect little valley—grass blowing, aspens whispering, and a stream winding through the meadow, catching the sun.

You find yourself saying to your own soul, *Wouldn't this be the spot! The perfect spot to live. To build a cabin...and a family...and a life.*

Sometimes, off the back roads of Oregon, I find hidden corners where others before me said the very same thing. And then they rolled up their sleeves and did it. Oregon is a state where pioneers followed their dreams; they visualized their paradise, cleared their land, raised their homes and barns, and planted their families.

The Oregon Trail drew so many dreams and dreamers a century and more ago. Homesteaders. Farmers and shopkeepers, ranchers and missionaries, husbands and wives and little ones, all hungering for a fresh run at life. People came in wagon trains by the hundreds to find their piece of heaven and put hammer, saw, plow, and ax into a home that had danced across their dreams along those long, sometimes merciless miles of the trail.

Then, strangely, so many of them just disappeared. Up and vanished, seemingly into the air.

So many plans. So many tears. So much energy and sweat and work. So much sacrifice and heartbreak. All gone. And people zoom by today on nearby highways as though these pioneer dreamers had never existed. The West is dotted with such abandoned homesteads. Small civilizations...come and gone.

Often, when I'm in need of some fresh perspective, I find myself driving toward the mountains. My way winds over the Cascade range and into the valleys of Central and Eastern Oregon. There, in the vast spaces of seemingly unlimited topography, I see them. Homesteads—dreams with boards on them. A cabin with the roof caved in, but her log walls still standing. A barn, long since abandoned. Tattered, but still reaching toward the heavens, refusing to collapse—in defiance of time and the elements.

But the people are no more.

You can no longer hear voices on the front porch or out in the little orchard. Nature has taken over again. A few of the old fruit trees, survivors of a bygone Eden, still drop their now wild apples on the ground. But no one picks them up. No one tastes them. No one is here anymore.

A small civilization has come...and gone. Only the thoughtful musing of the wind in the trees behind the once proud house still speaks. It says, *Something significant happened here. Something began. A family grew here. A small civilization grew on the unplowed ground among the virgin pines.* But the wind must add sadly, in a whisper, *And something significant has fallen.*

I strain to hear the voices of children in the wind. I try to imagine the man who broke the soil, cleared the rocks, and felled the trees for the walls of his new house. I try to picture the woman who turned those raw walls into a home. And I find myself wondering. *What were they like? What kind of man was he? What kind of woman was she? Where did they come from? What were their hopes? And where did they go? What happened to them? How did they end their life here? And what happened to the children? Did they grow up to maturity? Did they survive? Where did they go? What kind of people did they become? Why does this magnificent place seem a little like a burial ground? Where have the people gone?*

More than once I've turned to my wife, Linda, and said, "Big dreams.

Someone dreamed big dreams here, once. Life dreams. But they're gone now. We're actually staring at what's left of someone's dreams."

For a moment, something inside us makes us feel like intruders. Eerily, the words of Scripture come home once more:

As for man, his days are like grass;
As a flower of the field, so he flourishes.
When the wind has passed over it, it is no more;
And its place acknowledges it no longer.
(Psalm 103:15–16)

Then Lindy and I ponder our own lives. Will we be any different? What kind of a man am I? What kind of a woman is she? What kind of family are we growing? Will someone look over the remnants of our small civilization one day? What will they see? What kind of heritage will we have left? What difference will it make that we have lived?

I remember similar feelings years ago as Linda and I climbed across the last stone obstacles and looked out over the black basalt ruins of Korazin on the gentle slopes just above the northern shore of the Lake of Galilee. Once, a proud little community flowered here. Yet advanced and enlightened as it might have been, it too fell under the conquering heel of time. And now the once stately pillars lie broken in the dust and the scorching Middle Eastern sun. Where people had mingled and jostled in the marketplace, now an occasional scorpion wanders. Weeds lean in the wind. Disorder rules.

And I am reminded again that the only thing that lasts—that will, in fact, populate eternity—is people. Wooden walls may crumble and stone pillars may fall, but people are forever. And if life is to mean anything, building people must be what it is all about.

As someone has said, we can't do much about our ancestors but we can our descendants. We've got to build a family that outlives us. We've got to build a home that outlasts us. We've got to build a heritage that stands strong and firm in the winds of time. We've got to build a civilization that doesn't fall apart with the passing years. We've got to build a civilization on pillars that will not lean or crumble.

What kind of man builds a civilization, a small civilization, that outlasts him? What kind of man has shoulders broad enough to build upon? A four-pillared man:

—A man of vision and character...*a King.*
—A man of strength and power...*a Warrior.*
—A man of faith and wisdom...*a Mentor.*
—A man of heart and love...*a Friend.*

It is upon these pillars, the four pillars of manhood, that the small civilization we call "home" will either stand or fall. You can't support a roof, keep out the elements, and shield against things that go bump in the night with one or two pillars. Three pillars might hold up a roof for a while—but the structure is out of balance and always in danger of collapse. It takes four pillars to hold up a building, a temple, or a home.

And it takes four pillars to make a man. A man who will bear the weight, stand against the elements, and hold one small civilization intact in a world that would like nothing better than to tear it down.

What kind of a man am I? What can of a man are you? How can we become what we so deeply need to be?

Let's walk the path together, and see what we might find.

If there is a man who fears the Lord,
he shall be shown the path he should choose.
PSALM 25:12, NEB

CROSSROADS

I had a decision to make. And I had to make it that day.

Standing in front of Colonel "Iron Mike" Healy, the commanding officer of the 5th Special Forces Group (Airborne), my mind was racing even faster than my pounding heart. I'd been in Vietnam for nearly a year. I'd done my job. And God was doing His; He had moved my heart.

But the colonel, it seems, had other plans. And I have to admit, at that particular moment in time, it might have been a stretch for me to say who was the more powerful figure in my life—God, or the group commander.

In fact, some said the "old man" *was* God. He was certainly a striking figure. When he entered the room, men stood to attention for more reasons than simple protocol. Images of Caesar came to mind.

"Iron Mike" ran 5th Group. Every Green Beret in Vietnam answered to him. Even the commander of all U.S. forces in Vietnam, General Crieghton Abrams (no small man in his own right, and not one inclined to think highly of unconventional forces such as SF), had to admit that Healy was something else. In fact, he'd brought the colonel in specifically to clean up 5th Group. The previous group commander, a fine man in many respects, had ended up being court-martialed in the midst of an unfortunate scandal that made major headlines all around the globe.

Colonel Healy had a job to do and he was all business. I'd seen him, with fire in his eyes, relieve a lieutenant colonel and ruin a twenty-plus year military career with a single wave of his hand.

Come to think of it, at times we all thought he must have been God. Or at least a very stern archangel.

And now I stood braced in front of him.

The old saying goes, "A man's gotta do what a man's gotta do." I don't know where that saying originated, but it provokes a pretty basic question we should all probably ask ourselves: *What's a man gotta do?*

Really only one thing.

A man's got to decide who he's going to follow. A man's got to decide who he's going to listen to, who or what will be the authority in his life. A man must determine where he's going to get his orders. That's the question that stared me in the face that afternoon.

W H A T   R E A L L Y   M A T T E R S ?

When I had arrived in Vietnam nearly a year earlier, I was headed for a career in the United States Army. My father and grandfather, neither of them career military men, had answered the call to be citizen soldiers in their day. I had been taught at home to accept my responsibilities to my country—but found myself going a step further. Somewhat to my surprise I discovered I really loved the military and greatly appreciated its mission for our nation. I relished the healthy competition. I welcomed the affirmation for a job well done. And I believed a manly man ought to have a strong sense of "duty, honor, country."

Yes, I loved the military. More than that, it had taken hold of me. I had decided to stay in, make a go of it. Airborne. Ranger. Green Beret. The whole nine yards.

But all that changed midtour in Vietnam when God began to do surgery on my heart. Months before that moment in front of the CO's desk, I was crunched in a muddy little trench in the Central Highlands at Dak Pek, a Special Forces A Camp. That's where the new direction first began to take shape. Facing imminent combat and possible death, I'd begun asking myself some rather large, life-shaping questions. *What difference would it make if I died that day? For that matter, what difference would it make if I lived? What really matters in this thing called "life"?*[1]

Those frightening, soul-searching moments culminated in a decision to give my life to the two things on earth that really mattered to my Lord— my family and His family. My bride and kids, and His bride and kids— the local church. After all the smoke cleared, those were the only things that really counted. For eternity. When the long winds rustle the grass over my grave, only what I'd done for Christ and His kingdom would last.

I had decided to follow Jesus Christ without reservation. He would call the signals for the rest of my life. I determined then and there to resign my Regular Army commission and head for seminary and the ministry. In my mind, it was a done deal.

Or so I'd thought.

But that day, standing at attention in the "old man's" office, I realized that simply making a decision in your head and actually severing old ties and *moving* in that new direction are two different matters. I thought I had already passed the fork in the road, but now I knew I was only just approaching it.

TWO ROADS

The two roads swirled through my mind. *Two* roads? Hadn't I already gone beyond that? Hadn't I decided to leave the military and enter the ministry? I thought I'd heard God's heart. I thought I'd determined in my soul to follow His heart and values, not my own.

But standing in front of my CO, there it was again. Full in my face. A crossroads. Like a uniformed sorcerer, the colonel was spinning a future before my very eyes—a most appealing future. It was a little dazzling. He had my head spinning. Now I had to decide if I was really committed to that new direction. Had I meant what I told the Lord at Dak Pek, or was it just one more "fox hole conversion"? Would God truly call the shots in my life?

Choices. Decisions. Crossroads. You face them, too. Every man does.

Life is full of them. Every day and every hour is full of them. Options, alternatives, paths, and decisions. Lots of branching trails, each one encountering crossroads. But the Big One, the biggest fork in the road you'll ever come to, has a sign over it that reads: Who will be my authority? Whom will I choose to follow?

Let's think about that major intersection for a few moments.

TURNING THE CORNER

Some crossroads are large and obvious. You can see them a mile away. Others are subtle and seem small. Sometimes you don't recognize them when they're staring you in the face. But years later when you look back you realize—that "one little choice" on that single day determined the course of the rest of your life.

Sometimes it's a slow, well-thought-out, careful decision-making process over the course of months. Sometimes it happens in a flash, like a single lethal moment in the heat of passion in the back seat of a car. Sometimes it's the same choice made over and over and over again. But, boiled down—it's a decision...a commitment to a direction...a parting of the roads. And common to every crossroads, big or small, is that one over-arching question: Who will *truly* be the authority of my life? Me? Or God?

That choice, at every fork in the road, determines the road ahead for a long time. Possibly forever.

On that crossroads day in Vietnam, after months of processing in my soul, I stood in front of Iron Mike's enormous desk. For most of a year I had been his intelligence operations officer. Up well before dawn, I had briefed him and his senior staff every morning on enemy operations near our Special Forces A Camps across the country. It had been a significant and stretching year. Sometimes exhilarating, sometimes excruciatingly painful. I had grown a lot. It's a fine thing to know you've done your job, and that it's made a difference. All things considered, it had been a solid tour of duty for me.

And—there's no denying it—the vision he was conjuring before my eyes was incredibly alluring. My heart pounded in my chest; I could feel the throb of it in my temples. Still, I was already pointed in another direction. I was planning on something called "seminary" where, for all I knew, they made monks out of guys! A couple of weeks previously I had resigned my commission as a career officer in the Regular Army and made application to graduate school in the States. My feet were almost touching that new road. But there was Iron Mike, my all-powerful com-manding officer, trying with all of his considerable persuasive abilities to turn me back. To set before me that other road I thought I'd already shunned.

Others could do ministry, he told me. But I had the training, the ability, and the temperament to make significant strides in the military. The army was looking for more than a few good men. And from where he sat, the more obvious, more profitable, more *honorable* road for Captain Stu Weber would be to remain in my country's service.

I must have groaned inside. This was tough. But the colonel wasn't finished yet. (And in the army, you can't look at your watch and say, "Sorry, I've gotta run." You stay where you are until you are *dismissed.*) He told me he had received his orders for his first star. He was about to be promoted to brigadier general. He would be in a strong position to influence my next assignment, even my entire career. The details he outlined were staggering to a young officer. He told me, among other things, that if I would retain my commission and stay in the service, he would personally see to it that my next assignment would be *my choice*—any job, any location in the world that a captain could hold (including embassy duty or graduate school), and that I would have a career path that would delight any young officer.

What would my decision be? Which voice would command my heart? The colonel's? Or the Creator's?

About that time I heard my own voice speaking. Ever been in a room and heard someone speaking, and then realized it was your own voice? It sometimes happens to me in "tight" situations. And this one was tight. As though from across the room, I heard myself saying these words, "Sir, I cannot stay. I have orders from Higher Up. And though it may seem a bit corny—even imaginary—to you, it is a very real headquarters. It is, in reality, the throne room of the universe. I believe the King Himself has intentions for me. I believe He has actually guided me. I have clear direction in my soul. I have developed a sense of conviction from God. I must go this way. It's a matter of principle, faith, trust, and obedience. Sir, I *must* take this road."

It's the same today, these many years later. I must follow my Lord. No matter what. I must renew my allegiance every morning. It is His voice I must listen to, not the voices of those around me, however strident, however persuasive. It is His Word that must govern my life, not the words of others. God Himself has written a Book (think of it!) that must be the authority in my life. And in yours.

That day in the colonel's office, I finally turned the corner.

I knew Who I was going to follow.

NO TURNING BACK

As I look back over my life, I have to conclude that was the day I became a man. Turning twenty-one hadn't done it. A college degree hadn't done it. Even marriage hadn't made me a man. Nor having a son. Nor getting jump wings. Nor winning the Ranger tab. Nor wearing the Green Beret. But when I decided to follow Christ without reservation, I became a man.

I believe it's impossible to be a man—fully masculine—apart from bowing to Jesus Christ as the Lord of your life and submitting to His Word as the ultimate life authority. A man's man is a godly man. A man's gotta do what a man's gotta do. And a man's got to make some decisions. Especially that one.

Please hear me loud and clear on this, friend: As you read this book, you're going to have to make some decisions. We're going to talk about what it takes to be a real man. Some of what it takes is highly unpopular in our contemporary culture. But who are you going to listen to? The sages of political correctness, or the pages of biblical revelation? You must decide who you're going to listen to. If you don't, you won't follow Him. You'll waver. A double-minded man is unstable in all his ways. So what will it be? God, or the voices of a clamoring culture? Scripture, or the shouts of an eroding society?

I've always appreciated the words of a young man who had made up his mind to track with God's Word—no matter what would happen in his life. While history never records this man's name or tells us anything about the details of his life, no one reading his words could ever doubt his heart. Or his commitment. He, too, had turned the corner. Though life was far from easy, though his days were dogged by pain, loneliness, and blunt opposition, he had settled the authority question. Listen to these few notes from his personal journal:

> Though rulers sit together and slander me, your servant will meditate on your decrees. Your statutes are my delight; they are my counselors.... Direct me in the path of your commands, for there I find delight. Turn my heart toward your statutes and not toward selfish gain. Turn my eyes away from worthless things; preserve my life according to your word.... May those who fear

you rejoice when they see me, for I have put my hope in your word.... Help me, for men persecute me without cause. They almost wiped me from the earth, but I have not forsaken your precepts.... Trouble and distress have come upon me, but your commands are my delight.... I rise before dawn and cry for help; I have put my hope in your word.... Your decrees are the theme of my song wherever I lodge. In the night I remember your name, O LORD, and I will keep your law. This has been my practice: I obey your precepts. (Psalm 119:23-24, 35-37, 74, 86-87, 143, 147, 54-56, NIV)

Like that anonymous psalmist, I had committed myself to a direction that day, and there was no going back. It was a singular choice...on a single day...that determined the course of the rest of my life, and marked my eternal destiny. It also changed the lives of all those near and dear to me.

My wife's life changed that day. Her path was as irrevocably altered as my own.

The lives of my sons changed that day; one born, two yet unborn.

Even the lives of my friends changed, in the sense that it affected who would eventually become my closest friends.

Apart from that one choice, I would never have met many of the friends who mean so much in my life today. Without that choice I would never have preached a sermon. Nor lived in Oregon. Nor pastored a church. Nor stood in front of a massive stadium packed with Promise Keepers. It was a crossroads. And it was based upon my answer to that one, inescapable question—Whom will I choose to follow?

On a poetic scale, Robert Frost captured something of that crossroads moment that day in the colonel's office (and a thousand times ten thousand like it in your life and mine).

Two roads diverged in a yellow wood,
And sorry I could not travel both
And be one traveler, I stood
And looked down one as far as I could
To where it bent in the undergrowth;

Then took the other, as just as fair,
And having perhaps the better claim,
Because it was grassy and wanted wear;
Though as for that the passing there
Had worn them really about the same,
And both that morning equally lay
In leaves no step had trodden black.
Oh, I kept the first for another day,
Yet knowing how way leads on to way,
I doubted I should ever come back.
I shall be telling this with a sigh
Somewhere ages and ages hence;
Two roads diverged in a wood, and I—
I took the one less traveled by,
And that has made all the difference.[2]

William Bennett, former U.S. secretary of education, summarized that poem in a single statement when he said, "Courage does not follow rutted pathways."[3] Maybe that's why the road toward God's intentions is a narrow way, and there are few who find it. How about you? How will you decide?

THE VERY FIRST CROSSROADS

You and I come from a long line of men who made the wrong choice. That's why the pillars of manhood have fallen and so many homes and lives lie in ruin in these closing days of the millennium.

As a matter of fact, the ghost of one of your ancestors still haunts you right now. Look around you. See if you can catch the dark tones of his shadow. As you turn the pages of this book, a single choice of your forefather, Adam, casts a shadow over your future. One "little" choice on "just an average day at the office" can affect you and your family for generations. In Adam's case, it's been thousands of years of impact so far.

Adam stood at a crossroads one day. Adam, the only one of whom it could be accurately stated, "You're the man!" He was the first man, the original, straight from the hand of God. Pure masculinity, unadulterated and untainted. Your forefather and mine. Our model and prototype. Everything God wanted a man to be.

They don't come any better than Adam did when he arrived on the scene. A Real Man walked the fresh pathways of a new planet. But like all of his future children, Adam had a decision to make.

WHEN THE FIRST PILLARS FELL

As he stood there that day, that seemingly "ordinary" day in the garden, he held a piece of fruit in his hand. His wife had indicated it was a good thing. She should know, she'd already tasted it. And the evil one who would one day wear the title of "prince and power of the air" had done everything he could to make it appealing. No piece of fruit had ever appeared so luscious and desirable.

On the one hand, taking a bite made such sense to Adam. The voices in his ear were strong. On the other hand, he'd been told explicitly that he shouldn't touch it. By no less an authority than God Himself.

Adam stood at a crossroads. For the first time in his life, he was experiencing the tug of competing voices. Was he going to do what others around wanted him to do? Take the common route, the broad way? Or was he going to listen to the instructions of the Creator? Would he show some courage and do the right thing, choosing to take God at His Word? Would he listen to the perfect Father and Friend? Or would he take the road that others would choose for him, a road that would prove to be incredibly well traveled over the millennia? Would Adam calibrate the compass of his masculinity according to God's intentions or to his own appetites?

Well, you know the choice he made. He decided to go his own way. And that single choice, on that one day in history, affected every move he would make and every thought he would think for the remaining nine hundred or so years of his life. It impacted every single member of his human family. His wife. His sons. His daughters. Their mates. Their children. Their children's children...for thousands of generations.

Eden had been such a good place. Heaven on earth, so to speak. Just a small civilization nestled in one corner of a wide new world. Yet when it collapsed, the shock waves through space and time have sent billions reeling. When the original pillars of manhood fell in Eden, it started a falling dominoes chain reaction that has crushed life and hope in untold numbers of small civilizations through earth's sad history. Adam's simple, single, silly choice blew it 'til kingdom come.

What became of that beautiful Garden? Some say its location is now part of the sun-scorched, sandy wastes of the Iraqi desert. What a picture. Because of Adam's choice, the fossil remains of Eden would one day become the crude oil fueling Saddam Hussein's war machine.

Two of those people that Adam's choice impacted so profoundly are thee and me. Why has it effected us with such life-wrenching power? For one simple reason: Adam is our father, the head of the human family. That's the way it is in the Bible. God's economy is such that when the head of the family veers off course, the whole family suffers. When the head of the family is on target, the whole family thrives. Whatever the head of the home thinks or decides, however he acts or behaves, affects everybody in the home. And everyone else nearby as well. We humans are *not* islands. The acts of one *do* bear upon those nearby—sometimes around the globe.

It was a single crossroads, on a single day, that stretched across thousands of years. Evidently Adam didn't see it coming. But he should have. God could not have made it more clear. They had talked very specifically about it. The God of the Universe had walked with him and talked with him in the Garden. He should have known better.

THE LONG SHADOW

Adam's long, chilling shadow looms large over every crossroads facing you and me. His shadow stretches across our families. And our country.

America is at a crossroads today.

America's been such a good place to live for a couple of hundred years now, especially compared to the alternatives on this planet. On balance, among the nations, she's been a pretty solid family home. But she's falling apart as you read these words. Blowing herself asunder from the insides out. And she's destroying herself today because her men, standing at a crossroads without a map in their hands and only a broken compass in their hearts, are choosing their own way. It's the broad way, the way that seems right to a man but leads to death. And when a man decides to veer off course, everyone in his family pays.

America is paying a price today.

Since the class of 1965 graduated we've been careening through the years like an intoxicated driver, further and further off course. I was born on the front edge of the baby boom. We boomers have done just that—exploded—blown apart a lot of conventions, political and otherwise, including marriage, family, and male-female roles, to name just a few. Neither we nor our nation have ever recovered from our teenage years in the sixties.

In my short lifetime America has developed serious heart disease. Why? Because men have chosen a course for themselves and walked away from God's intentions. Men, even Christian men, aren't doing "what a man's gotta do."

Men aren't following Christ. And there is hell to pay.

FROM THE HEARTLAND

What do you hear from the heartland?

I'm reminded of the George Strait number, "Sing a Song about the Heartland." George nostalgically calls to mind a fading heritage. He reminds us that there are still a few places where a good man does a good day's work. He recalls a community where simple people still wave to their neighbors when they drive by. And he's glad there are yet a few places where people still know wrong from right. I love the song. And the nostalgia. But I weep inside because it's reduced to "just nostalgia" in so much of our land.

I didn't come from the plains of the American Midwest, but I still grew up in "heartland" kind of country. Our small coal-mining town in the Pacific Northwest was made up of hardworking, well-muscled, broad-smiling immigrants who loved their families. There were some unusual family names, too—Golubic, Klobucar, Butorac, Osmonovich, Katalinich, Javornik, Hrnjak and more. Like Aimone, Cappeletti, Arragoni, and Giaudroni. And Smith and Jones, too.

Looking back, it seemed like a little taste of Eden. The houses were in rows. Moms were moms. Dads were dads. Dads went to work in the morning with lunch pails. Kids played marbles and loved recess. Families ate dinner together in the evenings. We rarely watched TV, and then only at neighbors' houses, because there were few televisions in town. Life was healthy. Kids were happy. By and large, homes were stable.

But something's gone wrong in the heartland. Listen to the "songs" coming out of America's heart today and you will most likely hear discordant strains. The heartland is hurting. And the tune isn't pretty.

Since the class of 1965 graduated, the Scholastic Aptitude Test (SAT) scores have plummeted over 100 points. In the last couple of years they've even had to change the way they scale the test—so that we're spared the humiliation of comparing this generation with the scores of 1965. (Doesn't that sound like today's America? Don't admit slippage, lower the standards! Then declare victory.)

Since the class of 1965 graduated, illegitimate births have quintupled—multiplied five times in this so-called sexually sophisticated, birth-controlled culture!

Since the class of 1965 graduated, the number of children on welfare has tripled. Teenage suicide has tripled. Juvenile violent crime has increased six-fold. Between 1984 and 1994 alone, teenage homicide (that's murder!) multiplied several times. In one two-week period this last spring, in our small suburban town alone (!), two twelve-year-olds committed suicide in separate and unrelated incidents. Or were they related?

Something's gone wrong in the heartland. How are we to explain this rapid erosion of standards? How do we rationalize the breakdown of families; neighborhoods on edge; streets no longer safe; the death wishes of our children? What has happened? How do we account for this disaster?

With all my heart, I believe we can trace this disaster to failure in high office.

F A I L U R E   I N   H I G H   O F F I C E

Yes, I am referring to the highest office in the land; and no, I do not mean the presidency of the United States. Nor the presidency of any international conglomerate. Nor chairman of the board. I believe the greatest position a man can hold is his office as head of the home. A man's greatest title is not "Dr. So and So" or "Professor" or "General" or "Mr. Vice

President" or "Reverend." The highest office in the land is not in the White House. It's in your house.

In God's economy, a man will never get any higher, never have any greater influence, never wield any greater power than he does as the head of his own home. To fail at home is to have failed everywhere. And that's where men are made. I believe America shudders and is wracked with pain today because men have failed to be men.

An exaggeration? Listen to *U.S. News & World Report* in an article entitled "Lives Without Father": "Last year the nation's juvenile justice system spent $20 billion to arrest and jail children, only to see 70% commit new crimes."[4]

Time magazine gets even more specific: "Studies of young criminals have found that more than 70% of all juveniles in state reform institutions come from fatherless homes."[5]

David Blankenhorn, a well known sociologist, writes:

The United States is becoming an increasingly fatherless society.... Tonight, about 40% of American children will go to sleep in homes in which their fathers do not live.... Never before have so many children been voluntarily abandoned by their fathers.... Never before have so many children grown up without knowing what it means to have a father.

Fatherlessness is the most harmful demographic trend of this generation...It is the engine driving our most urgent social problems, from crime to adolescent pregnancy to child sexual abuse, to domestic violence against women....

There is debate, even alarm, about specific social problems. Divorce. Out-of-wedlock child-bearing. Children growing up in poverty. Youth violence. Unsafe neighborhoods. Domestic violence. The weakening of parental authority. But in these discussions we seldom acknowledge the underlying phenomenon that binds together these otherwise disparate issues: the flight of males from their children's lives....

In some respects it has been all downhill for fathers since the Industrial Revolution.... [Since that time] Increasingly, men

[have] looked outside the home for the meaning of their maleness. Masculinity became less domesticated, defined less by effective paternity and more by individual ambition and achievement.[6]

I agree with Dr. Blankenhorn that the root cause of the great bulk of our societal problems is fatherlessness. Another word for it would be a lack of manhood, for the term "father" is the consummate masculine word. It is applied masculinity at its best. True fathering has very little to do with biology, but everything to do with responsibly caring for others. Whether a man has biological children or not, he is to be applying himself to fathering functions. But men in America today seem to be looking out more for themselves than others.

That, my friend, is sorry manhood…and unworthy of the name.

As a culture we've lost our manhood. And our men, as a whole, are lost and confused—shell-shocked in the gender wars of the last thirty years. We've been told we've had it wrong for thousands of years. We've been told the man is not to be a leader. We've been told there are really no differences between men and women. We've been told that patriarchy is an evil that must be overcome by thinking men and women.

We've been told a lie.

We've been reading the wrong books.

We've been listening to the wrong authority.

We've been taking our cues from the culture rather than from the Book. We've accepted our marching orders from the faculties of our universities and the editorial pages of our newspapers rather than our Commander in Chief, the Lord of Hosts.

The question remains, *as it will always remain,* one of ultimate authority. Who are you going to follow in your life? Who will command your allegiance? Christ…or culture? You really can't have it both ways.

On the first night when newly appointed General Joshua had his troops camped within sight of their first major obstacle, the walled city of Jericho, he must have spent a restless night in his tent. At dawn, I can imagine him out with his sentries, peering through the eerie half-light at that ominous, seemingly impenetrable city in the distance.

When he saw a stranger suddenly standing in front of him with a drawn sword in his hand, the general took a deep breath and challenged the man himself.

"Are you for us or for our enemies?"

"Neither," he replied, "but as commander of the army of the LORD I have now come." Then Joshua fell facedown to the ground in reverence, and asked him, "What message does my Lord have for his servant?"

The commander of the LORD's army replied, "Take off your sandals, for the place where you are standing is holy." And Joshua did so. (Joshua 5:13-15, NIV)

I remember a sermon by my friend Luis Palau, where he paraphrased that Supreme Commander, possibly the Son of God Himself, like this: "I didn't come to take sides, Joshua, *I came to take over.*"

It's time Christ's men started remembering just who is calling the shots. It's time we took off our shoes in the presence of this Leader, and bowed before His authority. Did we receive Him into our lives as "just one more guiding voice," or as *Lord?* Are we ready to follow Him, even when He leads us directly across the grain of our culture?

The truth is, until we have settled the *authority* question, we cannot settle any question.

Yes, men in America today are at a crossroads. You're probably at one yourself. We've experienced the tug of God in our hearts. We've begun to sense His direction for us. We're beginning to move back down the trail He intended for us as His men in the first place. We're changing our priorities. We're determined to follow the King. We're going to be godly men. We're going to keep our promises.

No, it won't be easy. It's a road less traveled in our culture. But then, courage does not follow rutted pathways.

*"Be strong...and show yourself a man....
Keep the charge of the LORD your God."*

DAVID
1 KINGS 2:2–3

*Be on the alert, stand firm in the faith,
act like men, be strong. Let all that you do
be done in love.*

PAUL
1 CORINTHIANS 16:13

PLAY THE MAN!

P lay the man!
　　When was the last time you heard something like that spoken as positive encouragement?
　　Play the man!

I came across those words a couple of years back, and they still ring in my ears. I hadn't heard them for who knows how long. But they struck a chord somewhere down inside. They called something to the surface that all of us as Christian men need to think about carefully.

Manhood. It has been out of vogue too long.

My wife and I were visiting our son in England, where he was pursuing graduate studies. Late one afternoon I found myself wandering along the cobblestones of Broad Street in Oxford. There, imbedded in countless dark stones forming the road's surface, were twenty-four lighter stones. They stood out not only for their color, but for their pattern as well. They formed a simple cross on this thoroughfare of the western world's most prestigious university city.

As the bustling traffic surged by—heedless of crosses and white stones—my mind, recalling another day, sought to push back the years to the scene memorialized by the white stone marker. Such simple stones. Such an enormous event. Such profound instruction. And such a glorious display of manhood—a model for us all.

LATIMER'S LAST STAND

It was a crisp October day in 1555, a day that dawned like a thousand October mornings before, but a day destined to stand out among the thousands. Two men, refusing to recant their personal faith in Jesus

Christ, would die a terrible death that morning. They would be burned at the stake.

What crossed their minds, that fine autumn day, as these two men walked out of the doors of dreary Bocardo Prison and into the sunlight of their last moments on earth? We can't know all their thoughts, yet we have more than stones in the pavement to mark their passing.

We have a few of their words as well.

We know that as they approached the stake, Hugh Latimer turned to Nicholas Ridley and said, "Be of good cheer, Ridley. Play the man! We shall this day light such a candle, by God's grace...as I trust shall never be put out."

Play the man!

Three words. One point. Sound advice. As needed today, and probably more so, than it was on that day in 1555. In that moment, it was needed to lift one man's soul in a moment of personal crisis as he faced the fires of the religiously correct. Today it's needed even more, to lift an entire gender's collective soul as we face the firestorms of the politically correct.

Recently I came across those three words again, and I realized for the first time that Latimer had not originated that phrase. It suddenly seemed clear to me that the man had been doing some serious reading. In preparation for his appointment at the stake, he had evidently been immersing his soul in the words of a few warriors who had gone before him.

A WARRIOR'S HERO

Somewhere along the line, Hugh Latimer had evidently come across the account of a second-century martyr named Polycarp. Dying at his own stake in a Roman stadium before a bloodthirsty capacity crowd, Polycarp had literally blazed the path ahead of Latimer and Ridley.

An ancient account of that early martyr includes this extraordinary passage:

> But as Polycarp entered into the stadium, a voice came to him from heaven; "Be strong, Polycarp, and play the man." And no

one saw the speaker, but those of our people who were present heard the voice.[1]

When Latimer, in that moment of supreme crisis, repeated those words, "Play the man," was he remembering the noble Polycarp? Was he remembering the courageous believer who had died with such dignity before a jeering crowd in a stadium? Was he calling to mind those words of encouragement, spoken from heaven itself, to sustain him and his friend in that hour of their greatest trial?

Seems likely, doesn't it?

How long has it been since you've heard those words, "play the man"? Probably awhile back. A long while back. And what would you think if you did hear them? What does the term *man* mean anyway?

W H A T   M A K E S   A   M A N ?

It's been a long time since a man was allowed to be comfortable with his masculinity, since a man has been sincerely encouraged to...well, be a man. Our culture has struggled with the meaning of manhood for decades now. Today that culture is in serious crisis. And I believe our culture of crises is born directly out of a crisis inside men's souls. We haven't known how to act for more than a quarter century now.

I mused on Latimer's words to Ridley as the afternoon Oxford traffic flowed by, and the words drew me close to the hearts of those two men. Words are like markers, aren't they? Like shining cobblestones on a busy thoroughfare, they mark a man's passage. We see something of his journey into manhood, and in seeing, we better our own pilgrimage. The world's traffic rushes by, just as it always has and will, but our course takes a fresh track. We see the path a man has chosen, his spirit calls to ours, and we chart a better course.

I expect that happened for Ridley that day. Stop and think about it. Just what was Latimer trying to say to Ridley? "Play the man!" Say what? How so? Did Ridley catch his message? I'll bet he did. This, after all, was the sixteenth century; masculinity was not yet politically incorrect. While I think Latimer was mostly seeking to help Ridley "buck up," so to speak, by quoting an earlier warrior and martyr who had walked that path bravely before them, I also believe he repeated a theme that spans the centuries. There is a life message entwined in those three little words.

What was the intended meaning? Was Latimer calling Ridley to demonstrate certain qualities? If so, which ones? Courage, possibly. Strength, surely. What else? Integrity...loyalty...bravery...faithfulness... sacrifice?

What are the qualities of manhood? What should we consider masculine features? When you hear the term *man*, what images should it conjure up in your mind? While both genders are certainly capable of demonstrating all the qualities noted just above, are there elements more characteristically identified with one gender or the other?

What are the pillars of masculinity? What are the facets of femininity? What is the strength and splendor of manhood? What is the beauty and glory of womanhood?

Searching for answers, my mind scrolled back through the centuries from Latimer and Polycarp to a kingdom hero of an even earlier age. David! The son of Jesse was a man's man. David's heart called to the men around him—and to us. Even David's dying words ring like steel on steel. They sound a lot like Latimer, on a crisp October morning, walking toward his destiny.

> As David's time to die drew near, he charged Solomon his son, saying, "I am going the way of all the earth. *Be strong, therefore, and show yourself a man. And keep the charge of the LORD your God, to walk in His ways, to keep His statutes, His commandments, His ordinances, and His testimonies, according to what is written in the law of Moses,* that you may succeed in all that you do and wherever you turn." (1 Kings 2:1-3, emphasis added)

Look at those highlighted words. They provide us some clues, don't they? More than clues, there are instructions, expectations, even demands! Be strong; show yourself a man; keep the charge; walk in His ways; keep His commands. David said to Solomon, in effect, "Play the man!" And just in case young Solomon had any doubts about what a man was to be or do, David gave him some solid definition.

Let's wrestle with that definition as we think through the pages of this chapter.

T R A I L H E A D

After pondering the dying counsel of King David, my mind continued to scroll back through biblical times, along His ways. I began to pick up speed. I ran back along the trails of Scripture, all the way back to the law of Moses. And when I hit the trailhead, the beginning of the Genesis trail where it all started, I stopped and filled my lungs with the fresh air.

I camped there beside the headwaters of masculinity in the first chapters of the Genesis trail. I lingered for a long time. You can pick up the scent there, the scent of Original Man. There are words there at the trailhead, carved in the sights and sounds of the creation account. Like the time-worn stones in an Oxford street, those words serve as markers. They are God's words, and they mark a path, a way. His way.

Those Genesis markers stood up well for centuries, even millennia. But as the traffic in recent years has increased, we've lost sight of them in the blur. The high-speed traffic of our culture roars past them as though they do not exist. Consequently, by ignoring those ancient signposts, we've taken a number of serious wrong turns along the road. Some silly little rabbit trails, yes, but also some long, dark, tunneling detours—roads that can only end at a life-threatening, culture-destroying abyss.

These roads are man-killers. And Satan knows it.

D E F A C I N G   T H E   I M A G E

Satan loves dark tunnels. And he knows that *this* one, this gender-destroying detour from God's intentions, has the potential to do more damage than we can begin to dream. Our ancient adversary knows very well what most us have forgotten: Gender is one of the most basic and far-reaching expressions of the image of God. And the enemy loves nothing better than to distort the image of the God he hates.

As I write these words, I see the image of a hate-deranged child slashing a picture of his father to ribbons, then burning those fragments, one by one. But Satan is no child. The Book of Revelation calls him "the great dragon...that ancient serpent called the devil, or Satan, who leads the whole world astray." When he acts, it is according to an established pattern, old as Eden, old as the earth itself:

Distort the Word of God. Mar the image of God. And never stop attacking man, the creation of God formed in His very image.

God created mankind "in His image...male and female He created them." The image and glory of God on this planet is tied to our human masculinity and femininity. *Anything* Satan can do to bend, blur, or deface that image is a big-time coup for him. So he is at it with a vengeance today, in your lifetime and mine.

Could you pause with me a moment on this page? My heart's desire at this juncture is to convey the gravity of this matter to you. These gender battles in the cultural wars are not "faddish." They are not a "minor distraction" or a "cultural hiccup" to be lightly regarded or blandly accommodated. Hear me, please, when I say that these issues represent a rock-bottom, down-in-the-trenches, gut-tearing attack on our society's vital organs.

To tinker with the image of God, represented in male and female, is to slap God in the face. This is something more than politics, economics, social studies, or some bleeding-heart, feel-good crusade for "equality." This is a culture-killing disease. It also represents an ancient, long-simmering attack on the very person of God and His loving intentions for His children.

As you might expect, much of the Enemy's strategic missile force is directly targeted on our nation's capitol.

THE ATTACK

Some years ago, during those distressing congressional hearings over whether Clarence Thomas was qualified to sit on the Supreme Court of the United States, I came across the following statement from Chuck Colson. Chuck is a modern prophet, blessed of God with an unusually insightful discernment in seeing the big picture. Listen to his analysis of the hearings:

> It was a national real-life opera: 200 million Americans pasted to their television sets, mesmerized by lurid accusations of sexual harassment in high office. Center stage in the Senate caucus room was Prof. Anita Hill, doggedly asserting her claims. Judge Clarence Thomas issued angry denials....

Mercifully it is now over. Justice Clarence Thomas sits on the Supreme Court. Anita Hill is back in Oklahoma. Both will be shadowed by a cloud of suspicion for the rest of their lives....

But the damage has been done. The report was leaked; Hill testified publicly; and the Pandora's box of seething sexual politics, anger, resentment, and manipulation has been opened, spilling its contents all over America.

I reflected on this in an unlikely place. On the Saturday of the Thomas hearings, I was in a California prison. Under California law, there must be no sexual discrimination in hiring guards. Female correctional officers walk the cell blocks freely.

As I walked through the institution, I came upon an embarrassing scene. A young female officer strode into an exposed bathroom area, stood before an inmate seated on the toilet and ordered him to report to the cellblock.

Prison already strips a person of privacy. Now, because of antidiscrimination laws, inmates suffer the added shame of having the most intimate details of their daily lives invaded by members of the opposite sex.

Just then, across the cellblock, I saw a TV screen showing a sweating Judge Thomas being questioned for allegedly breaking the law by stripping an employee of her dignity through the use of indecent language. Yet here a female guard, by operation of the law, was stripping a naked man of his dignity.

Something was wrong with this picture. One law protects human honor in the workplace; another denigrates it. And both laws, I realized, are the result of militant feminism, a movement that might have begun with worthy intentions, but soon ran amuck.

...In the Thomas hearings, we saw the same women's groups who once proclaimed a woman's freedom to use explicit sexual language now righteously indignant in their claims that Clarence Thomas had allegedly spoken that way to a woman. The very people who once defended a woman's right to like pornography are now outraged if a man is vulgar enough to talk about such things to a woman. The very people who deliberately tore down older codes of chivalry and deference to women now want the protection they offer.[2]

Chuck's analysis is dead-on-target. What we are seeing is an incredibly ingenious scheme of the Evil One. The devil is attacking the image of God at its very heart. Read Mr. Colson's final paragraph. Let it sink in. Allow it to chill your soul:

The fundamental pillar of our society, the family, has been under assault for years, and its crumbling has long been of vital concern to Christians. *But do not miss the progression. The artillery salvos are escalating against something even more fundamental: the very notion of what it means to be a man, what it means to be a woman.* [3] (emphasis added)

"Sexual politics," so called, will be a key issue for many years to come. It was already an issue in the seventies. It was even bigger in the eighties. It is still huge today.

For the last twenty-five-plus years it has probably been the issue with the furthest-ranging implications. It's even affected our language. Just a couple of decades ago, words like "feminist," "women's lib," "male chauvinism," and "chairperson" were seldom heard. Today they are normative, appearing in the daily conversations of most Americans.

Gender issues will be a most significant issue, not only in a single election campaign, but well into the twenty-first century. So long as there is life in the image of God, and so long as Satan is free to go "roaming about on the earth and walking around on it" (Job 1:7), gender issues will be foundational.

So then, to put it in the words of the navy...

" N O W   H E A R   T H I S ! "

The gender issue is not primarily a political issue—though it certainly has tremendous political impact. Nor is it a social issue—though it affects society at its very foundation. Neither is it primarily an economic issue—

though it has great economic ramifications. It isn't even a primarily sexual issue—though sexuality is a central element.

The gender issues facing us today are primarily *spiritual* and *theological* at their core. Everything we do as humans is influenced strongly by our gender realities. Gender is a very basic element in dealing with our identity. In his or her soul, every human being asks a few basic questions: Who am I? Am I loved? Am I good or bad? Am I a boy or a girl—a man or a woman?

Gender is often the first question we ask at a human birth: "Is it a boy or a girl?" Incidentally, have you ever noticed that no one ever asks, "Is it a male or a female?" We are not looking so much for the child's sex as we are the child's *identity.*

Gender is primarily an issue of *theology.* And theology is the most foundational of all the sciences.

Gender is at the heart of creation.

Gender is tied to the image of God.

Gender is central to the glory of God.

And that is precisely why the armies of hell are throwing themselves into this particular battle with such concentrated frenzy.

Dr. Richard Halverson, former chaplain of the United States Senate and now with the Lord, beautifully captured the reality of gender centrality:

> Where can the enemy attack God most strategically? How most effectively destroy His relationship with mankind?
>
> *His masterpiece is to deface the image of God.*
>
> Image is indispensable in our Madison Avenue/Hollywood culture. It's the stock in trade of the public relations firm. Selling it is big business—billions of dollars worth. Bad image in our day is very costly. Which is precisely the point at which Satan makes his most strategic attack.
>
> God created man male-female as His image in history.
>
> Anything the devil can do to destroy the male-female union will mar God's image...anything that will alienate man from woman contributes to the destruction of a high view of God. The enemy has a multitude of tactics: premarital sex, extramarital sex,

sexual deviation, divorce, male chauvinism, feminism as an end in itself, and on and on…. Satan's effectiveness in destroying God's image through male-female alienation, by whatever means, has been incalculably costly to the human race.[4]

Halverson is right. So is Colson.

And we, as Christians, must address these gender issues with a whole heart and full energy. If we do not do so, we fail our Lord and His Word at the very point of the most basic contention in our culture. If we do not consistently address this issue over the years to come, we will be guilty of abandoning the Bible when our culture's very survival depends on it most. If we do not address it, we are guilty of the spiritual equivalent of sleeping on guard duty. Or, worse yet, simply going AWOL.

Martin Luther, the great reformer, and a warrior in his own right, said it this way: "If I profess with the loudest voice and clearest exposition every portion of the truth of God except precisely that…point which the world and the devil are at that moment attacking, I am not confessing Christ. *Where the battle rages, there the loyalty of the soldier is proved. And to be steady on all the battlefield (elsewhere), is merely flight and disgrace if he flinches at that point"* (emphasis added).

We who call ourselves Christian must be hard at it—in study, in understanding, in applying biblical principles of gender to our selves, our marriages, our families, and our daily lives. And we must address our culture. Or—listen—it will cease to exist.

The society that blurs gender realities cannot glorify God. The society that blurs gender realities simply dies. James Dobson, as usual, cuts to the chase on this issue in a recent remark:

In the thousands of years of human history and the thousands of different human cultures that have existed in human history, only a few have managed to blur masculinity and femininity. And every single one of them is extinct. According to Dr. Charles Winich of City University of New York, who has studied more than 2,000 cultures in world history, not one unisexual society has survived for more than a few years.[5]

In a society where men are confused about their masculinity and women are confused about their femininity, there is only disintegration, disorientation, destruction, and death. Ultimately the society collapses.

Such confusion in our society began, most noticeably, in the sixties, gathered momentum in the seventies, achieved "politically correct" status in the eighties, and is at the heart of unbelievable legal turmoil and in-your-face social engineering of the nineties.

We've got to address it. What is a man to be? What is a man to do? What are the pillars that stabilize and balance his heart? Our civilization, society, nation, families, and marriages depend upon a clear understanding of gender. These are foundational issues. The point should be clear to Christians, and to Christian men in particular. We cannot ignore these issues. There is too much at stake. And, heaven forbid, we cannot allow ourselves to passively buy into our culture's trends without holding them up to the light of Scripture.

CONSULTING THE OWNER'S MANUAL

I'm not particularly fond of manufacturers' manuals. Most of them sound as though they were poorly translated out of Swahili. But there is one owner's manual that speaks without stuttering. It sets forth the truth with stunning clarity. I refer, of course, to the Manufacturer's manual for humanity, the Bible. It's the owner's manual for both masculinity and femininity.

And, sure enough, the answers begin right there on Page One:

> Then God said, "Let Us make man in Our image, according to Our likeness; and let them rule over the fish of the sea and over the birds of the sky and over the cattle and over all the earth...."
> And God created man in His own image, in the image of God He created him; male and female He created them." (Genesis 1:26-27)

Doesn't it strike you as incredibly odd that a culture which so prides itself on "diversity" is working so hard to destroy it in its most obvious and beautiful form? That the politically correct buzzword, *diversity*, does not somehow apply to male and female differences? That somehow men and women must be the same? That God's chosen vehicle to carry His image, mankind as male and female, is the one form of diversity we seem bent not to accept? Dr. Halverson was right. It *is* devilish.

Are men and women really different? They are! They really are. Listen to one observer:

> Granted, men and women are different in physiological and sexual ways. The question is, are they essentially the same in all other areas? Feminists insist, "Yes!" A growing chorus of both secular and biblical researchers, however, respond with a firm "No!" Furthermore, a growing body of research indicates that these very basic differences are present from conception. These differences are innate. They are not learned.
>
> It is widely recognized now that the very brains of men and women are different. It is this structural, neurological difference that accounts for the many other observable distinctions. Women, for example, are generally superior to men in verbal abilities. Men are generally superior to women in mathematical abilities. Women are superior in sensory response. In men, the brain's hemispheres are separated in function—the right side for visual skills, the left side for verbal. In women these skills are controlled by both sides of the brain. These differences are primarily hormonal, due to the presence of testosterone in the male.
>
> One researcher summarizes the issue this way: "In organization, connection, and function the brains of men and women are appreciably different."[6]

It is overwhelmingly clear. Men and women are equal, but they are not the same. The differences in brain structure are present in the womb, and they are recognizable at every stage of human development—in the newborn infant, during early childhood, emphatically during puberty, and undeniably in adulthood. The feminist simply refuses to accept these realities. Feminists are forced to deny scientific fact in order to hold to their "socialization" theory, and in order to retain their dogged determination to engineer change. Feminists are hell-bent on destroying what they consider to be sexual stereotypes, on their way to creating a unisex society.

It will not happen, of course, but many individuals, marriages, and families will pay a terrible price in the unrelenting process. The winds will blow, the peoples will sway, but in the end there is no alternative to the divinely determined realities.

The key question we must ask ourselves is not, "Are there differences between men and women?" That is undeniable. What we must ask is, "How are we going to respond to the differences?" We can deny them and resist them, to our own pain. Or we can recognize them, accept them, and celebrate them to our own fulfillment and joy.

So how about you? Given the reality that gender differences are undeniable both scientifically and biblically, can we not safely conclude that God, the Creator Himself, chose to author these differences? Of course we can. And so we must if we hope to see health, life, and stability in our marriages, families, and churches.

There is something very profound here. It is deep. It is foundational. It is, by definition, essential. There is something here, related directly to the image of God, that will not go away with the rearranging of a few tasks or roles in society. It will not fade with the eliminating of a few words from our vocabulary. Gender differences are here to stay…by order of the Creator.

But many Christians have a tendency to drift with the sociological wishful-thinking of our culture which has been dominated by feminist thinking for nearly three decades now. Men have been relegated to something less than masculine. As C. S. Lewis stated so powerfully in *The Abolition of Man*, modernists "castrate, and bid the geldings be fruitful."

It is impossible. It is a tragedy. And our culture is in trouble.

WHEN A MAN'S A MAN

When men are not men, a civilization falls. When men let their masculinity drift with the winds of culture, everyone loses. When a culture is castrated, it dies. Let me tell you about one man who refused to become a gelding.

I'll never forget his words to me one evening.

"No, Stu, it isn't easy. But I'll do it and I'll keep on doing it, because it's the right thing to do…because I'm a man."

It was music to my ears.

I met Jim Manson (not his real name) in the course of our ministry years ago. Over a period of months, we spent a lot of hours together. Jim was in a difficult marriage. Of course, as in the vast majority of marriages, it hadn't started out that way. In fact, for more than a decade, Jim's marriage seemed to be a dream—one step after another, straight ahead. His career was a rocket. Financial goals were all met—and exceeded. The kids were beautiful. They owned a dream house in the right neighborhood. It was the best of everything.

But time has a way of taking the sheen off our dreams. And people have a way of forgetting what drew them together in the first place. Husbands and wives often grow distant without realizing it. Eventually couples "wake up" and feel like the only thing left of their dreams is the stagnant taste of morning breath. And they want something—or someone—better.

After marrying young and staying together for nearly twenty years, Jim and his wife had grown tired of and frustrated with each other. It had become a typical, but unusually intense, sparring contest. Cut for cut, stiffarm for stiffarm, issue for issue, insult for insult, it heated up. Nothing seemed to move them. They didn't like each other much, and their mind-sets had become so entrenched that neither could do anything right in the eyes of the other. Every attempt either of them made to change the stalemate seemed to turn sour. As another pained individual in a troubled relationship once said to me, "No good deed goes unpunished."

We all know that neither Jim nor Nancy was without fault. As is usually true in troubled marriages, both had contributed to the stony impasse. Both had blind spots. Both had stubborn streaks that went clean to the bone. And both knew how to hit the other's hot buttons.

Predictably enough, the marriage was in deep trouble. Like a small animal in the clutches of a predator, emotional energy was gone and they only had enough strength left for a few reflexive but hopeless kicks. It seemed they could do nothing more than give up and let the marriage die—like so many other marriages, every day of the year.

One more small civilization was about to crumble to ashes. This couple, like so many others before them, had moved beyond anger to that usually fatal cliff side you might call "numbed disinterest"—emotional apathy.

You may have been there yourself.

Divorce seemed the logical next step. And frankly, from our culture's perspective, that would have been a perfectly reasonable thing to do. After all, they weren't "making it" together. Love had flickered and seemingly died. They were bitterly unhappy. And they were still young enough to "find happiness somewhere else." It made perfect cultural sense to divide the money, find someone new, and spend the rest of their lives with new and more inviting partners. Perhaps someday they could even be "friends."

That was the cultural sense of the situation.

But biblically, it made no sense at all.

And Jim, believing that Bible, just couldn't let his family die. Here was a man who decided in his heart to be just that—a man. Here was a man who couldn't walk away from the small civilization God had given him to head. Somewhere deep down in his masculine soul, Jim couldn't do it. Couldn't sign the papers. Couldn't just "accept the inevitable." Couldn't walk away from the wife of his youth. Couldn't allow his family to become a statistic. And couldn't spit on his own word—the vows he had made to Nancy nearly two decades earlier.

Like the Rangers at the bottom of that cliff at Pont du Hoc on D-day in Normandy—in incredible pain, without hope, and up against a seemingly insurmountable obstacle—Jim swallowed hard through his agony, blinked back the tears, and determined to "play the man." Like Latimer, Ridley, and Polycarp, he determined to pay the price. If you have ever lived through the searing fires of marital warfare, you will understand that I am diminishing neither the courage of soldiers nor martyrs of the cross when I make the comparisons I've just made. The pain and desolation can be so intense that words cannot encompass it.

As I say, both Jim and Nancy had contributed to the deadlock in their marriage. Both had toxic attitudes and destructive habits to overcome. There was, however, one significant difference in their approach to their misery. To be sure, neither of them cared for the other much anymore, but Nancy had pretty well resigned herself to an inevitable divorce.

Jim would not.

Let me summarize his comments in one of our sessions together.

"I've been thinking about it a lot lately—in a fresh way. It's like the Lord is beginning to get through to me. I've come to realize that if I'm going to follow Christ, I need to follow His example. His Bride [the Church] didn't like Him much either. She didn't return His love. Didn't respond to Him at all like He'd hoped. But He loved her anyway, didn't He? And He *kept* loving her—even when it killed Him. Yet through it all, He never let Himself develop a bad attitude toward His Bride. He was willing to do whatever it took to make His marriage work. He knew that this life wasn't the end of the story. He knew that His dreams wouldn't be fulfilled in His lifetime on this earth.

"He decided to obey the Father. He decided as a mature man that He was willing to 'delay gratification'—until eternity, if need be.

"I guess I'm saying that I just need to be like my Lord."

Well said, Jim! And then he wrapped it up like this: "No, Pastor Stu, it isn't easy. But I'll do it and I'll keep on doing it, because it's right—and because I'm a man. I'm going to stay married and work at improving it, no matter what the cost, because I want to be the man Jesus wants me to be. I'm going to give myself to my marriage because of who I am, not because of who my wife is."

As Jim left my office that day, I found a smile on my face. And snatches of a few New Testament verses floated into my memory. Verses about love. Not the glandular, sentimental, Hollywood imitations, but the real thing. The kind of love so blended with courage and sacrifice that it's a three-fold cord…inseparable.

Husbands, love your wives, [exactly as] Christ loved the church and gave himself up for her…to present her to himself as a radiant [bride], without stain or wrinkle or any other blemish. (Ephesians 5:25-27, NIV)

This is love: not that we loved God, but that he loved us and sent his Son as an atoning sacrifice for our sins.... We love because he first loved us. (1 John 4:10, 19, NIV)

Jim Manson is no gelding. On the contrary, he's a stallion. In his own private battle, unheralded and unsung, one husband decided to "play the man." And by the way, he still is! Years and years later, he's still doing it. And he's glad he is. So are his children—and now, his grandchildren. And so is Nancy. Things have a way of getting better when hearts increase commitment.

Let's be men. Full-orbed, four-pillared men.

King. Warrior. Mentor. Friend. Four pillars in a manly heart. Every man is commissioned by his Creator…

to provide, *as a Servant-King;*
to protect, *as a Tender Warrior;*
to teach, *as a Wise Mentor; and*
to connect, *as a Faithful Friend.*

CHAPTER 3

FOUR PILLARS IN EDEN

Standing side by side in timeless symmetry, rising up together to uphold one unified whole, the four pillars reflect the light and majesty of the One in whose image they are made. In man, fallen creatures that we are, the pillars are often unbalanced, unstable, and unready to bear the weight of headship. In Christ, the Ultimate Man, they stand in perfect balance and regal dignity.

These four basic masculine functions appear both in the sacred Scriptures of God and in the secular history of man, whether we study history, anthropology, sociology, or psychology. To the degree that they conform to God's heart in each individual man, they represent God's intentions for the man and his manhood. The fact that these masculine qualities cut across the grain of history, race, tradition, and culture shouldn't surprise us at all. They are like fingerprints, the telltale mark of the Artist on the wet clay of the original.

Two secular psychologists, Robert Moore and Douglas Gillette, describe these basic kinds of functions as "blueprints" or "hard wiring" or "archetypes," deep in a man's insides. According to Moore and Gillette, these functions or potentials provide the very foundations of a man's behaviors—thinking, feeling, and reacting to whatever comes into his life.[1]

To the degree the pillars are balanced, God's image is clear, and the man and those around him flourish. To the degree they are abased and abused, the image is distorted, the man withers, and those around him experience imbalance, insecurity, and pain. That's why the adjectives—"servant," "tender," "wise," and "faithful"—are every bit as critical as the nouns—"king," "warrior," "mentor," and "friend."

A king who is not a servant is merely a tyrant.

A warrior who is not tender is only a brute.

A mentor who is not wise is just a know-it-all.

A friend who is not faithful is at best an acquaintance, or worse, a betrayer.

You might view these four fundamentals as the four points on the masculine compass. God has equipped every man with an internal gyroscope which gives his life purpose, direction, balance, and impact. Providing that it is calibrated to the "True North" of God's Word, a man may consult his internal compass for direction at any point in any situation on any given day.

Does this particular situation confronting me right now require the King, the Warrior, the Mentor, or the Friend?

Does my wife need the faithful Friend in me right now more than she needs the leader-King?

Does my daughter's dating relationship need a bit of the Warrior in me to weigh in at this point? Or does she just need a careful conversation with the Mentor?

Which pillar should bear the weight just now? Which of my masculine functions needs to seize this moment for my family's good? And which needs to take a back seat at the moment?

Balanced, the four pillars uphold the dreams of every man, woman, son, daughter, marriage, and family. Balanced, they provide security and significance for a man and his family. But if you let them lean, look out! Out of balance, leaning one way or the other, they will create havoc and pain, the opposite of everything you and your family desire. Out of balance and control they will destroy both the man and his family. When the pillars in a manly heart begin to lean and topple, everyone suffers.

Once upon a time those pillars were new, planted deeply in the virgin soil of a young planet. They stood tall and stately, majestic and clean, perfectly balanced in the heart of your father and mine.

Adam, the original. The first four-pillared man.

P I L L A R S   I N   E D E N

Masculinity did not evolve. It was *created.* There was a literal time and place when the Creator-God breathed it into the clay He had molded into man-shape. A moment before, there wasn't a man in the whole wide world. And then—snap!—just that quickly, there was a man in the house.

And what a man. In that creative instant, masculinity blazed forth in uneclipsed glory, and God's angels shouted for joy.

Have you ever walked through a brand-new house with fresh paint on the walls, new carpets on the floor, and shiny, just-out-of-the-box appliances everywhere? You can see your reflection in every piece of chrome. Counters and cabinets gleam. Windows sparkle. Lighting fixtures beam with golden, dustless splendor.

Have you ever slid behind the wheel of a brand-new car? There's nothing like it. Nothing that feels like it. Nothing that smells like it. The odometer reads 0000.03—the distance from the truck to the showroom floor. Flick a switch and the instrument panel winks to life with smudgeless radiance. Every fiber of carpet stands unbent, unbowed, and unstained. No wads of chewing gum, old M&Ms, used Band-Aids, or forgotten french fries lurk under the seats. No fingerprint has ever marked a window. No greasy hand has ever clutched the wheel. No little finger has ever traced a smiley-face on the windshield. And out under that flawless, sloping hood, a freshly assembled engine slumbers—lubricated with amber, unstained oil—waiting to flex its muscle, roar out its power, and prove the potential envisioned by its designers.

What do you suppose masculinity was like when it was brand new? What did it look like? What did it smell like, just out of the box? How did it perform when it was newly awakened, so fresh from the heart of its Creator?

The Book of Genesis gives us a tantalizing glimpse, however brief. Within those few sentences, we read what God had in mind for Man before Woman ever stepped so demurely off the design board. We hear God's instructions to Adam before there was Eve. And as the man walks through the morning splendor of a new planet, treading grass that has never felt the weight of man's foot, he casts the shadow of four pillars. An infant wind slipping through newly minted leaves whispers...*King... Warrior...Mentor...Friend.*

Right from the get-go, God had some specific intentions in mind for masculinity. Listen...

The LORD God formed *the man* from the dust of the ground and breathed into his nostrils the breath of life, and the man became a living being.

Now the LORD God had planted a garden in the east, in Eden; and there he put *the man* he had formed.... [Then] the LORD God took *the man* and put him in the Garden of Eden to work it and take care of it. And the LORD God commanded *the man,* "You are free to eat from any tree in the garden; but you must not eat from the tree of the knowledge of good and evil, for when you eat of it you will surely die."

Then, [and not before] the LORD God said, "It is not good for *the man* to be alone. I will make a helper suitable for him."... Then the LORD God made a woman from the rib he had taken out of *the man,* and he brought her to *the man....*

[There follows the account of the first sin, committed initially by Eve, then her husband. And then we read...]

The LORD God called to *the man,* "Where are you?"
(Genesis 2:7-8, 15-18, 22; 3:9, NIV, emphasis added)

Notice several standout principles from this account of the creation of masculinity and femininity:

God created the man first.
A prior order in creation? Yes, and it is no accident of sequence. It is rather a deliberate action on the part of the Creator, later appealed to in the New Testament as indicating a unique leadership role in God's economy for the masculine gender (1 Timothy 2:8-15). Having created the man first, and prior to creating the woman, God and the man engage in some key conversations.

While we have no indication of how many conversations or how long those discussions may have been, we cannot escape the fact that this communication took place *between the Creator and the man.* And specific responsibilities were at the center of those conversations. From the very onset, it is evident that God had some definitive intentions in mind regarding a man's priority role in leadership and headship responsibilities.

God created the Garden of Eden and, prior to creating the woman, directed the man to cultivate and keep it.

At this point in the creation account there was still only one human being. Adam was still flying solo. And to that lone man, God delivered a charge. It would be the man's responsibility in the garden *"to work it and take care of it."* He said to Adam, in effect, "Here is a garden, an environment, a realm. I want you to watch over it, superintend it, look out for it." God gave the man a specific charge regarding the realm. He was to cultivate it and to keep it. He was to be a provider and a superintendent.

In this charge, I believe, God was saying to the man, "There is something of a king inside your chest. I have placed it there. I have made you a leader and a provider." As Scripture unfolds it becomes patently clear that God's intention is not that the man be some swaggering monarch with an attitude, but a Servant-King.

God gave to the man (again prior to the woman's creation) specific instructions regarding the tree of knowledge.

God delivered to the man, while he was still alone, a specific and critically important body of information concerning the very nature of life itself. The subject of the conversation was the "tree of the knowledge of good and evil." Evidently God intended that the man become a steward, not only of the garden, but of this information as well. It is legitimate to draw the implication that the man was responsible to heed this information, to regard it carefully, and to steward it as information critical to life itself.

The further implication may be drawn that the man's stewardship of this information involves his carefully passing it along, or teaching it to others who may eventually live in the realm. I believe this is an early indicator of God's intention that a man know how life works. A man is to teach those near and dear to him the basic principles of life.

There is something of a Mentor in every man's chest. God's intention is a Wise Mentor.

God issued a clear warning of danger in the realm.
When God used the words *"shall surely die"* in his conversation with the man, His tone was necessarily ominous. He was warning the man of an enormous threat in the realm, saying in effect, "It is dangerous here. You (and, by implication, those you love) are vulnerable in this place. Though it feels like paradise, you could *die* here."

God clearly intended that Adam be alert, on guard, on watch. He intended that Adam protect himself, those around him, and the realm itself from the threat. I believe there is something of a Warrior in every man's chest. God's intention is a Tender Warrior.

In unmistakable terms, God said the man was never intended to live alone.
The Creator stated it clearly from the beginning: *"It is not good for the man to be alone."* While the immediate and obvious context of this statement is the marriage relationship (the very zenith of friendship), I believe it is also a statement of comprehensive principle found from one end of Scripture to the other. It is a sweeping life statement. Alone is not good. Together is better. Men were made to connect. There is a Friend in every man's chest. God's intention is a Faithful Friend.

When sin destroyed the peace of the realm, God came looking for the man.
Genesis 3:1-19 records the tragic account of the first sin and its catastrophic results. It is worth noting that while the woman sinned first, when God came to confront the sinners, He came looking for *the man.* Scripture says, "The LORD God called to the man."

I believe the question God asked Adam was more of an indictment than a request for information: *"Where are you?"*

The Lord wasn't inquiring about Adam's physical whereabouts. He knew perfectly well where the man was on the ground. The omniscient God has no trouble with geographical coordinates. What He was actually doing was demanding an explanation. He was reminding the man of his abuse of the stewardship responsibilities which he had been given.

Adam had failed his Lord, his wife, and himself. He had failed to steward his masculinity. I believe God was saying, in effect, "Adam, where *were* you?" God was demanding to know just what Adam had done with his masculine stewardship.

Where was the King in you, Adam? It appears you have not watched over your home. You have failed to superintend your realm. You have evidently failed to provide leadership to your family in the most basic area of all. It seems you were not looking ahead for those near and dear to you. Where was the King in you, man?

Where was the Warrior in you, Adam? When that snake invaded your home, were you asleep on guard duty? Why didn't you stand between your wife and the evil in your world? Did you expect her to protect herself? Why didn't you step into the gap?

Where was the Mentor in you, Adam? When your wife was taken in by that snake, where were you? When your wife conversed with that evil one, where was your influence? Was she not alert to what I told you earlier? Did you not communicate to her the information about life I gave to you? Where was the Mentor in you? Did you fail to teach?

Where was the Friend in you, Adam? When your wife was wandering off giving attention to evil influence, where were you? Were you aloof? Distant? Absent? Absorbed in your own stuff? Were you not with her? Where was the Friend in you, man? Did you fail to connect?

Please note that God holds the man responsible in a way in which he does not so hold the woman. Although Eve sinned first, it was Adam who God went looking for. It is apparent that God expects the man to have exercised some sort of corporate, overarching, family-wide responsibility reaching beyond his own personal responsibility.

Though Eve sinned first, God condemned the race for *Adam's* sin. The entire human race suffers because the head of the race fell short. This is clearly implied in Genesis, and explicitly confirmed in the New Testament: "Through one man sin entered into the world, and death through sin.... By the transgression of the one the many died.... Through one transgression there resulted condemnation to all.... As in Adam all die, so also in Christ all shall be made alive" (Romans 5:12, 15, 18; 1 Corinthians 15:22).

There are serious and humbling implications here for every man. Don't miss this principle, my friend: *The entire family suffers when the head of the family falls short.* When a man loses sight of his noble commission from God, he wallows, losing direction and perspective. When a man loses hope, his vision fades and his people perish. When a man loses direction, he tends to waste or abuse his God-given masculine energies and capacities on selfish and/or destructive pursuits.

It is this lack of manliness, this fatherlessness, that accounts for much of the chaos and so many of the social ills in our own culture—from drugs to gangs; from unfaithfulness to divorce; from unwanted pregnancies to single-parent homes; from simple selfishness to soaring crime rates. Masculinity off-course and run amuck is incredibly destructive.

But wait…there is good news!

Manliness on-course and in hot pursuit of God's intentions for masculinity enjoys an incredible power for health and healing. When Dad is following after God's intentions for him, everybody wins! It is on these positive, motivating implications that this book will concentrate. A man is motivated when he is pointed toward the high ground of God's intentions for him. And the whole family rises to a level of health, fulfillment, and happiness when the King-Warrior-Mentor-Friend is doing his job and living out God's intentions for his masculine soul.

When "the man" is at home, doing his job, living out the four pillars of his masculinity, and wrapping his arms around God's intentions for him, everyone wins.

JUST WAITIN' FOR YOU, MAN

Some years ago while speaking at a parenting conference with Dennis Rainey, FamilyLife's national director and the radio host of "FamilyLife Today," I heard Dennis tell a story which moved my masculine heart to intense emotion and determination. Maybe it will encourage you, too.

In the mid-1980s a missionary family serving overseas came home on furlough, needing a little R&R. Through the graciousness of friends, they'd been provided with the use of a summer home on a beautiful lake. For these tired, front-line warriors, it was like a little piece of Eden.

One bright summer morning, Mom was in the kitchen fussing with the baby and preparing a lunch for the family. Dad was in the boathouse puttering with something that needed some puttering. And the three children present were out on the lawn between the home and the edge of the lake. Three-year-old "little Billy" was under the care of a five-year-old sister and a twelve-year-old cousin.

When Sister and Cousin became distracted with some mutual interest, little Billy decided it would be an opportune time to wander down to the water and check out that shiny little aluminum boat that had been bobbing so temptingly beside the dock. The trouble is, three-year-olds have limited experience in getting from a stable dock to a bobbing boat. With one foot on the dock and the other stretching toward the boat, Little Billy lost his balance and fell into five or six feet of water beside the dock.

The splash alerted the twelve-year-old, who let loose a piercing scream. That brought Dad on the run. After scoping out the situation for a second or two, he dove into the murky water and began a desperate search for his little boy. But the lake water was murky, and Dad couldn't see a thing. With lungs desperate for air, he resurfaced, grabbed another ragged gasp, and plunged back under. Sick with panic, the only thing he could think to do was to extend his arms and legs as far as he could and try to *feel* little Billy's whereabouts. Having nearly exhausted his oxygen supply a second time, he began to ascend once again for another breath.

On his way up, he felt little Billy, arms locked in a death grip to a pier post some four feet under the water. Prying the boy's fingers loose, they burst together through the surface to fill their lungs with life-giving air.

Adrenaline continued to surge. Conversation would not return to normal for a long time. Dad just carried little Billy around, holding him close, unable to put him down for some time. Finally, when heart rates had returned to normal and nerves had calmed a bit, this missionary dad turned to his boy with a question.

"Billy, what on earth were you *doing* down there, hanging onto that post so far underwater?"

Little Billy's reply, laced with all the wisdom of a tot, reaches out and grabs us all by the throat.

"Just waitin' for you, Dad. Just waitin' for you!"

Just waitin' for you, Dad. I knew you'd come. I knew you'd be there for me. I knew you'd save me. You're my dad. You're a man. You're my king. I knew you wouldn't leave me.

G. K. Chesterton said it well, "The greatest political storm flutters only a fringe of humanity. But an ordinary man and an ordinary woman and their ordinary children literally alter the destiny of nations."

Friend, you and I need to play the man. Our kids, our wives, our friends, our neighbors, and our country are in desperate straits—they're just waitin' for us to be the men God intended us to be. Our culture is hurting. Too many dreams are four feet under water, buried in the mud and muck of the last thirty years of cultural storms. This country is suffering. Its dreams lay dashed in the dust of decay.

Let's get about rebuilding this place we call "home." One pillar at a time.

And what will it look like when we do? How will our small civilizations look different when four-pillared men stand balanced and strong? One recent incident comes quickly to mind.

A F O U R - P I L L A R E D   H E A R T
I N   A C T I O N

I have a friend who answered the phone one night to find his sister in distress, just beside herself. The pressures of life had been building for some time, and she was on the edge of falling apart.

Her husband had lost his job through no fault of his own. Both of their cars were breaking down. There was no money. On top of those things, their college- and high-school-age kids were wading through several heavy issues. When your kids are in pain, it kills you. It seemed like every person in the family was hurting somehow. There was no relief. It had been this way for *months*, and there seemed no end in sight.

She couldn't handle it anymore. There seemed nowhere to turn. And to add to the pressure, she did not want to "break down" and fall apart in front of her kids. In sheer desperation, she had called her brother. My friend could hear—could *feel*—the pain in her voice. It went far deeper than her words. It was more than desperation. It was more like whispered terror. If you've ever witnessed a person having a "panic attack," you have some idea of what she was experiencing.

My friend is no counselor, but he is a man. And the four pillars of his heart reached right through the phone line to his sister. This was no time for passivity. He had to do something. But what?

"Sis," he said, "can you drive?"

She thought she could. He said, "Jump in your car, Sis, and come on over to my place. Let's just sit together awhile and talk about it all."

When she knocked on the door, he simply opened his arms and embraced her right there in the doorway. She couldn't breathe normally. Her hands were trembling. Her tummy was hurting. Her eyes had the look of a young doe running before a forest fire.

They stood there in the doorway for a long time. Just hugging.

Eventually they sat down, just the two of them, in his living room. He made some tea. And they talked. He had no answers. But he did have a heart, and he gave it to her. In that moment, it was all she needed. A safe place. A place where she could just "crash." A place where, for a few minutes, she didn't have to "buck up" and be strong.

When she began to calm some, her brother asked her if she would like to spend the night at his home. At first she said no. She didn't think it was the responsible thing to do. But as they talked, she realized she really did need at least one good night's sleep. Her brother volunteered to call her husband.

Now, I know both of these men. They are good men. And the two of them respect each other a great deal. Neither would shame the other for anything. They stand beside each other, like family. And they both love this wonderful woman—one as a sister, one as a wife. Together, they agreed it would be really good for her to just sleep, care free. Her husband would take care of everything on the other end. She could just stay...and relax...and sleep. So two men, a husband and a brother, teamed up to provide for a lady.

That night she slept like a baby. And well she could. The men in her life were acting like men—four-pillared men. The next morning, as she prepared to leave and step back into her life, her brother slipped her some money with a wink and said, "This is just between you and me, Kiddo. It's mad money—just enjoy it."

What had happened there that night? It certainly wasn't some savior to the rescue on a prancing white steed. It wasn't some great counselor offering profound answers and a comprehensive plan for her life. But it was a couple of guys willing to do whatever it took to meet the needs of a woman they loved.

On the husband's part, it required some humility, some understanding, and a willingness to release and step into the gap. On the brother's part, it took asking some questions. And some serious listening.

Like most of us guys, these men didn't know just what "the right kind of questions" were. But they were willing to wade in and give it a try. Willing to ask, and willing to listen. Sometimes being a four-pillared man just means asking a whole lot of questions—and then *really* listening.

It takes a humble man to ask questions. Most men tend to think they have to offer solutions—an elaborate game plan. Not so. But what it does take is all a man's energy focused on entering into another person's world. In this case, it was a sister and a wife. Sometimes it's a child. Or a friend.

When all was said and done, neither man had a solution to all the pressures. They didn't have answers to all the questions. But these two men offered something greater than answers and solutions. They offered what they could: A hug; a reassurance of personal worth; and a commitment to stand beside, no matter what.

It was enough to make the difference. It was enough to calm the fears, to quiet the heart, and to allow one harried lady a chance to catch her breath and get back into the race. And you should see her today. She's running well. With smiles. And now and then, a wink.

When men are acting like kings—loving, calming, reassuring, sacrificing, providing—everyone flourishes. It is the king in a man—that first tall pillar of the heart—that longs to build peace and security for those around him.

It's a wonderful thing to behold…the pillars of a man's heart in balance.

It's like a little taste of Camelot.

FOUR PILLARS IN A MAN'S HEART

PILLAR	KING	WARRIOR	MENTOR	FRIEND
Scriptural Function	Provide (Gen. 2:15)	Protect (Gen. 2:17)	Teach (Gen. 2:16–17)	Connect (Gen. 2:18)
Secular/Historical Perspective*	*"The energy of just and creative ordering."*	*"The energy of disciplined aggressive action."*	*"The energy of transformation."*	*"The energy that connects men to others and the world."*
Core Characteristics	Cares Deeply	Contends Courageously	Communicates Transparently	Connects Deliberately
Common Results (When Pillar is leaning, absent, or abused)	1. Disorder 2. Chaos 3. Family dysfunction 4. Oppression	1. Fear 2. Abuse 3. Cruelty 4. Hatred	1. Lack of discipline 2. Personal immaturity 3. Disregard for Scripture 4. Spiritual insensitivity	1. Unavailability 2. Personal isolation 3. Emotional detachment 4. Illicit sensuality
Out of Balance (Right or Left)	Abdicator/Tyrant Passive— Failure to lead	Coward/Brute Passive— Failure to contend	Dunce/Know-it-all Passive— Failure to pass baton	Loner/Smotherer Passive— Failure to connect

*Moore & Gillette,
King, Warrior, Magician, Lover
Harper Collins, 1990

©Stu Weber, 1997

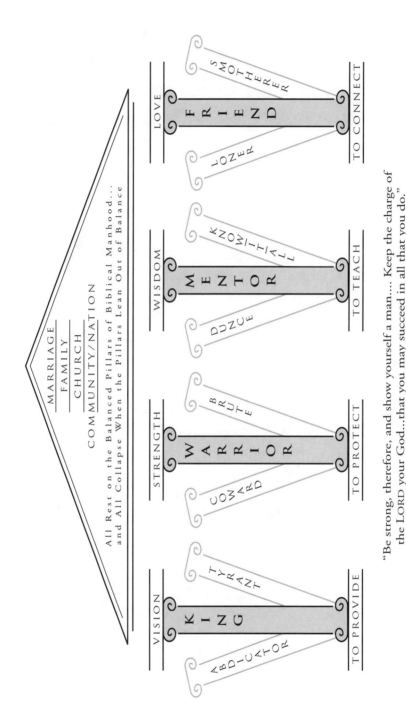

MARRIAGE
FAMILY
CHURCH
COMMUNITY/NATION

All Rest on the Balanced Pillars of Biblical Manhood...
and All Collapse When the Pillars Lean Out of Balance

LOVE — FRIEND — TO CONNECT
SMOTHERER
LONER

WISDOM — MENTOR — TO TEACH
KNOW-IT-ALL
DUNCE

STRENGTH — WARRIOR — TO PROTECT
BRUTE
COWARD

VISION — KING — TO PROVIDE
TYRANT
ABDICATOR

"Be strong, therefore, and show yourself a man.... Keep the charge of
the LORD your God...that you may succeed in all that you do."

1 KINGS 2:2-3

"Four mighty ones are in every man." —William Blake

THE KING PILLAR

"You know that in this world kings are tyrants, and officials lord it over the people beneath them. But among you it should be quite different. Whoever wants to be a leader among you must be your servant, and whoever wants to be first must become your slave. For even I, the Son of Man, came here not to be served but to serve others, and to give my life as a ransom for many."

MATTHEW 20:25-28, NLT

CAMELOT REVISITED

R emember Camelot?

Pristine. Pure rivers. Gentle breezes. Stable homes. Safe pathways winding between serene hamlets. Children at play. Happy citizens. The poets called it, "The kingdom of summer." It was a kingdom at peace.

Can you remember snatches of the musical by that name? What was it they said about Arthur's realm? *In short there's simply not, a more congenial spot, for happy-ever-aftering than here...in Camelot!*

The king made it happen. Arthur Pendragon, son of Uther, High King of Britain, delivered to his people their paradise. His courage and cunning as a warrior drove the raiding Saxon hordes into the sea. His skills as a negotiator united the petty regional kings, ended the constant bloodshed, and—for the first time since the Legions marched—brought the old Roman colony of Britannia under a single glorious banner. His leadership seemed nearly divine. It was a little bit of life "on earth as it is in heaven."

So long as Arthur occupied the throne and rode the king's highways with his knight companions, life was secure, carefree, and fulfilling. When the king was in his castle, the kingdom breathed a collective sigh of contentment. The only sounds of warfare came from the jousting tournaments where young would-be knights matched their skills and acquired the first dents in their armor. The only sounds that disturbed the night were the tramp of sentries on the castle walls and the occasional "all is well" of the king's household guards. Whether it actually existed in history or lives only in legend is a matter of conjecture. Nevertheless, Camelot was the idyllic realm.

And every generation since has longed for the same. A Kingdom of

Summer. Peace and sunlight, music and laughter. Everything at rest—and it all rides on the shoulders of the king.

CAMELOT ON THE POTOMAC

I was just a kid when John Fitzgerald Kennedy ascended to the Oval Office. With his queenly wife Jacqueline at his side and their young, beautiful children, they represented all of America. "John-John" played beneath his father's huge desk, and Caroline skipped about as the perfectly mature older sister.

It was idyllic. At last the White House looked like your house—it was occupied by healthy people, and led by a competent head. All of America (even Republicans, in their weaker moments) wanted to believe the kingdom had come. No one, at that point, knew about the president's reputed moral lapses. At that time, in that season, it was Camelot all over again—until a bullet shattered the dream. The Kingdom of Summer faded like a dream on a cold November morning.

America had so wanted to believe that, in Browning's words, "all was right with the world." Well, perhaps we've "grown up" enough to realize that nothing in this world is perfect. But when there is competent leadership at the head, things somehow seem better. People feel better. Spirits are up. Criticism is down. Cynicism slithers back into the shadows from which it came...and life is good.

Leadership is *everything*, whether it's Hitler's Germany, Kennedy's America, Khomeini's Iran, Arthur's Camelot—or your own home. As the leaders go, so go the people. Camelot is the responsibility of the king.

So how is your kingdom? How is the king in you doing? How's it going at your house, in your little realm? What kind of leader are you?

Is there a sweet aroma of contentment? Or is your home characterized by the sour taste of bitterness? Are the "citizens" secure? Is there peace? Is there laughter in the hallways? Is everyone glad to know the king is in his castle? Or would they, frankly, prefer a palace coup? Is your home a little taste of heaven, or is it hell on earth?

According to what we've already encountered in the Book of Genesis, the responsibility for choosing the direction rests squarely on the head of the home. Let's talk about the man as a leader.

There is a king in every man's chest. And that means...what? That he's "da Big Boss"? Don't be too sure. That depends on your view of authority.

THE GENERAL CLARIFIES REALITY

I'll never forget how quickly the tone of the meeting changed.

I was a young first lieutenant assigned to the brigade staff of 2nd Brigade, 3rd Armored Division. Standing humbly in "the gallery" that morning, I was privileged to observe the brass at their regular daily briefing.

These were the brigade's annual field maneuvers, during which we measured combat readiness—huge on the military's annual calendar. Tensions were always higher than usual. Competition stiffer. And, of course, those who tended to be prima donnas were always at their pompous best. Tank crews ran through their courses. Two battalions of mechanized infantry took to the field with an artillery battalion at their heels. And, of course, the Third Squadron of the Twelfth Cavalry strutted around wearing their colorful ascots and acting like they were still riding horses. Real pretty.

The day I attended the briefing was particularly important. The division commanding general was visiting. Major General Cowles, in field fatigues like his soldiers, sat in his chair at the head of the table. The brigade commander, a full colonel, took his place beside the great man. The battalion commanders and the Cav Squadron CO, all lieutenant colonels, were seated around the table. Each would have his moment in the sun, explaining the day's operations to the commanding general.

The briefing began routinely, unpretentiously. Pretty normal stuff, at first. No one could have guessed what was about to happen—or just how dramatically the meeting would turn. It would all hinge on a single moment, with a single statement from the general.

The presentation rotation came to the Cav Squadron CO. He took his moment in the spotlight to proudly announce a new policy he had instituted among his motor pool sentries. Now any military man can tell you that motor pools on field maneuvers are prime targets for "midnight requisitions" as competing units seek to keep their own equipment in top operating order. Any given unit will do whatever it takes to keep its own vehicles up and running. They will even resort to raiding parts from the next guy's motor pool in order to guarantee their own success and their competition's failure.

But old LTC Green thought he had the answer. In front of the general he announced, with obvious delight, how he had ingeniously "solved" the motor pool security problem. Seems the colonel had announced he would give any sentry actually catching a thief in his motor pool a three-day pass.

That's when it happened.

Whatever Colonel Green might have been expecting from the head of the table shattered as abruptly as a thin pane of glass. The division commanding general exploded! Now you need to understand that generals rarely resort to explosions. Generals have other tools, less public and more effective, in their arsenals. But Major General Cowles could stand it no longer. With red face and bulging veins, this normally genteel man dressed down the cavalry squadron commander in no uncertain terms.

"Do you mean to tell me, LTC Green, that you find it *necessary* as squadron commander to *bribe* your troops in order to get them *to do their jobs?* Listen to me! A soldier is a *soldier.* A soldier fulfills his duty. Sentry duty is at the heart of soldiering. A soldier is not some pre-pubescent junior higher that you should have to motivate by bribery. It's his *duty!* It's his *job!* And YOUR job as a leader is to see that he does his— without bribery! This is serious business, not some Sunday school picnic! And if any unit commander of mine has to drop so low as to bribe his men to be soldiers, it is evident that commander understands neither soldiering nor leadership. I will *relieve* him on the spot and replace him with a man who knows how to lead troops! Any questions?"

No, there were no questions. For a long moment, no one even breathed. No one moved in his chair. No one cleared his throat. The room went as quiet as a sub-basement under the pyramids.

The general's remarks were stunning, and totally unanticipated. And the point was painfully clear and powerfully obvious. Even a lowly lieutenant got the picture. There was no hedging; no beating around the proverbial bush. *In one brief emphatic statement, the general had clarified reality.*

T H E   L O R D   C L A R I F I E S   R E A L I T Y

Now imagine yourself in the gallery at a much earlier briefing, nearly two thousand years prior to General Cowles's comments. No generals attended this meeting. But there was a King present. The One in charge of the ancient briefing was the King of the universe, and He was recruiting leaders for His kingdom. He had carefully selected his "unit commanders," and He was in the process of training them in His own tactics. On this particular occasion, He was speaking with the twelve key leaders who would one day hold the highest seats in the kingdom. Undoubtedly, there was a prima donna or two present.

As you can well imagine, there was quite a bit of discussion among those senior leader designees about which of them was going to come out of this competition on top. None of them wore ascots or shiny boots, and none of them engaged in midnight raids. But there was plenty of small-minded jealousy. And more than enough selfishness to go around.

A couple of them, two brothers in particular, even resorted to a little after-hours lobbying. Evidently, they'd been raised that way. They pretentiously positioned themselves for what they thought to be the senior positions. And while they didn't resort to bribery or midnight requisitions, they did enlist their mother—of all people—to lobby on their behalf (self-inflated people have no shame). The other ten equally pompous would-be leaders were piqued. *(Why the NERVE of those sons of Zebedee!)* They puffed themselves up to the point of obvious indignation.

And that's when it happened.

The briefing changed...dramatically.

Everybody was caught off guard. Stunned. The Commanding General of heaven's armies looked them in the eyes and made Himself so absolutely clear that not even a child in their midst could have missed the point.

> "You know that the rulers of the Gentiles lord it over them, and their great men exercise authority over them. It is not so among you, but whoever wishes to become great among you shall be your servant, and whoever wishes to be first among you shall be your slave; just as the Son of Man did not come to be served, but to serve...." (Matthew 20:25-28)

In one emphatic statement, the King had clarified reality.

In one brief paragraph, just three sentences long, the Lord of the universe made His point. He settled the nature of authority. And He ought to know: He invented it! In no uncertain terms, He let them know that being "the leader" wasn't what they thought it was! Kingship, leadership, headship, patriarchy—call it what you want. Jesus Christ spelled it out in simple language.

It's not bossing...it's serving.

It's not demanding...it's caring.

It's not strutting...it's stooping.

It's not leisure...it's labor.

It's not a golden parachute...it's a cross.

Any questions?

Jesus Christ clarified reality for His followers as they had never understood it before. A leader is a *servant*. The one charged with authority must lead with love. Jesus did, and He is still changing the world. Perhaps he had even influenced Mohandas Gandhi, who said:

Power is of two kinds. One is obtained by fear of punishment and the other by the art of love. Power based on love is a thousand times more effective and permanent.[1]

Too often men miss that profound principle. And that's at least one major reason male headship in the home and church is under such fire today—men haven't got the message. We're still strutting about, demanding submission. We're still playing by the outdated rules of self-assertion, self-promotion, self-absorption, and self-elevation, which *never were* appropriate in God's kingdom. Jesus' point is clear—"IT SHALL NOT BE SO AMONG YOU!" There is no room in Christ's camp for those who "lord it over" others.

Leadership divine style, the only kind a Christian man is allowed, is servant hearted. All of Christ's lieutenants will lead like servants. Picture your own modern version of Camelot at your house. One modern man did. Listen to the peace in that man's castle, as described *by the queen*, his wife:

Sometimes, when my husband shares his big leather lounge chair with one of his children during a basketball game or the evening news, I can see they see him as a bulwark, an authority, a sort of deity. And a big kid. The kind of father who is strong enough to inform, secure enough to say, "I don't know," warm enough to kiss and cuddle, and wild enough to invent The Knuckle Machine tickling game.[2]

Sounds good, doesn't it? Leadership really is the power to evoke the best and right responses from others. You want that in your home, too? Let's get started.

T H E   K I N G   I N   E V E R Y   M A N ' S   H E A R T

Now that we've clarified reality—now that our Lord has stunned us into a new way of thinking—we're ready to take a careful look at the first pillar, the leader function that God placed deep inside every man's chest.

The KING pillar casts its long shadow across the length of Scripture. Our God is referred to as the King of kings. His Son, the second Adam, is destined to rule with "all power and authority." The first Adam, our masculine prototype, is instructed beside the Genesis Spring to "have dominion." The King function throughout Scripture is clearly an authority function. Let's think about authority for a moment.

Authority is the bottom line of the universe. It is the inevitable first question. *Who's in charge here?!* It is the first answer. Rebellion against it started the first war—on a cosmic scale—just as it has started every war since, whether global or local, physical or spiritual, marital or personal. Authority is the one element which, given our self-oriented depravity, chaffs us all. *But we will never escape it.* And it is particularly incumbent upon Christians to learn to live with it.

Someone is always in charge.

It goes without saying. It's axiomatic. We can try to deny it all we want to, but—someone is always in charge. It's the way God made this world, because it reflects the reality of His world. And when Satan tried to usurp a little authority for himself, he ended up on the ash heap of the universe.

Someone is always in charge.

I don't remember when I first realized that. But I'm sure it was early in life—somewhere between that instant of birth and the moment the doctor handed me to my mother. Every infant soon learns that someone is in charge. It was reinforced at home. It was reinforced again at school. There was no doubt that first day of kindergarten who was in charge. Our teacher, Mrs. Taylor! It was the same at recess; during the lunch hour; on the school bus; and, yes, even in the tree fort in the back yard.

Someone is *always* in charge.

It is true on the football team...in the marching band...in the fraternity house...and in the corporate board room. It is true everywhere.

Dennis Foley, a highly decorated career soldier, was struck with that reality early in his army career. He came face to face with it—in explicit terms—just after he bailed off the back of the truck, grabbed his duffel bag, and stood in formation in front of an experienced old NCO (non-commissioned officer). Smile at the picture as Dennis describes it:

> He (the NCO) didn't say a word. We lacked a little coordination and to him we must have looked like the Keystone Kops trying to build a military formation. He made a small gesture of impatience.
>
> "Who's in charge here?" he asked forcefully, tapping his swagger stick against his trouser leg. No one answered.
>
> "I'll ask again. Who-is-in-charge?" No one answered.
>
> Still standing at a perfect position of attention, he looked each of us in the eye for a split second and began our first class at the NCO Academy. "Everywhere and anywhere you are in the army—someone is always in charge."
>
> We weren't sure if that required a response. So we stayed quiet and listened.
>
> "If it isn't apparent just who is in charge—*take* charge. Organize and lead. I say again...organize and lead."
>
> We let that sink in.[3]

Yes, let that sink in, guys. Someone is always in charge. You've never been anywhere someone *wasn't* in charge. Or if by some chance you were, you didn't like it very much. It was disorderly and chaotic. This is not only true in the army, it's true everywhere you will ever go. It's true in life. It's true in your home. And the Bible is even more emphatic than that old NCO. When it comes to your home, *you* are in charge.

So *take* charge. Organize and lead. A very basic part of being male is taking initiative. Considerately? Yes. Thoughtfully? Yes. Lovingly? Yes. Putting the other person's interests above your own? Always. But doing it. Leading and organizing—taking responsibility and initiative.

THE MYTH OF "MUTUAL SUBMISSION"

There is a myth blowing in the winds across our evangelical culture. Myths are fun to think about, but they're not much good to found one's life upon. Myths are largely unfounded. They exist only in imaginary and unverifiable notions. "Mutual submission" is such a myth.

"Mutual submission" is not only an oxymoron, it is an impossibility. It exists neither in theory, nor in practice, nor in Scripture. It is a term used by "biblical feminists" to suggest that Ephesians 5:21 ("Be subject to one another") is intended to interpret 5:22 ("Wives, be subject to your own husbands, as to the Lord"). In actuality, it is quite the opposite of that suggestion. Ephesians 5:22–6:9 is an illustrative *amplification* of 5:21. The apostle is simply stating that there is to be clear order and authority and submission in the community of believers. He then illustrates the principle in actual practice. "For example," wives be subject to husbands, children to parents, slaves to masters, and so on.

The root of the verb "be subject" carries the idea of *serving*. If we are under the control of the Holy Spirit (5:18), one of the things that will begin to change in our lives is the way we relate to those around us, "being subject to one another out of reverence for Christ" (5:21). Paul then gives us three relational illustrations (5:22–6:9)—husband and wife, parents and children, masters and slaves—that should reflect this change in relationships. The bottom line: We must serve one another's needs in such a way as to enable us to become all God designed us to be.

He begins, not by telling the husband to be the head over his wife (he already is), but by calling her to recognize that God designed him for it, and that she needs to *serve* his mandate to function as the head of his marriage and family. Paul tells the husband to recognize his wife's sovereign appointment to be the most important person in all his life, and to *serve* that need by loving and cherishing her.

But to argue, as some Christian feminists do, that "being subject to one another" means that husbands are to be subject to wives is as nonsensical as parents being subject to children or masters being subject to slaves. It is not only conceptually wrong, it is exegetically wrong. The words "be subject to" and "one another" have specific usage patterns and context which absolutely prohibit this possibility.

The universe is subject to Christ (Ephesians 1:22), Christ is subject to God the Father (1 Corinthians 15:28), the Church is subject to Christ (Ephesians 5:24), Christians are subject to God (James 4:7), and wives are subject to husbands (Colossians 3:18).

None of these relationships can be reversed. Submission is always submission. It is always singular in direction when it refers to authority. It is never "mutual." The words of Scripture simply cannot be turned sideways and twisted to force the reverse. Nowhere are husbands told to be subject to wives. Everywhere husbands are told to take the lead.

To be sure, husbands are instructed to take that lead with great amounts of sober responsibility, tender sensitivity, and caring thoughtfulness. But they *must* take the lead. Wayne Grudem captures the need for bringing that strength into balance:

> Within a healthy Christian marriage there will be large elements of mutual consultation and seeking of wisdom, and most decisions will come by consensus between husband and wife. For a wife to be submissive to her husband will probably not often involve obeying actual commands or directives (though it will sometimes include this), for a husband may rather give requests and seek advice and discussion.[4]

Authority exists at every level of existence. It lives at every level of life. That's because authority is part of the very nature of God. And authority exists even *within* the Godhead. The Triune One Himself experiences clear lines of authority within the Trinity. So let's face it. Authority is an essential. It is part and parcel of life itself.

There is authority in the Godhead.
There is authority in the spirit world of angels and demons.
There is authority among nations.
There is authority in churches.
There is authority in homes and families.
And there is authority in marriage.

Life cannot exist without authority. So how do we deal with it? Some years ago an organization of psychologists, in order to help people learn how to deal with stress, did a thorough study of stress and its effects on human beings. When their study was completed, they announced their conclusion in straightforward terms: "Life is stressful. Get used to it."

We would do well to face authority in a similar fashion. We are forced to conclude, "Authority is life. We must get used to it."

And it isn't simply "getting under authority" on the "outside." It's an internal thing, an attitudinal reality that we're after here. It is becoming comfortable with the *principle* of authority, even if the *person* of authority isn't all we might wish them to be. And it is the role of the one in authority to unselfishly help those under authority learn to live at peace with it. Those who comply with authority without understanding the principles tend to become bitter and angry even when they are "coming under" authority. And that anger makes it hard for everyone.

On the other hand, those who understand and accept the principle of authority without "kicking at the goads" internally are more gracious, and therefore influential, in their homes. Before long that healthy attitude which understands and accepts authority turns everything into a "want to" rather than a "have to."

So let's get a grip on authority where we live. Starting at home. Few would argue with the statement that parents have authority over children. Although in our wild, crazy, "question authority" world, even something so obvious as parental authority is up for grabs. It should not surprise us then that authority in the marriage and family has become a matter of debate in our culture. We have become anti-authority across the board. And that, my friend, is at the very heart of ungodliness.

But no matter what winds are blowing in our contemporary culture, a man must make some decisions. Who is he going to listen to? Who is he going to follow? Once a man decides he will follow God and His Word, then all issues, most particularly authority issues, become noticeably more clear. Who will you follow? God, or the whims and fads of a changing society?

Hear this, please…

HEADSHIP IS LEADERSHIP

No ifs, ands, or buts. And no pompous jerks, either!

Both headship and leadership are frequently misunderstood in our "domination-sensitive" culture. The responsibility for leadership which God places upon a man is never to exalt himself over any woman. Pastor and author John Piper offers several descriptive statements that are extremely valuable in helping us define biblical masculinity. I have never seen a more carefully balanced description that captures the spirit of biblical headship and leadership. It is full, precise, practical…and worth the price of this book!

Mature masculine leadership, says Dr. Piper:

- *Serves and sacrifices for a woman's good.* A man is called to lead a woman by serving her—not demanding to be served.
- *Points the woman to Christ.* The husband's role is to help his wife learn to depend on Christ.
- *Makes the most of others' strengths.* A godly leader doesn't try to demonstrate his own superiority. Instead, he brings out the strengths of others. A man should treat his wife like a fellow heir, not like a servant girl or a child.
- *Takes the general responsibility to initiate.* "General" is the key word. In some areas, the wife will take the initiative, according to her gifts. The man, however, has the general responsibility for his family's spiritual welfare. He is not to be passive while his wife shoulders the burden.

- *Expresses itself romantically.* In the sexual relationship the mature man is alert to the romantic gestures that bring his wife joy.
- *Takes the initiative in disciplining the children.* The wife has both authority and leadership over her children along with her husband. She can rightly discipline them in her husband's absence. When both parents are present, however, the man should take charge of discipline rather than watching passively.
- *Finds appropriate ways to express masculinity.* Mature men practice those manners that are associated with the role of a man, such as opening the door for a woman, seating her in a restaurant, and so on.
- *Knows that leadership requires repentance and humility.* Men need to be willing to humble themselves before God because of their failures and their bent toward either avoiding or overstepping their responsibilities.[5]

There is no room in biblical headship for self-inflated big shots. Still, God's Word makes it undeniably clear that "the man" is the head of his home. The man is held responsible for the leadership of his marriage and home! The two words that describe his role most basically are "husband" and "head." These two words are good words—benevolent words—intended to provide our homes with leadership, authority, order, and direction. Rightly understood, they are Camelot-inducing words. If you'll allow me, I'll borrow a couple of definitions from my earlier book, *Tender Warrior,* to nail these terms down.

HUSBAND. The noun form of the word means "manager." A husband is a steward. He is a caretaker and caregiver. He is the man held responsible. In its verb form the word means "to direct, to manage." Those are strong terms that imply effective and responsible leadership.

HEAD. "Head" means director. It means chief. As in headmaster. Principal. Foremost. "Head" equals leadership and authority, as in the head of the class, head of the military, head of the company, head of the church, head of the home, or head man. Head means head.

You see, words mean something. But many Christians today are so shaped by their culture that they actually undertake a few "midnight raids" of their own on the text of Scripture. Under the guise of "cultural context" they seek to disarm the reality of words like "head." But no amount of pseudo-scholarly linguistic gymnastics can change it. Contemporary "biblical feminists" attempt to disarm the meaning of key passages either to promote their own agenda or to make it more palatable to our politically correct culture. But the text will not be denied.

These Christian feminists are finding their task tantamount to holding thousands of ping pong balls below the surface of a swimming pool. Now and then they think they get a couple of them handled. But they no sooner get several of those white balls submerged than a dozen more slip through their fingers and join the myriads which have sprung to the surface and refuse to be submerged.

God's Word will not be denied.

Ironically, as I write these words I am also preparing to speak at an upcoming Promise Keeper rally in my own state of Oregon. The rally is still a week away but the politically correct of Eugene, Oregon have been at work for weeks. Protests have been organized. The media have been alerted. Even the University of Oregon student body president is up in arms. Over what? A clear-cut on the hills south of Eugene? Some newly discovered lethal public health epidemic? A hazardous waste spill?

No, nothing like that. The young student body president has bought into the winds of culture. Evidently he thinks men have no business meeting together. He's indignant that some men are gathering in his own community to help themselves become better men, better husbands, and better fathers. Bottom line, he's upset because women aren't invited.

Now doesn't that strike you as a bit absurd? *Inviting women to a seminar on becoming better men?* Might as well invite me to a seminar on becoming a better giraffe or ballerina. What are these kinds of protests about, really? What's the root problem here?

In a word, *fear.*

Fear of self-centered tyranny. Fear of Hitleresque headship. And that fear is not without some basis. Given how tyrannical many men have acted in the past, I can understand at least some of this fear in our culture. So what's the solution? Where do we go from here? What can you and I do about all this confusion?

The solution is manly love. You and I as Christian men must develop and practice a thorough-going, Bible-grounded, masculine-flavored love. We must embody the spirit of Paul's instructions in Ephesians 4:1-2, to "Walk in a manner worthy of the calling with which you have been called, with all [meekness] and gentleness."

"M E E K"   I S N ' T   W H A T   Y O U   T H I N K

Meekness is a marvelous word, though greatly discredited in our culture. At its core, meekness requires great strength. In fact, a careful distilling of its background often conceptualizes it as "strength under control." Meekness has to do with responsiveness to authority. Southern horse breeders, for example, are known to hold to the premise that "the meekest horse wins the race." By that they mean that the true champion is the horse, well bred and muscular, who has most clearly responded to his training. He is the picture of strength under control.

The same may be said of human beings. The meekest man wins the throne. The humble man makes the finest leader. The most effective leader is the man—strong in his soul and muscular in his spirit—who is most responsive to his Lord. For example, Moses, perhaps one of the most reluctant but effective leaders in human history, was described as "the meekest man on the face of the earth" (Numbers 12:3, paraphrased).

If meekness is *weakness*, the word could never apply to Moses. The man was a superb leader. Think about it! He led more than two million people on a forty-year camping trip without any showers! Any man who can successfully move two grumpy complainers two feet in two hours is something of an accomplished leader. Moses moved two million for four decades. If there ever was to be such a thing, the guy should receive the Nobel Prize for Leadership in all of human history! And he was a meek man.

Phillip Keller captures some of the spirit of meekness as an essential leadership quality:

Meek men are not weak men...they refuse to shove, push, and throw their weight around. They do not win their wars with brutal battles and fierce fights. They win their way into a hundred hearts and homes with the passport of a lowly, loving spirit.

Their unique genius is their gentleness. This quality of life does not come from a position of feeble impotence, but rather from a tremendous inner strength and serenity. Only the strong, stable spirit can afford to be gentle.... This quality is much more than a thin veneer of proper propriety or superficial politeness.... Rather, it is the epitome of a laid-down life, poured out, laid out, lived on behalf of others.[6]

Indeed, the solution to the exaggerated fear of, and disrespect for, headship in our day is a manly love. Around your home, another word for thorough, biblical, manly love is *headship*. It is the king in your chest. It is the king in a man living biblically. It is King Jesus, alive in the hearts of His sons, living out leadership, divine style.

In a word, it is "sacrifice."

Headship, you see, is linked directly to savior-ship. And savior-ship is self-sacrificing. The Bible says so in one incredibly emphatic clarification of reality. "Husbands, love your wives *just as* Christ loved the church *and gave himself up for her"* (Ephesians 5:25, NIV, emphasis added).

There you have it. Headship is always "giving up" one's self. Headship is never "lording it over" another. So, Christian husband, your kingly crown is a crown of thorns. In describing the headship of the Christian husband, C. S. Lewis said:

Christian law has crowned him in the permanent relationship of marriage, bestowing—or should I say, inflicting?—a certain "headship" on him.... The husband is the head of the wife just in so far as he is to her what Christ is to the Church. He is to love her as Christ loved the Church—read on—and gave his life for her (Ephesians 5:25). *This headship, then, is most fully embodied not in the husband we should all wish to be but in him whose marriage is most like a crucifixion;* whose wife receives most and gives least, is most unworthy of him, is—in her own mere nature—least lovable. For the Church has no beauty but what the Bridegroom gives her; he does not find, but makes her lovely. The chrism of this terrible coronation is to be seen not in the joys of any man's marriage but in its sorrow, in the sickness and sufferings of a good wife or the faults of a bad one; in his unwearying (never paraded) care or his inexhaustible forgiveness; forgiveness, not acquiescence. As Christ sees in the flawed, proud, fanatical, or lukewarm Church on earth that Bride who will one day be without spot or wrinkle, and labours to produce the latter, so the husband whose headship is Christ-like (and he is allowed no other sort) never despairs....

The sternest feminist [Lewis wrote this prior to his death in 1963!] need not grudge my sex the crown offered to it either in the Pagan or the Christian mystery. For the one is of paper and the other is of thorns. The real danger is not that husbands may grasp the latter too eagerly; but that they will allow or compel their wives to usurp it.[7] (emphasis added)

Think about it. Christ did not come to earth for Himself, but for you. Your marriage is not given to you for you; it is given to you for *her*. Your marriage is not a gift for your satisfaction; it is a labor for her development. She is not a gratuity to you; you are a sacrifice for her. You are not drawn to her for her beauty; you are to render her beautiful through your own pain.

The Christian husband works at great length to actually produce a beauty in his wife. He prays, "Lord, help me to make my wife the most beautiful woman in the world to me." And he puts the feet of mature, humble sacrifice to his prayers.

THE HEART OF THE MATTER

So let's take a good look at the heart of the King that God intended to thrive behind every man's rib cage.

The heart of the king is a *provisionary* heart. A man is intended to be a provider. As I explained in an earlier book, the key part of the word is "vision." The "pro" part of the word indicates "before" or "ahead of time." "Vision" obviously speaks of sight or seeing. *Pro*-vision means "vision before hand." The king in a man looks ahead, anticipates needs, spots potential dangers, defines direction, and charts a wise course. He is an overseer, in the truest sense of the word.

This is no king who lounges in a La-Z-Boy recliner throne with servants bringing him sandwiches and ale all day. No, this is a king who's on his horse, riding the borderlands of his realm, checking the supports of the bridges, chatting with his troops, and scanning the horizon for potential enemies.

Out of the heart of the king flows a sense of purpose, stability, and justice. The king in a man possesses strong qualities of order, establishing reasonable patterns and structures, and maintaining a sense of calm. Moore and Gillette call it "the energy of just and creative ordering." Listen to their description of the king's heart. According to them, this kingly energy...

> brings maintenance and balance.... It looks upon the world with a firm but kindly eye. It sees others in all their weakness and in all their talent and worth. It honors them...it guides them and nurtures them...it is not envious because it is secure, as the King, in its own worth. It rewards and encourages...others.[8]

Sound like Anyone you know?

This is the kingly trait in a man's heart that expresses itself when he takes all the necessary steps to see to it that his wife and children prosper—mentally, emotionally, and spiritually, as well as financially. This is the strength to reassure others. It is the power to calmly turn chaos into order. This is the energy that longs to build peace and security. This is the biblical shepherd-king.

Hopefully you have been able to see this kingly masculine heart in operation in your extended family. Ideally you saw it in your dad. Perhaps you saw it in an uncle or a grandfather. Or a brother. Or a boss. Or a friend, neighbor, teacher, or pastor.

Unfortunately, the king pillar can slip out of balance. It can lean left or right. When it leans right, it gives birth to tyranny. No one wants to live near a tyrant. When it tilts to the left, it caves in to passivity and weakness. No one wants to live with a weakling. The tyrant and weakling know only fear, and envy, and hatred. They are the craftsmen of abuse and exploitation. And yes, it *is* a fine line, sometimes, between these extremes.

The king disciplines his children by spanking; the tyrant assaults his children by beating. The king encourages his employees with recognition; the weakling controls his by belittling. The king out of balance is overly sensitive to criticism, and finds no joy in others' successes.

As with Herod, it is the tyrant who destroys his own sons (and daughters). Today few men would actually kill their own children as Herod did. But many maim them for life by verbal assault, by depreciation of their aspirations, or by simply ignoring their accomplishments.

When the king is balanced, when the king is truly "at home" with himself and his responsibility, the realm flourishes. When the king is home the castle is secure. When Dad is functioning rightly, everyone enjoys stability.

When the king function is out of balance in a man, everything is shaky. People tremble. Relationships totter. Finances crumble. Stomachs churn. Hopes fall low. And the home feels more like an abandoned hospital ward than a secure castle.

A true king is neither a tyrant nor a weakling. And never a passive "victim of circumstances." Perhaps the only thing worse than a dictator is a leader who refuses to lead at all. The king is never passive. For when the king fails, the kingdom falls. When the king is absent or abusive, the family experiences utter dysfunction. The climate grows oppressive. Disorder and chaos rule.

But when Dad is dad, when the man is the man, there is peace, prosperity, justice, and love. As another described it, home is but an earlier heaven. Eden arrives at your address. What *confidence* that kind of leadership brings to any realm, whether to a nation, a business, a church, or even a family of two.

A provisionary king keeps the larger issues before his family (or organization) so they won't be overcome by temporary setbacks or the disorienting fog of daily circumstances. Clarity of vision is critical to health, and the king lives with his eyes on the horizon, always asking the right kinds of questions in order to secure, as best he can, the future for his family.

Bottom line, the king provides a climate in his realm where all can exercise their gifts and flourish. The king gives definition to life.

Such kingly moments of clarification cannot be programmed or scheduled. They don't rise from a formal agenda. They are the quality times that rise spontaneously out of deliberate quantities of time spent in relationship.

Admiral Richard Byrd, one of American history's foremost explorers, said it for all of us when he reached the end of his illustrious life. On his deathbed, he put it all in perspective for every man who would be king:

> In the end, only two things matter to a man, regardless of who he is, and they're the affection and understanding of his family. Anything and everything else he creates are insubstantial. They are merely ships given over to the mercy of the winds and the tides of prejudice. But the family is an everlasting anchorage, a quiet harbor where a man's ships can be left to (ride) the moorings of pride and loyalty.[9]

In these next couple of chapters, we're going to study the heart of the king in action. You'll be a better man for it. Say a prayer, and let's drive on.

Like a roaring lion or a charging bear
*   is a wicked man ruling over a helpless people.*
A tyrannical ruler lacks judgment.

PROVERBS 28:15-16, NIV

"The God of Israel spoke,
*   the Rock of Israel said to me:*
'When one rules over men in righteousness,
*   when he rules in the fear of God,*
he is like the light of morning at sunrise
*   on a cloudless morning,*
like the brightness after rain
*   that brings the grass from the earth.' "*

THE LAST WORDS OF DAVID THE KING, C. 1000 B.C.
2 SAMUEL 23:3-4, NIV

Live as free men, but do not use your
freedom as a cover-up for evil; live as ser-
vants of God. Show proper respect to
everyone.... Be considerate as you live
with your wives, and treat them with
respect...not lording it over those entrusted
to you, but being examples.... Humble
yourselves, therefore, under God's mighty
hand, that he may lift you up in due
time.... To him be the power forever and
ever.

PETER THE APOSTLE, C. A.D. 65
1 PETER 2:16-17; 3:7; 5:3,6,11, NIV

CHAPTER 5

A REALM AT RISK

There are a lot of impostors out there; have you noticed?

One of the best was Fred Demara. Check that—I actually mean Ferdinand Waldo Demara, Jr., alias Martin Godgart, school teacher. Or was that Dr. Robert Linton French, also known as Brother John Payne? Then again, the name might have been Ben W. Jones, the Huntsville Prison warden. Or was it Dr. Joseph Cyr, Royal Canadian Navy surgeon?

In actuality, it was *all the above*. The guy did it all. He went where he wanted to go and played the role he wished to play. Demara successfully masqueraded as a teacher, a monk, a physician, a prison warden, and a *surgeon*. Fred pulled it off—surgery included—with aplomb.

By gathering official stationery, writing a few fake letters, manufacturing some credentials, and playing the role with consummate acting skill, Fred continually appeared to be something he wasn't. He will forever be known as The Great Impostor.

But Fred the Fabulous Fake isn't alone. Too many men are great impostors—some even "greater" than he. By gathering some professional credentials, collecting a wife, manufacturing a few children, and playing a role, they appear to be something they aren't—real men.

I see them every day in my ministry. Claiming to be the heads of their homes, they act more like banana republic dictators than kings. Masquerading as kings, they are actually nothing more than schoolyard bullies who never grew up.

They're pretend men. Impostor kings. I watched one in action the other day.

He sat in my office next to his wife. Ostensibly he was there for marriage counseling. On the surface, he was "trying to make (my) marriage better." In actuality he was trying to enlist my help to beat up on his wife. His fake plea was for "more communication." But the poor fool had no idea what that term meant. He thought it meant everybody doing what he wanted. There in my office, with veins standing out on his neck, he pounded his fist and shouted, "We've gotta get some *communication* going here!"

The word was ill-fitted for his mouth. What he was really shouting for was not communication at all. It was old-fashioned, even primitive, *domination.* Actual communication—the developing of a common understanding—was the furthest thing from his mind. He was a fake. Nothing more than a gorilla in a man-suit. All he wanted was to bully "the little lady" into "meeting his needs."

He was no more a pro-visionary king than Hitler was a Sunday school teacher. He was what some have called a "highchair tyrant." Like the spoiled child banging his spoon on his highchair and demanding to be fed, he was an infant, albeit in a thirty-something body.

Men throwing their weight around are not kings. They're as phony as a gold ring out of a gum-ball machine. *Real* kings love. Authentic kings care, provide, serve, and sacrifice. True kings give themselves away.

And, in the process, kings lead.

But impostor kings are none of the above. Impostor kings see themselves as the center. Impostor kings are little boys trying to wear man clothes, but they are too small to fill them out.

A wife beater is an impostor. A drug dealer is a pretend man. A vacillating politician is a fake. A pompous minister is a masquerade. The flirting playboy is a charlatan. The father who never manages to attend his kids' events is a pretender. The boss who ridicules is an impostor. So is the coach who belittles his players. None are men. None are kings. Their "crowns" are of the cardboard variety given away at hamburger stands.

Listen…the king in a man is that inner driving sense which compels him to provide for others. The king in a man understands that his headship assignment is to lead his marriage and family in the kind of united partnership that glorifies God and builds people. The king in a man does not see himself as the center. He exists for others! And he sees himself as providing order, justice, mercy, and stability so others can thrive.

K I N G M O S E S

Moses, one of the largest figures in the Old Testament, was a king. He was the most powerful man alive among the millions of his people. Oh, like most of us, no one was actually calling him "king." He would have been the first to remind you that he had spent most of his life as a back-country shepherd, and would have remained so, had God not tapped him on the shoulder.

Moses' great moments as a king came as he was carefully providing ("looking ahead") for his people. With the King of kings beside him, he scanned the horizons of the Promised Land from the top of Mt. Sinai. Moses was at his kingly best when, under the inspiration of the Almighty, he was recording "the law of Moses." Together, a man and his Lord laid out the most beautiful set of family values the world has ever known. Representing the Lord as the head of the family-nation, Moses articulated laws, principles, and values which would govern the people for their own good and development. Up until the last few decades, those laws were *still* posted in classrooms and meeting halls across our land.

That is the way of kings. Whether serving kingdoms or companies or churches or families, the king in a man's chest beats to secure justice, establish order, ensure stability, and provide structure. The king in a man develops what one rather kingly document called the United States Constitution, calls "domestic tranquillity."

It is the way of kings and fathers. For the king in a man is most like a wise father. Both firm and gentle. Loving and disciplining as the situation requires, but always benevolent over the long haul. And always giving himself away and "sacrificing" his resources for the good of his people.

Unfortunately the king in a man is a dying breed in our culture. The men who wrote our constitution were kings. They looked way ahead. And for two hundred years now this nation has enjoyed the fruit of their provision. But by contrast, some of the men who today *interpret* our founders' constitution cannot see beyond the end of their own legal noses. As a result, justice is fading. Security is eroding. Kingly leadership is in short supply. And the nation is adrift.

But far more devastating than the disintegration of our justice system, is the utter deterioration of our family system. And here again, men are at the heart of the issue. In our society we see everywhere the absence of the king. With our general rejection of authority, and our repudiation of male headship in particular, we have let our homes fend for themselves.

It doesn't take a rocket scientist to observe that the most common element in America's most dysfunctional homes is a father who is immature, passive...or simply not there. The result is disorder, chaos, and unspeakable unhappiness. In past years, this has been particularly obvious among our black families. But the problem is fast approaching epidemic proportions across *all* groups comprising our society.

Whatever the race, nation, culture, or neighborhood, it is axiomatic: When the king pillar crumbles, civilization falls in upon itself. The resulting devastation is much deeper and more far-reaching than the fall of any silly stock market.

After years of careful research, Rutgers University sociologist David Popenoe summarizes the calamity with clarity:

> The decline of fatherhood is one of the most basic, unexpected, and extraordinary social trends of our time. The trend can be captured in a single telling statistic: in just three decades, from 1960 to 1990, the percentage of children living apart from their biological fathers more than doubled.... If this rate continues, by the turn of the century nearly 50 percent of American children will be going to sleep each night without being able to say goodnight to their dads.... Father absence is a major force lying behind many of the attention-grabbing issues that dominate the news: crime and delinquency; premature sexuality and out-of-wedlock teen births; deteriorating educational achievement; depression, substance abuse, and alienation among teenagers; and the growing number of women and children in poverty.... The United States...may be the first society in history in which children are distinctly worse off than adults.[1]

The experiment has been run, the results are in, and the bottom line is this: If we men don't get our act (and our masculinity) together, there is no hope for our country. As we used to drill in sophomore typing class: "Now is the time for all good men to come to the aid of their country."

It is time for the men in our country, and the king in our men, to be the provider-leaders God intended them to be. It's time to shore up and balance the king pillar in a man's heart. But how do we go about it?

WHAT DO KINGS DO?

The role of masculinity in the home and in society is indisputably foundational. When manhood runs amuck, everyone suffers. When the king in a man is fully functional, the home (and therefore the neighborhood, community, nation, and culture) will experience greater calm. When a man is the capable, caring leader he should be, people can flourish. Emotions are stable. Out-of-control behaviors fade. And people grow into love and trust. When the king is in his castle, so to speak, his wife is energized, his children are purposeful, and the relationships within the family become the springboard from which the challenges of life are successfully met.

- *It is the king in a man* that encourages his wife to "go ahead, Hon," and get that Master's degree.
- *It is the king in a man* that climbs out from behind his office desk and slips into a chair at the back of his child's piano recital, or patrols the sidelines of a soccer game, or takes his young teen to the youth group.
- *It is the king in a man* that appropriately confronts injustice at work in a manner that can be respected by his superiors and accepted by his subordinates.
- *It is the king in a man* that reaches out to lift up—to empower a struggling alcoholic to seek help or to encourage a failing husband to get counsel.
- *It is the king in a man* that keeps his cool when everyone else is losing theirs. His is the voice that affirms with authority, calms with understanding, and controls with wisdom. His is the decision

that, after thoughtful deliberation, cuts through the mess and provides a direction that allows each family member to feel respected and directed. His is the hand that administers punishment appropriately. And his is the voice that issues praise lavishly.

Most of us have experienced a king in action along the way. We've noticed a positive change in atmosphere when he walked into the room. We've felt his presence, and it made things better. Without noticing all the details, we experienced a calm. It was a relieving, satisfying, "It'll be okay" kind of peace. His words were creative, constructive, and comforting. Maybe it was only a couple of words of comfort after a child sustained a skinned knee...or a broken heart. Maybe it was his encouragement after the big game was lost. Or his healthy, balanced perspective after a key victory. But somehow, his very presence made it "all right."

By contrast, many of us have also experienced the king pillar leaning way out of balance. When a tyrant walks into a room, everyone tightens. Shoulders shrink, eyes narrow, minds close, and fear reigns. Tyrants are destructive. They breed discomfort, paranoia, and rigidity. People around them rarely experience calm. Imagine living with Saul, the spear-throwing schizophrenic. Or Herod, the paranoid baby killer. Or how about sitting in a war council with Saddam Hussein? One wrong word and you'll leave the room with your head tucked neatly under your arm.

The tyrant breeds fear because he is himself afraid. His insecurity exploits and abuses others. Full of bluster and bravado on the outside, he is most often a shriveling coward just under the skin. For all his huffing and puffing, his angry tyranny is a self-protective facade. To maintain that facade, he dominates his wife, abuses his daughters, and denigrates his sons. His tools run the gamut from the largely psychological and verbal, all the way to physical abuse. That is no man at all. That is a wimp, a pitiful bully-boy with a paper crown.

I know of a great impostor in our community who dresses like a model for *GQ* magazine. He enjoys a smooth and effective gift of gab. He is an exceptionally capable and talented athlete. He attends a church, listens to the sermons, and probably takes notes. And he claims he wants to walk with God. But he also hits his wife!

Sorry, fella, that's no man. Any male who raises so much as a finger to strike a woman is not a man. He is a pathetic, self-absorbed wuss. He thinks he is a powerful man, but he is not even strong enough to control his own emotions. He is the greatest of impostors.

That kind of man makes Fred Demara's act look like dress-up day in kindergarten. And if you watch carefully, you can see that same pitiful self-centeredness carry over from his family into all of his life. Such an impostor king abuses his employees, raids his company for his own profit, and lords it over his community in various forms of manipulation. No one wants to live with such a man. He is a highchair infant trying to bully his way into a place at the table of manliness. But he will never make it. He will never find a seat among those truly confident in their manhood. Those who know him will know him for what he is—just one more childish tyrant. A counterfeit man. An impersonator.

Never abuse the power of the king in your chest. Biblical servant-kings are just that—servant-leaders. Never abusers of any form of power. Possibly the most grave danger attached to the opportunities and responsibilities of a king is the risk that men will see the power in their hands as a *weapon* they can use for their own benefit, at the expense of those under their care. This is precisely the heart of the outcry of the feminist movement. *And they have a point.* I believe the feminist movement was birthed by the unmanly abuse of power on the part of impostor men.

Be extremely alert to it in your own life. From time to time it bites all of us, and we've got to get over it. This abuse of power can show itself in you in a variety of forms, all incredibly destructive:

Emotional abuse
Emotional abuse is using the power of a king to ignore or squash the emotional needs of those under his care. It translates in a variety of ways. An unwillingness to spend time with someone who longs to spend time with you. Deliberately ignoring someone who speaks to you. Treating others with contempt, as though they were somehow less than you, or unworthy of your notice and attention. Approaching situations with neither justice nor mercy in your heart. Abandoning someone who depends on you.

Verbal abuse

Verbal abuse is using the verbal power of a king to wound, disable, or dishonor those under his care. This includes speaking in dishonoring, cold, callous, or demeaning ways to those we are responsible for. It shows up when we use words to hide from our own hurt, pain, or insecurity in such a way that we hurt or disarm those around us. It takes place when we hurl words as weapons, rather than giving them as gifts.

Physical abuse

Physical abuse is using the physical power of a king to pound others into servanthood, for the king's sake. Men tend to be physically stronger than women and children. When this position of strength is used against those in our care and not for them, it is abusive. Whatever the reasons or excuses (and I've heard some wild ones), this is *never* justified.

Sexual abuse

Sexual abuse is using the sexual power of a king to control some or all under his care, for his personal sexual pleasure and fulfillment. Men who use their wives as sex toys or mere playful objects of pleasure, just to fulfill their sexual needs, are not functioning as kings but are rapists loose in the kingdom. True kings look out for the sexual fulfillment of their wives, and leave other women alone. And men who use children or other helpless victims for their sexual pleasure are madmen who need help of the sternest kind.

Spiritual abuse

Spiritual abuse is using the spiritual power of a king to "lord it over" those under his care, rather than serving their needs. Men who use the Bible as a weapon against those under their care, to get what they want for their own benefit or ego satisfaction, are not functioning as kings but as spiritual bullies. Kings teach and live the truth, they don't wield it as a threatening club or try to cram it down people's throats. The Word of God is intended to be a lamp, not a Molotov cocktail lobbed through a window. It is a mirror to stimulate personal change. It was never intended to be used as a ruse to create a house of horrors.

And one more thing while we're talking about masquerades. There is yet another breed of king impostor. And, in the long run, I suppose he is every bit as destructive as an abuser.

The Overly Passive Leader

The overly passive king is an impostor, too. No, he doesn't rant and rave, throw his weight around, or domineer. Truth is, he doesn't do much of anything. And that's just the problem. While occupying the office of a king, he is nothing more than a figurehead. He doesn't lead at all.

He goes to work, eats and sleeps, and manages to bring home some kind of check once or twice a month. (Give him credit for that.) But with that check, he evidently thinks he's off the hook. As if bringing home the bacon was the consummation of his responsibility, or that he'd somehow "done enough."

Just as difficult to live with as the tyrant, in many respects, is the impostor whose king pillar is out of balance in the opposite direction—leaning into passivity and weakness. Too many husbands and fathers, like the thumb-sucking Prince John of Disney's *Robin Hood* fame, simply live off their position while refusing to exercise any real leadership. In the process, they allow their passivity to undermine the well-being of their family and their entire community.

This kind of king is an abdicator. Abdicators are as bad as, possibly worse than, simple impostors. And today, men are abdicating in droves, tossing off the God-given mantel of masculinity and opting for a life of their own.

Nobody said it was easy being a real man in today's world. It is flat tough to walk the line. On the one hand, we're to be strong. On the other, tender. And with our culture nipping at our ankles, and hostile voices shrilling in our ears, it isn't easy to find the balance.

C. S. Lewis, as always, said it clearly:

It is painful, being a man, to have to assert the privilege, or the burden, which Christianity lays upon my own sex. I am crushingly aware of how inadequate most of us are, on our actual and historical individualities, to fill the place prepared for us.[2]

Oh, how right he is. Left to ourselves we are totally inadequate. But "the place prepared for us" is still there, and it must be occupied. As Christian men, we must throw ourselves at the feet of the King of kings, and beg His wisdom, insight, grace, and blessing. Still, *the mantle must be worn.* When a man refuses it, everybody is the loser for it.

Whatever our frustration—a culture that bites us, wives who won't follow us, kids who won't cooperate with us—we do not have the option of just tossing up our hands and walking away. God-honoring men don't quit. God-honoring men don't abdicate, or try to hide in the baggage from God's anointing, like the pitiful king-designate Saul.

God-honoring men stay at it. And stay. And stay. And stay. Growing and improving. Taking the hits and pushing on down the field. Moving in one direction over the long haul. Many times it's two steps forward, one back. But it's still movement; it's keeping on keeping on.

Too many of us men, however, are just tossing in the towel. Too many of us run the risk of abdicating to our wives. When we as servant-kings do not assume our responsibilities, probably the most common shift that occurs in the home is that the wife assumes the role of leader. Whether it's based in her own strong personality as compared to ours, or in our refusal to accept the headship, she takes over. (Hey, *someone* has to do it!) As time goes on, this usually kindles resentment on her part because she is left alone to make all the tough decisions. And it causes resentment on his part because "she's bossy" or "taking over." More often than not she is one very frustrated lady, waiting without much hope for her man to *be* one—after God's design.

Sometimes we abdicate to our children. Disaster! A growing pattern in homes today is for dads and moms both to abdicate their roles in the family to the kids, allowing the children to become their own "leaders." Too many families are child-centered and child-led. Increasingly in my counseling office, I am hearing engaged couples talk about growing up in situations where dad, and even mom, left them to lead their own lives from a very early age…and therefore, in effect, to lead the family by their choices for themselves. These essentially parentless men and women become adults who are used to making decisions, but have no history of guidance to know how to make *good* decisions. Usually, they are frustrated and angry to the core.

Possibly the most common abdication today is our tendency as men to abdicate to our culture. Television, radio, schools, and youth and adult clubs are probably dictating more direction in many homes in America than the God-designated head of the home. There isn't anything necessarily wrong with any of these influential factors in our homes—unless the man is using them as an excuse to abdicate his responsibilities as family leader and head.

When you're up against it, man, and tempted to walk away from it all, take a few minutes and remind yourself of your heavenly Father's presence with you. He didn't commission you to do a job and then leave you dangling to figure out where He went.

> And Jesus came up and spoke to them, saying, "All authority has been given to Me in heaven and on earth. Go therefore and make disciples of all the nations, baptizing them in the name of the Father and the Son and the Holy Spirit, teaching them to observe all that I commanded you; and lo, *I am with you always,* even to the end of the age." (Matthew 28:18-20, emphasis added)

When Jesus promised, "I am with you always," He was saying, "I am with you each step of the way." He is the ultimate King of kings. And He has not called us to be or do *anything* in life but that He will be right there at our sides as a strong Helper, Advocate, and Mentor. He has promised to be there—in the face of each agonizing choice, in the pressure of each challenge to our leadership, in the thick of every battle that rages across our personal landscape. It is indeed "lonely at the top"...but we are not really alone.

And don't get to feeling sorry for yourself. It's a temptation every man faces— "the lonely howl of the top dog." It is so easy for us to have the attitude, "Hey, I never volunteered for this job! I didn't even have a vote in being chosen. I don't *want* this responsibility; it's not fair that I have to bear the weight of all this stuff."

Your emotions may tell you all that and more. But friend...that's *life.* And if we persist in feeling sorry for ourselves we are going to end up trying to buck God and His design—and life doesn't work too well that way. James says, "Humble yourselves before the Lord, and he will lift you up" (James 4:10, NIV).

If we are finding ourselves in a nonstop pity party, we need to come back to the bottom line of bottom lines: Am I bowing the knees of my heart before almighty God or not? Only in that position can I accept what He has designed for my life, whether I feel like it or not. Only then can I accept what doesn't seem "fair" in human terms. Only then can I get on with my life and accept the mantle of king that He has given me. Only then will those under my care be able to begin to flourish toward their full potential by God's design. When we humble ourselves before Him, He will exalt us. He will lift us up.

Speaking of doubt, don't spend a bunch of time doubting yourself either. It's a dead-end. Admittedly, it's pretty easy for a man to look at all the talented and knowledgeable people around him and say to himself, "Criminy, *who am I* to be wearing this mantle? I'm not qualified for this." As you well know, you are not the first (nor will you be the last) to think such thoughts. As a matter of fact, there will be those around you who may seriously question or challenge your right to sit in that kingly chair in which God has placed you. You will hear these questions both from your own mind, and from the lips of others:

"What makes you think you are better than anyone else?"
Of course, the question *assumes* that men who lead do so because they think they are better qualified than anyone else around them. (Just see to it that you don't give anyone a justifiable excuse to think you really are stuck on yourself!) In reality, the only reason in the world men must act as the heads of homes is because that is what God decided. It has nothing to do with being "better," but rather with being chosen by the One who has the right to choose. Begin to believe that; let the truth of it humble you and keep you on your knees—the most kingly posture of all.

"Who do you think you are, anyway?"
Ouch! That stings, doesn't it? Again, it assumes you are leading because you have somehow "earned" a right to lead. Not so. You don't "deserve" anything—except the wrath of a righteous God, along with the rest of

sinful humanity. You were just *appointed.* Frankly, on your own individual merits, you may not *be* the best in your home. But you're the only one God assigned to the job. So you need to get used to it. It's nothing less than your "calling" from God.

"What gives you the right to sit up there in the head seat?"
Nothing. Not one darn thing. But God is not a "thing," He's a person. And what He has given you as the head of your home is not so much a "right" as a full-orbed *responsibility.* The question is not "what" but "who." And that answer is clear. God determined the chain of command. I may not like it any more than my wife or kids, but that doesn't change the reality. God seldom determines His design on advice from me or anyone else.

"Do you really think you can do this king thing better than someone else?"
Not particularly. In fact, I'm pretty sure there are numbers of others who could do just as well or better at it. But the issue, again, is not ability. It is accountability. I am accountable to the One who is the King of kings. And He told me to do it. Period. I certainly hope to do the best job possible, and I will greatly benefit from the gifts and skills of others around me. But I can't transfer the accountability! I'm going to answer to God for this.

The toughest objections, however, usually don't come from others. They come from within. How many times have you complained…

"But I'm not a natural born leader!"
So, who is? We all sound a lot like the reluctant Moses, don't we? Yes, some have the opportunity and encouragement to move in that direction sooner and faster than some others, but the most effective leadership is a learned skill, not a "natural" ability. And never forget—the Bible insists God never calls us to what He does not enable us to do.

And then there's that voice in the back of each of our minds, filling us with fear, saying…

"Okay. Say I give it my best shot and no one follows?"
Welcome to the club. We've all entertained thoughts like that. "This job is way over my head, and I'm going to look pretty foolish when no one

accepts my leadership. This is all ready to backfire." Yes, fear is real. It is also an incredible debilitator. We've simply got to push through it by faith, and pursue God's stated intentions.

Paul, perhaps dealing with some fears of his own, gave us these words to cling to:

> I don't mean to say that I have already achieved these things or that I have already reached perfection! But I keep working toward that day when I will finally be all that Christ saved me for and wants me to be. No dear friends, I am still not all I should be, but I am focusing all my energies on this one thing: Forgetting the past and looking forward to what lies ahead, I strain to reach the end of the race and receive the prize for which God, through Christ Jesus, is calling us up to heaven. (Philippians 3:12-14, NLT)

Let's work, for a bit, on this fear of "no one following."

Some wag has said, "If you think you are leading and turn around to find no one there, then you're merely taking a walk." Sometimes it feels that way. Many men have tried their hand at leading at some point and found no one in the family following. So, the next time they strike out in the lead position, it is awfully easy to do so with some serious hesitation in their step. It doesn't take long before that fear can become *paralyzing*. Fear is potent stuff. But if we don't keep working at it, we will never develop our ability to lead effectively.

Guess what? It's back to the bottom line again: I lead because God appointed me to do so and will hold me accountable for it. Who *follows* is another issue. But that which stares me in the face is the responsibility to lead. God didn't call me to lead *only* when someone else decides to follow. I am to lead, and in the process, to make it as easy as possible for others to follow my lead. But no matter what, come Hades or high water, I am to LEAD.

We live in a culture that breeds contempt for leadership in certain arenas, and unfortunately, men leading in the home is one of the most obvious of those places. We should never stop leading if others are not following, but we should ask ourselves if the way we are leading is hindering those under our care. God-ordained leaders are to serve the needs (not wants) of the followers. It is much easier to follow someone who is devoted to serving you than someone who is leading for his own benefit and glory.

My friend, it can be done. I read recently about one man who decided he was going to "go for it"—in spite of whatever response or lack of response there was to his attempts. He was determined to take responsibility for setting the direction in his home and marriage, even though no one was willing to follow at first. A woman by the name of Larsen wrote up his story:

> Larry and Jo Ann were an ordinary couple. They lived in an ordinary house on an ordinary street. Like any other ordinary couple, they struggled to make ends meet and to do the right things for their children.
>
> They were ordinary in yet another way—they had their squabbles. Much of their conversation concerned what was wrong in their marriage and who was to blame.
>
> Until one day when a most extraordinary event took place. "You know, Jo Ann, I've got a magic chest of drawers. Every time I open them, they're full of socks and underwear," Larry said. "I want to thank you for filling them all these years."
>
> Jo Ann stared at her husband over the top of her glasses. "What do you want, Larry?"
>
> "Nothing. I just want you to know I appreciate those magic drawers."
>
> This wasn't the first time Larry had done something odd, so Jo Ann pushed the incident out of her mind until a few days later. "Jo Ann, thank you for recording so many correct check numbers in the ledger this month. You put down the right numbers 15 out of 16 times. That's a record."
>
> Disbelieving what she had heard, Jo Ann looked up from her mending. "Larry, you're always complaining about my recording the wrong check numbers. Why stop now?"

"No reason. I just wanted you to know I appreciate the effort you're making."

Jo Ann shook her head and went back to her mending. "What's got into him?" she mumbled to herself.

Nevertheless, the next day when Jo Ann wrote a check at the grocery store, she glanced at her checkbook to confirm that she had put down the right check number. "Why do I suddenly care about those dumb check numbers?" she asked herself.

She tried to disregard the incident, but Larry's strange behavior intensified.

"Jo Ann, that was a great dinner," he said one evening. "I appreciate all your effort. Why, in the past 15 years I'll bet you've fixed over 14,000 meals for me and the kids."

Then "Gee, Jo Ann, the house looks spiffy. You've really worked hard to get it looking so good." And even "Thanks, Jo Ann, for just being you. I really enjoy your company."

Jo Ann was growing worried. "Where's the sarcasm, the criticism?" she wondered.

Her fears that something peculiar was happening to her husband were confirmed by 16-year-old Shelly, who complained, "Dad's gone bonkers, Mom. He just told me I looked nice. With all this makeup and these sloppy clothes, he still said it. That's not Dad, Mom. What's wrong with him?"

Whatever was wrong, Larry didn't get over it. Day in and day out he continued focusing on the positive. Over the weeks, Jo Ann grew more accustomed to her mate's unusual behavior and occasionally even gave him a grudging "Thank you." She prided herself on taking it all in stride, until one day something so peculiar happened, she became completely discombobulated:

"I want you to take a break," Larry said. "I am going to do the dishes. So please take your hands off that frying pan and leave the kitchen."

(Long, long pause.) "Thank you, Larry. Thank you very much!"

Jo Ann's step was now a little lighter, her self-confidence

higher, and once in a while she hummed. She didn't seem to have as many blue moods anymore. "I rather like Larry's new behavior," she thought.

That would be the end of the story except one day another most extraordinary event took place. This time it was Jo Ann who spoke. "Larry," she said, "I want to thank you for going to work and providing for us all these years. I don't think I've ever told you how much I appreciate it."

Larry has never revealed the reason for his dramatic change of behavior no matter how hard Jo Ann has pushed for an answer, and so it will likely remain one of life's mysteries. But it's one I'm thankful to live with.

You see, I am Jo Ann.[3]

It's only one example, but you get the picture. Larry swallowed hard, and took the plunge. He decided to lead. Like a servant-king. Sure enough, no one followed for a long time. But he kept leading. And slowly, ever so slowly, his home began to take on a faint resemblance to Camelot.

Only this was no legend. And Larry was no impostor.

"Now, therefore, fear the LORD and serve Him in sincerity and truth; and put away the gods which your fathers served beyond the River and in Egypt, and serve the LORD. And if it is disagreeable in your sight to serve the LORD, choose for yourselves today whom you will serve…but as for me and my house, we will serve the LORD."

JOSHUA 24:14-15

CHAPTER 6

THE KING
PROVIDES DIRECTION

For the last few years the phone has been ringing more insistently in my office.

Prompted by what they read in *Tender Warrior*, men from across this country have been calling with questions. Those questions have caused me to wake up to a strange reality: We men need the most basic of instruction.

Our culture has been awash for so long that, like the physicist who can create cold fusion in a laboratory test tube but can't scramble an egg to feed himself, we're out of touch with the basics. We've got all the psychology in the world and little of the biblical reality. We may have managed to put a robot on Mars, but life is here! Now! On your street. In your home. Today. We men need to get our minds out of space somewhere and plant our feet firmly on the ground—*where we live*. We need to become brilliant in the basics.

One recent letter really touched my soul. It was from a guy longing to be the man God made him to be. While he struggles with balance in his masculinity, just as most of us do, his angle on the problem is a little different from that of many of us. This man was in touch with his sensitive side; he was developing the mentor and friend pillars.

But he still recognized something was missing.

Shaped, perhaps, by our feminizing culture, this young husband felt deficient in his strength pillars. He wanted to see more evidence of the king and the warrior in his life. As I read his letter several times over, I deeply appreciated his authenticity and honest heart. And I believe that recognizing the problem as he has is at least half the cure he's seeking. Listen in for a moment to this good man's heart:

Recently I have been seriously struggling with my masculinity. The struggle has been very difficult for me, because I'm not your "typical male." Your book stressed a man's need to balance the four pillars of his being—the king, the warrior, the mentor, the friend. Whereas the typical man is naturally strong in the first two categories and weak in the latter two, I am exactly the opposite. I find it very easy to express my emotions, and I do it frequently. It comes natural to me to "speak woman" with my wife. But I am severely lacking as a provisionary and protector.

For years I thought I had a healthy sense of masculinity. I'm seeing now that I never have. I've been hiding behind a facade of tough talk and physical strength. I've always counted myself privileged that it comes easy for me to express emotion, but I'm beginning to see that my lack of kingly strength oftentimes leaves my emotions unchecked.

When I ask my wife why she loves me, a typical answer might be, "because of your tenderness" or "because you make me laugh," or "because you make me feel loved." These are good things, but she never says "because you make me feel secure." Nor does she say "because I would follow you anywhere."

The emotion she says she loves is the same emotion that, because it is not balanced by manly strength, often sends me into fits of rage or depression.

My lack of emotional control is just one aspect of how this affects our marriage, and my life.... I'm also very self-conscious; I'm afraid to do things because I don't want to look stupid. I feel that I'm an intelligent person; I get straight A's in all of my college courses. But I'm often too full of self-doubt to express my opinions. I feel my wife is the more confident and competent between the two of us; I feel like she is the provider and protector and I'm just her teddy bear. I feel as if I've let her down....

I have been able to find plenty of reading material on how a tough king and warrior can learn to balance his spirit with his mentor and friend side. But I'm not finding much about how a mentor and friend who feels like a wimp can learn to be a warrior/king.... Stu, how does a man who seemingly doesn't have the strength to be a warrior, get it? If I feel like a wimpy little lamb, how do I get the lion inside me to roar? I don't want to be lovable to my wife just because I'm "sensitive." I want her to look up to me and respect me as a man.

Wow. What a letter. What a heart. And what a *man*. I think he's well on the way, don't you? And with an attitude like that, by God's grace he'll get there. Especially if he can find some healthy mentoring men with whom to lock arms. He reminds us of the careful and necessary balance—Jesus was both the Lamb of God and the Lion of Judah. As the lion, He knew when to roar and when not to roar. Jesus roared about the right things—always kingdom issues and righteousness issues, never petty personal frustrations. Too many men just roar when the kids are too noisy, or the wife is late, or the television is unavailable, or.... There is no merit in "roaring" unless it is for the right reason.

Let's work on it. After laying a foundation in the previous chapter, how do we frame this king function? How could we offer more help to that young husband who opened his heart in that letter? Let's take a good look at one of the primary strengths of the king pillar—providing direction.

THE KING PROVIDES BASIC DIRECTION

Stories based on the legend of King Arthur speak of the driving passion that brought him as a young man to the throne of the High King of Britain. As an island realm, the old Roman colony of Britannia was open to attack from all directions. And after the Roman Legions set sail back toward the east, there didn't seem to be an internal will or an internal force great enough to stand against the barbarian invaders: wild bands of Irish raiders from the west; savage Saxons from the east and south; howling, blue-painted Pics, Ingles, and Scotti to the north. Even among the Britons themselves, the bloody internecine border battles and boundary feuds threatened to transform "the Island of the Mighty" into easy pickings.

Arthur's burning passion to unite the British kingdoms under one noble banner and one High King seated in Camelot made the stuff of legends. It took a great king to provide a vision large enough to move and inspire a people to draw together for a common cause.

Whatever you might have thought of his politics and policies, Ronald Reagan did something similar for America in the 1980s. Yes, the political battles were white-hot and he had many bitter opponents. But something about the man...something about that endearing smile and wink...some larger-than-life quality brought Americans together under this former actor as they had not been together since John Kennedy's brief moment in the sun. President Reagan *stood* for something. He came into office as a tax-cutter, a strong advocate of national defense, a fierce anti-Communist, and a man who believed his nation needed a moral awakening to regain her greatness.

And even those who had honest disagreements with his plans and policies had to recognize that the Gipper restored some luster to the office of president that had been missing for a long while. America regained something in those days. Stood a little straighter. Walked with a little more spring in her step. Felt a little better about herself. Under Reagan's watch, the Berlin Wall crumbled, the Soviet Union disintegrated without a shot fired, and the Iron Curtain collapsed across Europe. And everyone in America knew that their president was truly *leading* from the heart, even if it wasn't in the precise direction they wanted to go.

In his landslide reelection bid, he won the votes of thousands from the opposing party who probably would have *never* described themselves as "conservatives" or "Republicans." But they recognized that this president was really *going* somewhere, and they stayed on board for the ride.

It takes a great leader to inspire a diverse and multi-hued nation such as America has become.

That is the way of a king. With God's help, he sets a general direction for his family. He pulls others along by the strength of his vision. He's the one who says, "This is where we need to go. This is the sort of family we need to be. These are the things we need to stand for and value." With Joshua of old, he says, "As for me and my household, we will serve the LORD."

Of course it is wonderful when you can *begin* a marriage, *begin* a household, and *begin* a family with those convictions standing in your heart and ringing in your ears. But life doesn't always work out that way, does it? Sometimes a man comes to his senses a little (or a lot) later in life. Sometimes by the time he finally picks up the crown, his little kingdom is in disarray. Some of the ways of his family are set—and they may not all be healthy. He'd love to go back and undo some of the things he's done, and *do* some of those things he left undone…but none of us has that opportunity.

Nevertheless, at whatever point in life we wake up to our responsibilities as kings, God calls us to take a stand and, in His strength, to point the way. Not everyone will follow. There will be opposition. There may be outright rebellion. But it is never too late to begin doing the right things.

My mind gravitates to the life of Jacob. Talk about a man who kicked over the game board of his life! He made so many serious mistakes and so infuriated his family and friends, that he spent a great deal of his life listening for footsteps behind him and looking over his shoulder—a rotten way to live. His "king" pillar was so unstable and out of balance, people probably wanted to duck whenever they saw him coming.

Jacob hadn't acted anything like a king in his youth. He'd grown up as a mama's boy while his more manly brother, "a man of the open fields," hunted meat for the family table. As the character of his life took shape, he looked less and less like a man of integrity and more and more like a cheat and a coward.

But then one night, all by himself by a rushing stream in the backcountry, Jacob had an encounter with the living God. Never one to do things the easy way, Jacob wrestled all night with the Lord. Finally, after God put a couple of moves on him and took him hard to the mat, a few basic truths began to sink into this man's awareness.

The old rascal had amassed quite a store of practical knowledge during his exile years. He raised healthy stock to provide for his family both food and shelter. Like many of us, his early years were spent chasing "success." But where was his life headed? What was his family's future if he stayed where he was, hiding from his past in a foreign country?

Jacob began to realize, again like many men at mid-life, that "those who bring trouble on their families inherit only the wind" (Proverbs 11:29, NLT). It occurred to him that providing a great lifestyle didn't necessarily provide a great and meaningful *life*. It began to dawn on him that the whole point of "bringing home the paycheck" was to provide for healthy life and relationships—not to pile up a bunch of stuff. To use Bob Buford's words, Jacob's emphasis began to shift from success toward significance. Jacob began to get some bearings. Family and relationships began to mean what they should have meant in the first place.

So Jacob decided he'd been on the run long enough. It was time to restore some broken relationships. It was time to go home to the Promised Land—and take his family with him.

Picture the scene…

It was a hot and dusty day on the trail, herding flocks of critters that had minds of their own—all the while keeping one eye on his energetic children who played care free, with no awareness of the dangers encircling them. But Jacob saw and lived with those dangers on a moment by moment basis. While some were oblivious to them and others were distraught over them, Jacob sat tall in the saddle, knowing they were there—and his to deal with.

Besides the heat that could kill the newborn among his livestock, and strays that could become prey to wild animals, there were always the bandits who roamed and plundered little caravans such as his. But the most pressing danger on Jacob's mind was neither heat nor cold, predators nor bandits.

It was one man, and one man only—his older brother, Esau. Jacob was about to face up to his past and try to make amends. He was tired of living a lie; really, it was no life at all. He wanted to move his family out from under the shadow he'd walked in for so many long, weary years.

It had been years since he'd last seen his brother, and their parting wasn't exactly what you'd call "brotherly." In fact, Jacob had fled for his life from the understandable anger of his sibling. This, after using trickery to rob Esau of both his birthright and his father's blessing, the eldest brother's rightful inheritance.

Since those days of treachery, Jacob had added a couple of wives to his family in Haran (a story in itself), and more children than he'd probably ever intended. Now, at the head of his little wagon train, he was rolling west to plant some roots where he truly belonged—even if it meant risking his skin to do it. Esau was a strong and powerful man, and Jacob could only expect the worst. That was the danger that haunted Jacob's every waking moment.

Scripture shows him looking ahead to this uncertain meeting, as a servant-king looks ahead for the well-being of those for whom he cares.

> Then Jacob sent messengers before him to his brother Esau.... And the messengers returned to Jacob, saying, "We came to your brother Esau, and furthermore he is coming to meet you, and four hundred men are with him." Then Jacob was greatly afraid and distressed; and he divided the people who were with him, and the flocks and the herds and the camels, into two companies; for he said, "If Esau comes to the one company and attacks it, then the company which is left will escape."...
>
> So he spent the night there. Then he selected from what he had with him a present for his brother Esau....
>
> Now he arose that same night and took his two wives and his two maids and his eleven children, and crossed the ford of the Jabbok. And he took them and sent them across the stream. And he sent across whatever he had....
>
> Then Jacob lifted his eyes and looked, and behold, Esau was coming, and four hundred men with him. So he divided the children among Leah and Rachel and the two maids.... But he himself passed on ahead of them. (Genesis 32:3, 6-8, 13, 22-23; 33:1, 3)

When the long-dreaded meeting finally took place, Esau shocked Jacob by running to him and embracing and kissing him. He even went so far as to offer Jacob and his troop a safe escort on his trip back home. But the new Jacob was thinking about his family—still looking ahead for those under his care:

But he said to him, "My lord knows that the children are frail and that the flocks and herds which are nursing are a care to me. And if they are driven hard one day, all the flocks will die. Please let my lord pass on before his servant; and I will proceed at my leisure, according to the pace of the cattle that are before me and according to the pace of the children, until I come to my lord at Seir." (33:13-14)

Whether it is Jacob almost 4,000 years ago, or the wagon master leading a wagon train across the western wilds 150 years ago, or the man today leading his family through the treacherous terrain of urban society, God has equipped and charged "the man" to use his God-given abilities to survey the approaching horizons. The Lord calls upon the family's head to calculate potential dangers, and take appropriate actions to move toward his God-given destination.

The God-prepared heart that "looks ahead" beats within every man, no matter in which century or which part of the world he is born.

Old Jacob had had to ask himself some tough questions. And because of the wild oats he'd sown, he didn't like all the answers. But he swallowed hard, tightened his belt, set his eyes on the course, and started putting one foot in front of the other. And his family followed. Jacob would probably have to admit that his two closest companions, Fear and Trembling, dogged his steps every inch of the way. But so what? Jacob went ahead with Plan A. Instead of working in Haran for his manipulative father-in-law for the rest of his life, he asked the tough questions, climbed a tree for perspective, and took a good long look at the horizons of God's intentions. Then he climbed back down to reality, put the mantle firmly over his shoulders, and set a course.

He followed it. And today the God of the Universe, the Almighty One Himself, loves to be called "the God of Jacob." If a guy as fouled up as Jacob could recover from the errors of his ways, don't you think there is hope for you? You betcha!

Maybe it's time for you to step back from routine. Take a day or two off. Head for the hills, or the beach, or whatever your favorite retreat might be. Take the time you need to clear your head. Climb a tall tree, and let the king in you ask a few penetrating questions. Then climb back down from that tree—come on back to face reality—and be the man God called you to be.

Here are a few "king pillar questions" for guys like Jacob, and you and me. Remember that the king function is pro-visionary, looking ahead for the good of his people. God calls upon us to ask, struggle through, and eventually develop answers to questions like these. Take a moment or two to read through them. Do any of them touch a nerve?

- How am I going to provide financially for my family when I get married?
- How am I going to provide enough living space for the children we want to have?
- How am I going to balance the pressures of work and family as they each develop?
- What will my wife's emotional needs be when the children are all in school; as we face an empty nest; as she enters into menopause?
- How can we raise our children so they are increasingly "responsibly independent" of us as parents, and at the same time increasingly "humbly dependent" on their heavenly Father?
- What do my children need to know from me before they enter elementary school, middle school, high school, college or career?
- What adjustments do I need to make financially to meet the coming needs of my family and church?
- How can I best serve the needs of my church family so it will not become stagnant and root-bound?
- How can I help my wife continue to grow as a person of beauty and impact?
- What will my family's needs be for college, the empty nest, and our retirement?
- What will it be like for my wife and me when the children are gone?
- What will our children need from me when they become independent adult children, and how will my role need to change?

And here are a few more questions we each need to ask ourselves as pro-visionaries. A wise king is always checking his own pulse and the pulse of those around him. He does indeed scan the horizon for any dangers lurking there in the valleys and shadows. Consider some "potential danger" questions like these:

- Are there tendencies from my past that (if I'm not careful) could eventually affect my relationship with my wife and children?
- If I keep on the present track of growth in my relationship with the Lord, will I be where I need to be to lead my family in three years? Five years? Ten years?
- If I keep on this same track at work, is it going to rob me of the richest years with my family?
- Is my wife growing as a woman of beauty, or is she constantly coming to the end of her rope?
- What influences is my wife facing at work or in the neighborhood that might change her way of thinking in an unhealthy way?
- What if my wife ever falls for another man?
- What influences are my children being exposed to at school and in the neighborhood that might change their way of thinking in an unhealthy way?
- What if one or more of my children chooses to rebel against our family and the Lord?
- What if a woman starts making passes at me?
- What if I find a pornographic magazine in the men's room at work?
- Am I living and growing the way I want my wife and children to live and grow over the next few years?
- Are my children learning the things they need to be learning right now to face the challenges of their next stage of life?
- What will high school be like when my children get there, and how can I help them be prepared for those crucial years?
- What if something fatal happens to my wife, or one or more of my children; how will I deal with that?

- What if I lose my job or the economy takes a sudden, harsh turn for the worst?

The more we look at these potential dangers at face value, the more we realize why it is so easy to keep our heads down and our eyes closed. Hopefully we also realize why it is so important to keep our heart soft and tender before the Lord, learning to trust and depend upon Him more and more in our lives. You and I never know what the coming day, or hour, or *minute* holds for us. Yet God has given us the promise that He will never allow any trial or temptation in our lives that He won't at the same time give us the ability to face and defeat. But we need to be aware that He has given us that ability—and use it courageously.

Serving as the provider may mean many things. Let's start with the most basic.

Like getting a job. Any job.

It may mean starting at the bottom of the heap with a "blue collar," minimum-pay job (but even the fast-food restaurants provide healthy benefits). It may mean taking a second minimum-paying job. And it may mean working some of the hours that are least desirable. Too many young men today want to start somewhere near the top. They want to start where their dads started after twenty years. So they hold off, hold out, hold up, and pretty much live life on hold. "All hard work brings a profit," wrote Solomon, "but mere talk leads only to poverty" (Proverbs 14:23, NIV).

Okay, so the job isn't the greatest and the pay ain't anything to write home about. Nevertheless, the king in you says, *Start somewhere.* Work hard. And stay at it. Climb a tall tree or high hill now and then to get your bearings. Focus on Christ and His values, and watch what happens.

As I write these words, I'm picturing a young man who became the first custodian for the church where I pastor, Good Shepherd Community Church. He swept and mopped, took out the trash and swabbed the toilets. He worked hard at it, keeping one eye on the horizon. The king in him kept saying, *"This is fine, Lord, I'll give it my best. But is there something else out there? Do You have anything else for me out on the horizon?"* Through a series of remarkable events, he eventually became the founder, owner, and president of Questar Publishers, Inc., a company with annual sales in the multiple millions.

He's my publisher. The publisher of this book.

Don came a long way by working hard and faithfully, and so can you. Do it, man!

Being a provider may mean giving up some hobbies for a season in order to make the budget stretch a bit more. Does your family really need you to play more golf, attend more sporting events, ride a snowmobile, or hang around the health club?

Being a provider may mean taking care of possessions, including your wife's car. Changing the oil. Adding antifreeze for the winter. Watching for tire wear. Rotating the tires.

Being a provider means filing taxes year after year after year.

Being a provider means looking over your home and yard in order to provide a safe environment for your family.

Being a provider means taking responsibility for your own emotional and physical needs in order to be even-keeled and healthy at home and work. It means dealing honestly with your anger. It means facing up to your depression and getting help for it. It means getting a prescription for your high blood pressure and taking it, so that you'll be there for your kids and *their* kids. It means finding friends to spur you on to become the best you can be.

A king who is burned out, beat up, and run down is no good to anyone. Being a provider means taking appropriate self-care so you can care for others.

If the king is to survive and flourish for the sake of the people, then he is going to need to be replenished as well. When those under his care know where he is at and how he functions, then they will be better able to help him and "fit" with him. Teams are formed around leaders. As the leader leads, then all team members can more easily and quickly find out where they fit on the team and how they can support the leader so he can keep leading.

Any servant-king who thinks he doesn't need help is deceiving himself. We do need help, truckloads of it. Remember, it was God who said, "It is not good for the man to be alone." But unless the burden of ultimate leadership falls on the man, then a man's wife and even his children are not sure what role he is playing and how to support and help him. However, when the servant-king is clearly on his throne of accountability and responsibility, then those around him can better determine how to serve his need to be and function as God designed. But when he is on the throne, then off the throne, on and off, leading and then not leading, it becomes almost impossible for those around him to know how to help him.

It is much easier for a team to work together and support the leader when there is a consistent, serving leader. But he must give them *consistent* leadership with which to cooperate! He must show respect if he is to receive it. He must encourage the achievements of others, if they are to encourage his. A true servant-king positions himself to be helped to be an even better servant-leader.

Being a provider means working hard at creating a home environment that says, "Everything's okay...Daddy's here." How does he do that? How does he bring that smoothing of troubled waters when he walks through the front door? Well...by controlling his anger for starters. And smiling more. And playing catch, riding bikes, reading stories, helping with homework, helping in the kitchen, not expecting the kids to be adults, not allowing the kids to remain infants, spanking sometimes, encouraging always. And oh, yes, did I mention *smiling* more? And how about some good long, rafter-shaking laughter now and then. Go ahead, try it! I promise it won't break your face—just that too-serious, all-business concrete mask you wear too often.

Being a provider means having a healthy understanding of authority, so your family can, too. It means refusing to bad-mouth your boss. It means refusing to cut down the pastor, the kids' teachers, the school principal, the PTA leader.

Being a provider means leading your family in the non-negotiables, such as church attendance, for example. For some reason, many men seem to look for excuses not to go to church. How many times have I heard it said, "Oh, our church is all messed up, so we can't really look there for growth." Say what? You're just kidding yourself. You get back there and participate with a good attitude. Or find a church where you can. But get to it. Jesus never gave His men permission to forsake the assembly. If you can't get along at church, what are your children learning?

There are a lot of questions for would-be kings of all ages. The king in your chest will *never* outgrow the need to scan the horizon and ask the questions. In so many ways, even at my rapidly advancing age (chuckle), I'm beginning to feel like I'm just getting *started* with questions.

CLIMBING THE TREE AT FIFTY

I've passed the fifty-year mark now. My sons are raised and out of the home. Linda and I are entering a new phase in our pilgrimage together. We needed some direction. I needed to do some serious thinking about our future, both professionally and personally.

So, after nineteen years in ministry at the same local church, I took a sabbatical. For a couple of months I got to take my head out of the daily grind and look up a little harder and longer than usual.

I realized that at fifty I only had "so many more years" ahead for me and my family with its expanding generations. We had all changed and our horizons were changing daily. I was able to sit down and write about some of the adjustments we needed to be making as a family. A new set of questions emerged and a fresh set of ideas and plans for the future began to unfold. Someone rightly said that by the time we get a plan on paper, we're halfway to accomplishing our goal.

At age fifty I began to feel the very real need to re-calibrate my life compass for the next season of life. Twenty-five years earlier, at age twenty-five, I had committed my life to ministry. Through some experiences in Vietnam where I was faced with the possibility of dying, I began to ask, "What really matters?" in life. I remember thinking, *Now that I've lived twenty-five years, how might my life count if the Lord gave me another twenty-five?*

Through a process of asking those key questions together while on R&R from Vietnam, Lindy and I devoted the next twenty-five years of our lives to the two things we thought mattered most to the Lord—our family and His family, the Church. That was 1970. We left the army, enrolled in seminary, and started a new church in the suburbs east of Portland. And the rest, as they say, is history.

Now our family is grown, our sons have direction of their own, and Good Shepherd Church is established, happy, and healthy.

My fiftieth birthday brought with it the completion of our "twenty-five-year vow." With our nest empty and the church family well established, Lindy and I set our two-month sabbatical aside to deal with the question, "If our Lord gives us yet *another* twenty-five years, how might we finish well?"

The question of "finishing" was a new one to us. But a realistic one. The first "trimester" of life was largely preparation. The second trimester was spent in raising the family and in energetic ministry. What should the third trimester look like? It was time for the king pillar to develop a careful balance for a new phase of life in our home now that it was just the two of us.

In this new season of our lives, we asked many questions—some personal, some professional, some familial, some financial. How should we regard our role at Good Shepherd Church? Nearly twenty years is a long time; should we stay? Move on? Should the ministry be broader? How do I retain the "fire in the belly"? And how should we be alert to each other now that we are empty-nesters? With the kids gone, is there a danger of losing each other in a slough of new opportunities? How should we regard our role in the lives of our adult children? What preparation should we make to become grandparents? Our own parents are beginning to age now; still healthy, but well into their seventies. What kind of provision do we need to be considering for them?

The questions poured out of the recesses of our minds and hearts. For weeks, even months, we considered them. We read books. Prayed. Sought counsel. And we presented the fruit of our thinking to our church elders for their consideration.

Together, we decided to take kind of a midcourse "first aid" approach to our lives. We wanted to:

1. "Stop the bleeding"—This area was primarily concerned with our schedule and finances. Linda and I have never really laid out a "plan" for our lives. Welcome to the club, eh? We were just "too busy" raising kids, ministering in the church, removing obstacles, and "getting on." But now we felt the need to become more naturally alert to our mortality

(smile), bring the pace of our lives and the demands upon them under more careful scrutiny and control, and plan more intelligently in our budget. We decided we needed, from this point forward, to become more thoughtfully pro-active and less habitually re-active—both with our time and our money.

2. "Get it breathing"—This area had to do with giving attention to our personal life in the present. I needed to find some diversions in order to enjoy life—to experience some good old-fashioned, systematic refreshment. Too often we had ended up using our vacation time for extended ministry opportunities—all valuable, but not vacation. As it was, I had come to the place where I was *talking* more about hunting and the outdoors than actually experiencing it. We needed to inject into our lives, at fairly regular intervals, time for personal rejuvenation and ministry reflection.

3. "Set the broken bones"—This area had to do, in our case, with a careful "retirement" program for our senior years. Our pension plan at the church had been in place for only a few years. How could we be available to our adult children and grandchildren if we became unable to support ourselves? We decided we needed to develop some kind of comprehensive approach to retirement that would allow Linda and me at least some degree of freedom in our later years.

In my effort to "finish well" I then divided my life into seven quantifiable roles—my personal life, my marriage, my family, my friends, my church, my broader professional life, and my financial life. Believe me, it was not an easy thing for me to do. I'm not by nature a goal setter. I'm not a detail-oriented person. But we worked hard at this, and we did it! We set some goals, laid some plans, and made some decisions in each of the seven areas.

I hadn't climbed that high in a tall tree for a quarter of a century, and it winded me a little getting to the top. But the view! Magnificent. As never before, I could see how my Lord and Friend has been with me along every trail and at every crossroads. Seeing His faithfulness to me and my family as I looked back encouraged me to lean on Him even more through the uncertain years ahead.

You should try it.

Just a brief closing word here, if you'll allow it. Should you live and should your family survive intact through the coming years, you are the only "king" and "head of the family" your wife and children will know. In other words, when God in His grace and kindness provided your family with a king, *you were IT, friend.*

What kind of king are they experiencing right now? What kind of king will they remember in the coming years? Will it be a tiny taste of Camelot, or some years they'd just as soon forget?

Perhaps, just about now, you're feeling a little inadequate for the job. Welcome to the club. A sense of personal inadequacy is *required* in this position. So let's walk together into the presence of the Great King for some of that on-the-job training.

And the strength of the King loves justice...and righteousness.

PSALM 99:4

"Your servant has been keeping his father's sheep. When a lion or a bear came and carried off a sheep from the flock, I went after it, struck it and rescued the sheep from its mouth. When it turned on me, I seized it by its hair, struck it and killed it.... The Lord...delivered me from the paw of the lion and the paw of the bear."

DAVID
1 SAMUEL 17:34-35, 37, NIV

THE KING
AS SHEPHERD

I t was just another day on the job. One like virtually every other day under the baking sun of the Judean hill country.

Yet hot and still as it was, David couldn't afford to be drowsy. Those sheep still required attention. They *always* required attention.

He was situated on a large, shaded boulder at one end of a meadow, not far from the edge of the trees and undergrowth. Rolled back on his haunches, one knee bent to relax, the teenager's eyes dropped from the lazy, drifting clouds to a quick scan of the meadow before him. He had just spent a good chunk of the morning leading the flock to this place, with its good, lush grass.

Young David knew his responsibilities well. As shepherd, he was charged to watch over the sheep, keep them together, and make sure they had all they needed to stay healthy and growing. To his mind, the task was nothing extraordinary. That's just what shepherds did.

Relieved that the hard, hot work of the morning was finally over, it felt good to sit down in the shade for a bit. But David knew all too well that his day's work wasn't done. In reality, it was *never* "done." Day and night, sunlight and storm, hot or cold, the shepherd's job was to stay alert to danger. And how quickly that danger could take shape out of seemingly thin air!

His memory drifted back to a hot afternoon not unlike this one. In fact, it was in this very meadow. He'd been looking in another direction, but caught—or rather felt—some motion just outside his range of vision. A dark smudge where it didn't belong.

A bear. With a lamb in its jaws.

The lamb, of course, was totally helpless; clubbed into unconsciousness from just one swipe of the big predator's paw.

David had to grin at the memory. Oh, he'd been quick to his feet that day! When had he ever run so fast? Like a gazelle! He'd neither paused nor hesitated. In fact, he hadn't thought much about it at all. He'd just reacted. He had to chuckle at how he had surprised even himself. But he'd done it. In the moment of crisis, somewhere from down deep inside, character had exerted itself and answered.

Thinking back on those moments gave him an involuntary shudder. He could so easily have been overpowered that day. But God had been good, sovereignly involving Himself in the encounter.

The old bear had seen David's approach. Dropping the lamb, he whirled to face this brash young challenger. Up on his hind legs, the bear towered over what seemed rightly to him to be his next victim. He'd let out a woof as he wagged his head to the right and then the left, as though staking claim to the lamb and warning the intruder all at once.

David smiled as he remembered. Would he do the same thing again? Charge straight into that bear like there was no tomorrow? Yes, he mused, he probably would. He'd probably do it all over again.

True, the youngest son of Jesse was a bit older and wiser now. But that had only increased his zeal for his Lord—and the empowering sense of His presence. More than ever, David burned with an inner passion to fill his responsibility. Yes, that old bear had easily outweighed and outmuscled him—and most certainly had the sharper claws! But the sheep were David's responsibility, and he was willing to go down hard, if necessary, to provide for them and protect them.

It had all happened so fast it was hard for him to reconstruct those furious twenty seconds. He did remember the rod in his hand. He did remember mixing it up so close that his left hand had actually grabbed the bear by the beard. He remembered the musty, musky smell of the animal. And then it was over. It was hard to remember the details, but if the Lord gave him a hundred years of life, he would never forget the sensation of deliverance. And the rush of battle won.

Now this day, as the adrenaline of memory pulsed again through his veins, David welcomed the cooling touch of a slight breeze and the gentle rustling of the leaves behind him. He was thankful his father Jesse had entrusted such a special responsibility to him. Yes, it was work. Hard work. He could say with his ancestor Jacob, "This was my situation: The heat consumed me in the daytime and the cold at night, and sleep fled from my eyes" (Genesis 31:40, NIV). And though he seldom heard a "thank you" for the daily grind of shepherding, he did have a fierce sense of pride about doing his job well, no matter what it took. There was something inside of David that made him glad he was a man. He was invigorated by it. And he resolved to be the man God intended him to be. That resolve would come in handy in many a valley yet future—and with opponents deadlier than the bear.

It was during those days of running his father's flocks that David began to understand what it meant to shepherd those under his care, to watch over them. It was during those times, including that skirmish with the bear—and yet another with a lion—that David personalized the reality of God's watch-care over his own life.

The heart of a future shepherd-king was taking shape back in that lonely hill country. Out with the flocks, David jotted down notes to himself. He worked through those notes under the vast panoply of stars…and under his Father's watchful eye. Through the long, silent afternoons, he began to weave music through those thoughts…strum the notes with his little harp…sing them out loud and strong, to the echoing hills.

Many of them would become the psalms of Israel. Let's take a closer look at one of David's most famous. This short little number has been at the top of the charts for centuries now. Psalm 23 is also one of the most instructive to men who would become the kings God intends them to be. It is the psalm of a provisionary, and it gives color and definition to the "watch over" function of the family shepherd.

> The LORD is my shepherd, I shall not be in want.
> He makes me lie down in green pastures,
> he leads me beside quiet waters,
> he restores my soul.
> He guides me in paths of righteousness for his name's sake.

Even though I walk through the valley of the shadow of death,
I fear no evil, for you are with me;
your rod and your staff, they comfort me.

You prepare a table before me in the presence of my enemies.
You anoint my head with oil; my cup overflows.
Surely goodness and love will follow me all the days of my life,
and I will dwell in the house of the LORD forever.

(Psalm 23, NIV)

David knew it! Believed it with everything in him.

God was watching over his life! It had become personal. The King of kings was shepherding him—providing for him and protecting him in oh so many ways. And under the inspiration of God's Spirit, David wrote that little song down for you and me. Let's look at these familiar scenes painted by the shepherd-poet; let's use them to get a grip on becoming the provisionaries God wants us to be. Familiar as it may be, think of Psalm 23 in a fresh way for a few moments. Think of it as a *fathering* psalm.

The Lord is my shepherd, I shall not be in want.
He makes me lie down in green pastures...

My King watches over me. He provides for all my needs—and so many of my wants, as well. Life is good—and fun!—with Him.

He leads me beside quiet waters...

This King of mine provides security and rest for me. He gives me confidence to face whatever life throws across my path.

He restores my soul...

He fixes my insides. Touches the wounds no one else can see. He listens. Hears. Understands. Helps. Builds me up in the deep places of my soul.

He guides me in paths of righteousness for his name's sake...

He has truly thought through His plans for me. He communicates His heart to me. He builds on the good things in me and points out those needing adjustment. And best of all, He lets me wear His own name!

Even though I walk through the valley of the shadow of death, I fear no evil, for you are with me; your rod and your staff they comfort me.

How I love His sovereign, providential watch-care! My confidence in Him surrounds me like a cloak. I know right down to my core that nothing will ever happen to me that He and I can't handle together. Bear, lion, or giant. The darkest moments; the heaviest weights; the greatest pain— I don't fear *any* evil. I can look death right in the face. Whatever touches me, He can use it all for my good. I can walk without fear. From one end of His Word to the other, He tells me, "I will be with you!"

You prepare a table before me in the presence of my enemies...

You, my Lord and my Friend, are so incredibly creative, caring, and providing that—even when I am faced with the cruelest of realities—life is a feast at Your hand.

You anoint my head with oil...

You have marked me out as Your own. Your healing touch is wonder-full. I am proud to be Yours. You bless me as Your son and heir, and fill my days with appointment and purpose.

My cup overflows. Surely goodness and love will follow me all the days of my life, and I will dwell in the house of the LORD forever.

Wow! This is too much! All You are in Your great heart pursues me. It's as though You have chosen me as Your son. And You have! You constantly assure me of Your loyal love. Nothing I could ever do could be bad enough to turn You away from me. I can't wait for forever—and Your good house, my new home. Surely, the best is yet to come!

David had caught it. Life with the King of kings and Shepherd of shepherds was fulfilling beyond words. He was overjoyed. Having caught a picture of his Father's provisionary intentions, David would fashion himself into a servant-king after God's own heart. Yes, his humanity was full of flaws and warts, just like yours and mine. But for whatever mistakes he would make and sins he would commit in the future, it must be said that David kept a firm grip on the reality of God's intentions. It pleased the King of kings to have David leading His people.

> He also chose David His *servant*, and took him from the sheepfolds; from the care of the ewes with suckling lambs He brought him, to shepherd [Israel] His people.... So he shepherded them according to the integrity of his heart, and guided them with his skillful hands. (Psalm 78:70-72, emphasis added)

Wouldn't you love the Lord to say similar things of you? "He is My servant. I chose him to lead his wife, his kids, his church, his fellow workers." Well, He *has* chosen you, my friend. It's as clear as anything in the Bible! So let's get to it. Let's develop the servant-shepherd king in our chests and become the men He has anointed us to be.

P R O V I D I N G   F O R   P E R S O N A L   N E E D S

David learned well that providing, though it involved food and shelter, was a whole lot more comprehensive than that. He learned that his needs as a person were far more than just physical needs. He was deeply moved by the knowledge that his Father in heaven understood *all* his needs—and supplied them so richly. Some of the needs David mentioned in his psalms included...

Physical needs

When David alludes to green pastures and quiet waters, he is saying, at a minimum, that God made sure his daily physical needs for food, drink, and the like were taken care of. God created us as human beings who have physical needs. Shepherding, watching over, involves making sure that needs and provision come together for those under the shepherd's care.

Now consider this: As those who have been given the ability and the responsibility to "watch over" others (as God watches over us), we should be asking and answering questions regarding the physical needs of those who look to us as shepherd. Questions, perhaps, like these...

- Is my wife getting the rest she needs? Am I?
- Is my pregnant wife getting the prenatal care that both she and the baby need?
- Is my wife getting a regular female physical, as prescribed for her age? Am I getting a regular physical, too?
- Am I fulfilling my wife's sexual needs? Am I asking her opinion and giving her freedom to be honest?
- Am I, and the other members of my family, getting the balance of diet, exercise, and rest that is healthy for us?
- Are my children being given opportunities to develop their basic motor skills—such as climbing trees, participating in sports, ballet, dance, gymnastics, or playing catch?
- Am I taking time to do these things *with* my kids?
- Do we have a doctor, or doctors, for the family that we know, trust, and feel comfortable and confident with?
- Am I certain in my heart about those who watch the children in our absence—even if they are family members? Have I carefully questioned the kids about that care?
- Do my children know how to be safe around strangers?
- Am I making sure that questions about physical and sexual abuse are being raised at my church? (If I am abusing my wife or children, am I willing to admit it, and get what help, counsel, and accountability that I need to change my ways?)

Not only did God provide for David's physical needs, but also for his...

Emotional needs

David says that God led him beside the *still* waters and *restored his soul.* David recognized that God was the Source of refreshment and restoration in his life. As he would later acknowledge, "You chart the path ahead of me and tell me where to stop and rest" (Psalm 139:3, NLT). David realized that God gave him a place and an opportunity to "catch his emotional breath" from time to time.

Here are some important questions we might want to consider as we watch over our own flock's emotional well-being:

- Am I, my wife, and our children all so busy we don't have time to stop and get some refreshment together?
- Are we assuming that intense busyness in "good things" is always the best choice?
- Do we have time for significant vacations?
- Do we take time to get away for weekends occasionally?
- Is there opportunity and a place for each of us to be alone and quiet in our house?
- Am I reading materials that will refresh my soul? Are we encouraging and helping the others in our family and church to do the same?
- Am I helping my family realize the emotional value of meditating on God's Word?
- Am I expressing my emotions to my family? Do they see me laugh, cry, hurt, and rejoice?
- Am I giving them the opportunity and encouragement to express their emotions to me and the rest of the family?
- Is my wife growing weary from disciplining the children without much response? Does she need some help from me?
- Are there responsibilities that my wife has taken on around the home that are weighing her down, that I could possibly take over for her or get taken care of some other way?

Yes, God provided for David's physical and emotional needs, but He also provided for his...

Spiritual needs

David sings the words, "He guides me in paths of righteousness for his name's sake." God guided David in the way he ought to live life. He gave him spiritual guidelines or markers along the highway of his life. Just as God watched over David—and you and me—in this way, so we should be concerned with watching over those under our care.

We ought to be thinking about these kinds of questions for those entrusted to our keeping:

- Am I spending regular time alone with the Lord, opening my heart to Him in prayer and listening intently to Him through the Word?
- Are my wife and I praying together regularly?
- Am I helping make sure my children learn how to read and understand the Bible? Do they understand how to pray?
- Am I seeing to it that my children hear voices other than just mine by taking them to church on a regular basis and helping them be involved in children's or youth activities?
- Am I helping my children find the Christian music and books they are most responsive to, even though it may not be what I am most responsive to?
- Am I appropriately and skillfully asking my children how their walk with Jesus is going? Am I doing anything to motivate them in that direction?
- How can I help my wife keep growing spiritually?
- Am I making sure there are good Christian books around the house for the family to pick up and read?

Did you happen to notice from Psalm 23 how "justice" and "mercy" (or loyal loving kindness) just follow around people who are under the care of the King? In the same way, the man of God's intentions is a benevolent servant-king who provides a clear, consistent system of justice. He is a man who strives to be honest and fair in his dealings with his wife, children, and comrades.

S E R V A N T - K I N G S   P R O V I D E   J U S T I C E

If a man is to uphold a standard of justice in his own family, he must *be* just in his dealings with those under his care. As a pastor, I've often noticed that men tend to be *least* fair and honest in dealing with their own wife and children. Too many men have one set of standards for themselves and another for those under their roof. The man who comes home expecting to be served (the paper, the easy chair, dinner on time, peace 'n' quiet, etc.) but not demanding of himself the same standard of service for those under his care, is an unfair and selfish man. The man who demands honesty of his wife and children but cuts himself all kinds of slack in his own personal habits and pleasures, is not being honest and just with his family.

A servant-leader must not have double standards…one for himself and another for those around him.

> If he wants respect, he must give it.
> If he wants forgiveness, he must extend it.
> If he wants consistency, he must show it.
> If he wants promptness, he must demonstrate it.
> If he wants enthusiastic love, he must be an enthusiastic lover of others.

The implication of the golden rule, in its context, is that we should treat others the way we expect to be treated—because in all likelihood, the way we treat others is the way they *will* in turn treat us.

I may complain to my buddies that "my wife and kids just don't understand me," but how far am I going out of my way to truly understand them?

To be fair and honest with my wife, children, and comrades, I must be willing to set aside my own stuff long enough to pay attention to them. I must be willing to ask questions that help me understand them and their situation well enough to offer a fair response.

Being fair and honest with others is, at the root, the result of being fair and honest in our relationship with our God. When I cheat Him, I cheat myself and others around me. When I lie to Him, I lie to myself and others around me. When I am fair and honest with Him, I can be fair and honest in my relationships with others. In the life of David himself, you can see that his drift from the passionate love for God he'd had as a simple shepherd boy went hand in glove with his cold-hearted abuse of people in his later years. When the prophet Nathan finally nailed him to the floor as a selfish, heartless deceiver and murderer, David immediately responded, "I have sinned against *the Lord.*" He recognized that his nightmare of adultery and betrayal had begun right there—with a year-long neglect of his walk with the loving Father of his youth.

A servant-king does serve justice. He is responsible to establish, develop, and—yes—enforce the family rules. But a servant-king only makes rules for the *benefit* of others. Moses is a fundamental example. He did not establish rules for his own good, but for the good of the people.

Rules are for the good of others, not the good of the leader. Rules are never to be established in order to make the leader feel important or so that he can somehow establish himself as The Big Man. Ask yourself, as head of your home, *How many of our household rules are (really) for me? How many are for the good of the family?* Too many rules are unlivable, even unbearable. A servant-king realizes that while there must be *some* rules, they must be tailored for the well-being of those entrusted to his care—even at his own expense.

I'm reminded of the local deputy sheriff I recently saw on the nightly news. The poor guy was in a hurry to get home after his shift and he had to make a quick stop on the way to pick up a few groceries. In his haste, he pulled his squad car up to the curb and dashed into the store. What he hadn't noticed was that he'd parked his car in a "no parking" zone. Moments later, when he came out of the store, he sheepishly noticed the sign. What to do?

No hesitation in this good man! He simply pulled out his pad and, there in front of the smiling passersby, wrote himself a seventeen-dollar ticket. The passersby, buoyed by his consistency, applauded. And you've got to believe they will more readily accept their own lumps from this authority figure whose justice is consistent—even when it hurts.

Since rules are for the benefit of others, it is important to make sure those rules are clear and understandable. And let me make a suggestion: The most basic rule must have something to do with authority. One of the greatest gifts we can leave our children is a basic understanding that *authority is to be obeyed.* Children will sometimes feign misunderstanding of a rule. At other times, they may not understand or agree with the *reason* for a rule. Nevertheless, understand it or not, like it or not, agree with it or not, they must OBEY it. That lesson is one of the most basic realities in the universe. Its violation in Eden has spelled disaster for the human family from the very beginning.

A servant-king is consistent with the rules. Consistency is not optional if we are to provide justice. Without consistency, we're like a local government that is constantly changing the speed limits, but not changing the signs. When we communicate standards to those around us, we have put up a sign. If we don't stick with that, others will become frustrated and angry, because the signs said one thing, but they are being judged by another set of rules.

And certainly, *one* of those signs or rules ought to be an immediate admission and apology for our own lapses in consistency!

S E R V A N T - K I N G S   P R O V I D E   M E R C Y

The benevolent servant-king has the responsibility and unique opportunity to be compassionate to the guilty. He realizes that every one of us human beings has a propensity to sin. As Paul tersely noted, "For all have sinned and fall short of the glory of God" (Romans 3:23).

A servant-king's motive is always to help and never to deliberately hurt the guilty. He is firm, but also compassionate.

When Fiorello LaGuardia was mayor of New York City, he would from time to time sit as magistrate for the evening court. One night as he was doing so, a man was brought before him accused of stealing food. When LaGuardia asked him if it was true, he admitted that indeed he had stolen the food. As the questioning continued, it became evident the accused man was utterly destitute, and had no money even for food. He had stolen in order to stay alive.

Being the firm yet compassionate man that he was, LaGuardia fined the man ten dollars. But then, after passing sentence, the mayor stepped down from his high office and paid the man's fine out of his own pocket.

A servant-king actually looks for ways to show compassion to the guilty under his care, without being cruel to them. He doesn't rub things in their faces. He doesn't get even. He is just, but not a bully or a braggart. The servant-king reads the heart and ministers to it. Realizing that every one of us has flaws and limitations, he has the responsibility and unique opportunity to be compassionate to the helpless.

A SERVANT-KING PROVIDES HONOR

The benevolent servant-king has the responsibility and unique opportunity to give honor to those under his care. He realizes that by God's own design we *all* need to be honored, and that those who are consistently denied this will either rebel, or just wither away at the roots.

He realizes that he is in a unique position to *give* honor like no one else, and that no one can truly replace that responsibility for him. He avoids sarcasm, put-downs, belittling words, and ways that diminish the honor of a person.

What would happen in families across our land if dad-shepherds began to literally heed Paul's command to the Ephesians?

> Do not let any unwholesome talk come out of your mouths, but only what is helpful for building others up according to their needs, that it may benefit those who listen. (Ephesians 4:29, NIV)

The shepherd-king looks for ways to publicly lift up and commend those who are under his care. Demeaning jokes about your wife or children—even though they may garner a cheap laugh or two—are never appropriate.

A SHEPHERD-KING NEVER, NEVER ABANDONS HIS FLOCK

How many times have I seen it in my ministry? Innumerable! A man decides to leave his wife. He "explains it all" to the children. But somehow, they "just don't get it."

The tragic reality is, they never will.

Hear me carefully, please. For all our wishful thinking, children *never* fully recover from the divorce of their parents. It does not "strengthen them for life in a tough world," nor does the adversity "build character in their lives." Believe me, I've heard all the lines, *ad nauseam*. Divorce is abandonment, pure and simple. And children abandoned by divorce are no more "strengthened" or "matured" than sheep abandoned by shepherds. Both tend to be vulnerable to marauding wolves.

To be abandoned is the most "cruel"—though certainly no longer the most "unusual"—of human punishments. It is utterly devastating. This same deep sense of desolation, however, can still happen with the family shepherd who comes home every night and sleeps under the same roof with his wife and children. It is the emotional distancing caused by a parent, most often a dad, who is still in the home but not in the heart. Abandonment is a dad who is "there without being there."

The resultant sense of loss is so deep and so far-reaching, it can impact the family tree for *generations*. When a human being grows up with a sense of emotional distance, he or she is (usually unwittingly) motivated to do all kinds of "crazy," irrational things that push people away—including overindulgence in food, alcohol, sex, or even nonstop talking.

No, a shepherd-king never, never abandons his flock. Let me tell you about a friend of mine who walked right up to the edge of that cliff.

BACK FROM THE BRINK

Dyrk Van Zanten had a rough marriage. Dyrk's a big, strong man with a full dark beard and a mechanic's grip. The kind of guy you wouldn't want to meet alone (or even with two or three friends) in a dark alley. But a number of years ago he came to the point where he felt he couldn't handle the pressure of his marriage anymore—and he decided to bail.

He'd thought about it often. Now he thought about it long. And he determined to go through with it. So late one afternoon, he collected a few of his things, tossed them in his car, told his wife Jamie and their firstborn son he was through, and headed north from Portland.

Just like that, he was gone. For good. Or so he intended.

He landed in a Seattle motel for the night. Tossing and turning, unable to sleep, he eventually crawled out of the sheets and ended up in a phone conversation with his dad. Now, Roger Van Zanten is just as big and burly as Dyrk, and had endured a few rough roads of his own through the years. This road-wise older man heard his distraught son pour it all out on the phone in the middle of the night.

And then, in a quiet voice, he told the younger man what he already knew in his heart.

"Dyrk, you can't run. There's a better way. God would want you to stick it out."

Dyrk hung up. He wrestled with himself; and wrestled with God. He didn't want to go back, but he did want to do what is right. Dyrk paid his motel bill, climbed back into his car, and headed south down I-5 toward Portland. Not long after this, he wandered into Good Shepherd Church as a visitor. That was eleven years ago. During that time, Dyrk's made some friends—man-friends, the kind of guys who will go to the wall with you. He's gotten some good, solid marriage counseling under his belt. He and Jamie are making it. And you should see their boys. Two happier lads you can't imagine.

Every time I drive into the church parking lot on a Sunday morning and see Dyrk standing out there in the rain directing traffic, my mind wanders back through his journey. I love that big man. So godly, so mature in his faith. And because he chose to return to his little flock and wear the mantle of a shepherd-king no matter what, there is a woman who can trust her husband. And boys who admire their father. And a church which thrives because a family is ministering—together. Wow, it's enough to make a full-grown man cry.

And I am. Right now.

Some time ago Dyrk stood up in front of the whole church and told his story of pain and flight, of redemption and growth. He thanked the body for their support. And then this huge man, with tears in his eyes and a smile on his face, proposed a new name for our church. He said, "How about calling it Good Shepherd Family Recycling Center!"

And Dyrk continues to minister, far beyond the rainy parking lot. Just a few weeks ago, he and one of our elders called on another man who had decided to abandon his family. The jury is still out on that one, but the verdict is clear in the Van Zanten family. They're together and growing. And the big man, his wife, and his kids, are building a legacy of love and commitment, "that the generations to come might know."

A shepherd-king never, never abandons his flock. Not for a lion. Not for a bear. And not for a pain with a bite bigger than both. He stays even when all hell breaks loose. Like Moses. Like David. Like Dyrk. Like Jesus.

THE WARRIOR
PILLAR

And I saw heaven opened; and behold a white horse, and He who sat upon it is called Faithful and True; and in righteousness He...wages war.... And the armies...[of] heaven...were following Him on white horses.
REVELATION 19:11, 14

CHAPTER 8

BRAVEHEART UNTAINTED

D ave Barry is a kick. When he lays a spoof on you, you've been spoofed! But there's always just enough truth mixed in with the levity to make you nod (or wince) with recognition. Whenever I'm caught in traffic and feel the "macho" in me wanting to kick up its heels, I rethink my way through my all-time-favorite Barry column. He called it, "Guys aren't stupid; they just *act* that way." It's classic:

One recent morning I was driving in Miami on Interstate 95, which should have a sign that says: WARNING! HIGH TESTOSTERONE LEVELS NEXT 15 MILES!

In the left lane, one behind the other, were two well-dressed middle-age men, both driving luxury, telephone-equipped German automobiles. They looked like responsible business executives, probably named Roger, with good jobs and nice families and male-pattern baldness, the kind of guys whose most violent physical activity, on an average day, is stapling.

They were driving normally, except that the guy in front, Roger One, was thoughtlessly going only about 65 miles an hour, which in Miami is the speed limit normally observed inside car washes. So Roger Two pulled up behind until the two cars were about one electron apart, and honked his horn.

Of course, Roger One was not about to stand for *that*. You let a guy honk at you and you basically are admitting that he has a bigger stapler. So Roger One stomped on his brakes, forcing Roger Two to swerve onto the shoulder, where, showing amazing presence of mind in an emergency, he was able to make obscene gestures *with both hands*.

At this point, both Rogers accelerated to about 147 miles per hour and began weaving violently through dense rush-hour traffic, each risking numerous lives in an effort to get in front of the other, screaming and getting spit all over their walnut dashboards.

I quickly lost sight of them, but I bet neither one backed down. Their co-workers probably wondered what had happened to them. "Where the heck is Roger?" they probably said later that morning, unaware that, even as they spoke, the dueling Rogers, still only inches apart, were approaching the Canadian border.[1]

That old warrior in each of us sometimes gets twisted around a bit, doesn't it? Every one of us has been a "dueling Roger" at one point or another. The warrior in us becomes so heavily engaged in a short-sighted and foolish skirmish that we end up exhausted, way off course…and no good to anybody. The "braveheart" in every man is easily tainted. Our world needs the braveheart untainted. The warrior pillar must never be allowed to lean to the left or to the right, but must stand straight and tall.

True warriors face off with evil. True warriors protect, even at the cost of their own lives. Like Jesus.

The final pages of Scripture describe Jesus at the end of time. The picture is not soft. The colors are not pastel. This is not a portrait of "gentle Jesus, meek and mild."

Our Lord sits astride a mighty white war horse. His eyes are a flame of fire. His robe is spattered with blood. His own. He carries a sharp sword. On His thigh He has a name written: "KING OF KINGS AND LORD OF LORDS." He is called "Faithful and True, and in righteousness He wages war."

Jesus, the ultimate Warrior, came from a long line of warriors. On the first page of the New Testament, in the first verse, He is called the Son of David. I think Jesus loved that title—probably for a variety of reasons. He certainly loved David's heart, and it was the heart of a consummate warrior. David developed that heart, alone with his Lord, facing the beasts of the wilderness in hand-to-hand combat. David had the heart of a lion. And, on at least one occasion recorded in Scripture, he took the heart right out of a lion.

L I O N S :   U P   C L O S E   &   P E R S O N A L

I faced off with a lion once. It wasn't a matter of bare-handed combat (I carried a .300 Winchester Magnum that day), but all things considered, I wouldn't care to do it again.

It was elk season. Several of us were camped on the rim of Hell's Canyon, six thousand feet above a wild stretch of the Snake River. I and my hunting partner, the son of a good friend, had left camp in the murky pre-dawn and stationed ourselves high on a hog's back ridge overlooking some promising terrain. Elk sign was plentiful. And we anticipated them moving through the ravine below en route to cover and shade once the sun climbed higher in the sky.

It was a delightfully crisp fall morning, and we had a good day of it. We spotted a number of elk moving, but no big bulls. Earlier that same morning, in a box canyon just off to our north, we had heard the telltale chirping sounds of a small herd already settled into the shade to beat the heat.

When the action in front of us slowed, I decided to slip quietly into the box canyon, hoping, at worst, to move the elk out of there. In so doing, I might open up a shot at a big bull for my partner, who remained high on the ridge.

The canyon wall was steep, but it was a north slope covered with fir and pine clinging precariously to the mountainside, so I was able to descend it. I went down in what I call a "five-point descent"—both feet, both hands, and one behind always in contact with the ground. It's the only way to handle the slippery patches of grass on such a steep incline.

Moving slowly and silently, I made my way into the canyon, always alert to the wind's direction. The herd continued their occasional contented chirping some distance to the west and just ahead of me. Oh, this was great! Everything was developing perfectly. It was going to be an exciting morning. Little did I realize just *how* exciting.

At that point, with the herd still relaxed and grazing, something really strange happened. They spooked! Big time. And believe me, when a herd of elk spooks, the whole world knows it. Down in the bottom of the canyon, it sounded like the *end* of the world. Rocks rolled. Hooves thundered. Branches cracked. Dust exploded against the hot canyon wall.

And right in the middle of it all, a calf screamed—really screamed. The unmistakable cry of an animal in serious distress raises the hair right off the back of your neck. *What in the world?* I thought maybe a rolling boulder had broken its leg.

Why had they spooked? I couldn't figure it. Certainly I couldn't have spooked them. The wind had been with me all the way. I'd been perfectly silent. I hadn't even moved in some time. And the herd had still been a hundred and fifty yards ahead of me in heavy timber.

I just shook my head. The woods can be crazy—and critters sometimes do things that only makes sense to them. For lack of knowing anything better to do, I continued to move toward the area where the herd had been. Not that it would do any good. Those elk were probably scattered across three states by then.

I approached a dry wash at the bottom of the canyon, overgrown with underbrush. Real dog hair stuff. It was going to be tough maneuvering for a ways. Up ahead of me, however, I noticed a huge wind-felled ponderosa pine down across the wash. Its position would allow me to cross without fighting the heavy underbrush. Grateful for small favors, I headed toward it.

I walked into a ten-foot-square clearing, still a dozen or so feet away from the big log. Suddenly, in the hollow beneath the fallen pine, my eye caught a flash of movement. I was looking at something, but my mind didn't register. What was it? At first, I thought it must have been a piece of yellowed bark, fallen from the tree's underside.

But no, it looked more like—*Holy cow!* It was the forepaw of a huge mountain lion. He looked up from where he crouched under the deadfall with his prey, and I think he was almost as surprised as I was.

Even as I froze in position, my mind instantly told me what had happened. I hadn't spooked that herd at all! This oversized party crasher had done it. That helped my hunter's pride a bit, but it didn't calm my heart rate. That cat was fully mature and a good eight feet long—four feet of body, four feet of tail. His tawny bulk was astride the young elk calf. Neck broken, the calf was big enough to feed the big fella for some time.

Now, stumbling across a mountain lion in the wild is one thing. But a mature cat on a fresh kill is something else. And I was messing with his lunch! His big yellow eyes narrowed into slits as he regarded me. I'm sure his pulse rate was up, too. Big cougars will normally spend a lifetime without being seen by a human, let alone one at a range of ten feet—during lunch hour! The cougar's eyes betrayed no fear, only seething hostility. His dusty yellow ears had dropped down flat to his skull—like a tom cat in an alley fight. Only I didn't feel like any threatening tom. I felt more like an itty-bitty kitty, wishing to be excused from this unwanted encounter. And I really didn't want to fight. Yeah, I had a rifle. But at that range, I figured I might have time for just one shot.

With ears pasted flat, his huge head took on the shape of an oversized football. We stared at each other, neither moving. The smell of dust hung in the air. I've really no idea how long we stayed in that position. A few seconds? A minute? More? However long it was, I'll never forget those eyes, taking my measure. Intelligent. Focused. Threatening. Wild as a canyon wind.

If he moves toward me to pounce, I recall thinking, *I'll wait until my rifle muzzle is buried in his chest before I pull the trigger.* That way, I could figure on one shot hitting home. I knew full well I wouldn't get another.

In that same instant, I remember calculating how long his forelegs were and whether he could reach around the rifle barrel and nail me before I could pull the trigger.

It's amazing how fast the mind works in a circumstance like that! I'm not saying my life flashed before my eyes, but I did manage to scroll back through what little reading I'd done about the big cats. It didn't seem nearly enough! But I remembered some old boy writing that if a man remains upright, doesn't run or give in to panic, and acts somewhat loud and aggressively, it's unlikely a mountain lion will attack.

"Unlikely"? That was small comfort in that moment. Besides, the book wasn't talking about a hungry lion astride a fresh kill.

I decided to call loudly to my partner up on the ridge to let him know just what was transpiring down in my little canyon. It was an assertive move—and something of a bluff. But I also figured it wouldn't hurt to give my partner a "heads up" and let him know I might need some serious aid and comfort in a minute or two.

Looking back now, I believe it was the shout that delivered me. As soon as I called up the hill, the big lion decided to cash in his chips. Slowly and methodically, his eyes never leaving me for a second, he circled slightly to my right, worked his way out of the clearing, and without a sound, melted into the brush.

He never ran. He just slinked away and disappeared—mad, disappointed, and still without his lunch.

Whew! I felt my muscles begin to relax, leaving me a little weak and shaky. I walked over to inspect the calf's body. Not a drop of blood. Just a broken neck, and a wet nape where the lion had been dragging it. I was left thinking about the sheer raw power it required to break that neck in an instant.

Slowly working my way back to the head of the canyon, I engaged myself in a debate. Should I have shot him? No, it was against the law. But wasn't it legal in cases of self-defense? And what else could that little encounter have been called? Man, what a beautiful mount he would have made! Darn it, I could have taken him! Why had I hesitated?

Clambering back up the slope to the top of the ridge, I knew deep down I was glad I'd let him go. And even more glad that he'd returned the favor! Besides that, this was going to make one great campfire story when we hiked back into camp that evening.

Since that encounter in the wilderness, a verse from the Old Testament has meant just that much more to me:

Benaiah son of Jehoiada was a valiant fighter from Kabzeel, who performed great exploits. He struck down two of Moab's best men. He also went down into a pit on a snowy day and killed a lion. (2 Samuel 23:20, NIV)

And I can never read about David's eyeball-to-eyeball encounter with the lion without remembering that terrifying moment in the valley near Hell's Canyon.

David said to Saul, "Your servant has been keeping his father's sheep. When a lion or a bear came and carried off a sheep from the flock, I went after it, struck it and rescued the sheep from its mouth. When it turned on me, I seized it by its hair, struck it and killed it." (1 Samuel 17:34-35, NIV)

That was bare-handed combat. David didn't even use his sling. I've often wondered if his sling was a .300 Ebenezer Magnum reserved just for giants. Maybe, maybe not. But I have no doubts at all about David's heart. He was a *warrior*, pure and simple. He shouldered his responsibility as a man and stood ready to protect whatever was in his charge. His father's flock depended on him. And you and I must follow in the footsteps of David, and the Greater Son of David, Jesus Christ.

Think of your biblical heroes. Most often one of the things they had in common was a warrior's heart. Check it out.

- With 318 men of his own household, Abraham pursued four kings and *four armies*, divided his forces, struck his enemies by night, thoroughly routed them, and rescued their hostages.
- Joshua led his green troops against walled cities, populated by giants.
- Caleb, eighty-five years young, didn't want to sit around in a deck chair drinking Ensure. He pleaded for the opportunity to drive God's enemies out of a chunk of rough hill country. And then went out and did it.
- Nehemiah sent his men out to rebuild Jerusalem's shattered wall with trowels in one hand and swords in the other.
- Stephen stood toe to toe and all alone against the whole ruling body of Israel, condemned them from their own cherished history, and pointed to the Christ they'd killed, now sitting in glory at His Father's right hand.

There are many others, too, who were willing to be the men of the in-between. They were men who walked with God. Men who were willing to stand between their families and whatever lions threatened them.

There are lions out there who would devour our little flocks, too. Satan is roaring every day. Satan is devouring every day. And he will roar louder and devour more as we enter the twenty-first century because he knows his time is short.

In this battle-torn world, a man must find his warrior's heart. Families without warrior pillars are in deadly danger in this culture.

David's exploits as a young man rate our strong attention. Did you ever think about him as a model for your own life? You should. He was some kind of man. After all, even our Lord enjoyed being known as "the Son of David."

SOME KIND OF WARRIOR

I've always loved David. When I think about him, I get a mental picture of a bulldog—albeit a puppy bulldog at times early on. Yet in the end, he became the underdog who whipped the whole pack and sent 'em howling.

In some ways, he didn't have much of a background. He grew up in the backwoods, far south of the big city (the one that would someday bear his name!). His dad's acreage in Judah's hill country was off the beaten path, populated with witless sheep.

David, the sheep guard. Can you close your eyes and see him? Chewin' a stem of grass, tossin' rocks, rolling boulders off cliffs, watching clouds, wandering up nameless ravines, exploring caves, counting stars, strumming his harp, and—oh yeah, rasslin' bears. And choking mountain lions now and then.

The shepherd's life: weeks of sheer boredom, punctuated by minutes of total terror. A guy could go crazy with no one to talk to. But David *did* have someone to talk to. He talked with the Lord, the God of Israel. And he played his harp for an audience of One. All alone—plucking his strings; humming his songs, new songs composed of sunsets, starlight, dewy mornings, stormy winds, and untainted passion; and all for the Lord's own ears.

And it grew a heart in the man! A warrior's heart with two huge chambers, pumping the passionate blood of a man in love with God, and with God's people. What an incredible combination. It would shake his world. And it would touch the Heart of the universe. God would call it a heart after His own.

Out there in the nowhere, left to himself with only the whisper of the wind, the beating of his own heart, and the still, small voice of the living God, young David came of age. But no one knew it except the Lord.

Then came the day when the Lord directed the boy onto the pages of history. It all started in a small valley west of David's hometown. No one but the One could have guessed what was about to happen.

A N   E R R A N D   B O Y   W I T H   H E A R T

The incident began with a simple errand. Old Jesse asked his youngest son—the kid with the bronze skin and bright eyes—to pack up a lunch and carry it on down to his brothers who were serving in the military at the time. It wasn't a good time to serve in Israel's army. Morale was low. Equipment was sub-par; there wasn't a working smelt producing swords or spears in the whole nation. The red threat to the west, Philistia, completely intimidated the little nation. And it was painfully obvious that Israel's General-King Saul had no stomach for combat.

But the kid with the heart didn't know about all that.

David knew just two things as he carried those cheese sandwiches over the hill into the Valley of Elah. Number one, he knew he loved God. Number two, he knew God had a heart and plan for His people.

The scene he encountered in the valley made no sense to him at all. It was like a crazy dream, yet—it was real. Here were the armies of the living God slumped in their camp on one ridgeline while the armies of pagan Philistia blustered and swaggered across the valley on the opposite ridge. And in between there was some character, a so-called "Champion of Gath," who looked to David more like some kind of weird mutant. And this grotesque tower of a man was actually taunting—literally tormenting—the cowering legions of Israel! Goliath rubbed it in their faces, his great belly quivering with laughter. He continually challenged Israel to send out a champion of their choice to face him in the "land in-between."

It was a winner-take-all proposition. But there were no takers. The official "Champion of Israel," the man who stood head and shoulders above his own people, had lost his heart for the Lord—and for the Lord's battles. King Saul could not bring himself to square off with the evil giant who screamed and belched and spat out taunts and curses.

Israel and the armies of the living God had no champion. But whether they knew it or not, they had a boy with heart—a double-chambered heart that loved God and His people. And God's warriors cowering before the uncircumcised armies of idolatry was more than David could stomach.

So he put down his cheese sandwiches, rolled up his sleeves, and *handled* it.

The youngster had already faced a few giants of his own, all by himself, out in the wilderness, with only One watching. And that One had delivered him every time. What was this drooling Philistine mutant compared to a lion or a bear? David immediately volunteered to venture to the valley floor and shut the blasphemer's mouth.

You already know the rest of the story if you know your Bible. If you haven't read it lately, take a break from this book and read the Good Book. Take it up in 1 Samuel 17. David proved his warrior's heart on that remarkable day—as he would on many more days to come. He was a man who could bear up under tremendous weight and pressure.

THE WARRIOR PILLAR WILL HOLD A TON

He carried his father's flock. He endured his brother's mockery. He weathered Saul's jealousy and death-dealing treachery. He shouldered the pain of Jonathan, his best friend. In time, he would wear the weight of the kingdom on his broad shoulders. And in the long years to come, he would feel the crushing weight of his own great sin and folly, and the agony of death, rivalry, and rebellion within his own family.

David would carry it all. And he knew precisely where to carry it: *straight to his Lord's feet.* When he was discouraged, he poured out his heart. When he was in danger or afraid, he called out aloud. When he was overwhelmed by his own weakness and felt pulled down by his own sin, he reached his arms around the Rock, and held on for dear life. Whether a shepherd, a soldier, or a king, he continually felt inadequate for the calling on his life. He just didn't feel up to the task. But with

God's help, he did it anyway. He was always ready to run, even in tears, to the Lord.

David became "the man of the in-between." He stepped forward, descended the hillside, and shouted to the champion of the evil empire, "This day the LORD will deliver you into my hands and I will strike you down and remove your head from you...that all the earth may know that there is a God in Israel.... The battle is the LORD's" (1 Samuel 17:46-47).

And the young warrior went forth to conquer.

A thousand years later, the Greater Son of David—with similar words pulsing in his heart—met the Champion of Evil on a hill called Golgotha. Like His father David before Him, His shout of victory was simple and to the point: "It is finished!" He had accomplished all that the Father had sent Him to do. He served His people as the champion of the in-between. He stood between them and all that would hurt them. He took the hurt and the wounds and the abuse that belonged to us.

How about you? Are you a man of the in-between? Do you stand between those you love and all that would harm them? The Creator placed a warrior in every man's chest: one who remains alert on his post, vigilant and protective.

We happen to live in a day when many people are uncomfortable with the warrior in a man. Generally speaking, our feminist-influenced culture is opposed to anything strong in a man.

Still, the warrior is here to stay. C. S. Lewis recognized that noble reality when he said, "We have discovered that the scheme of 'outlawing war' has made war more like an outlaw without making it less frequent, and that to banish the knight does not alleviate the suffering of the peasant."[2]

The warrior is to be one who shields, defends, stands between, and guards. The warrior is a protector. According to Moore and Gillette, he invests himself in "the energy of self-disciplined, aggressive action." A real warrior does not love war. He draws no sadistic pleasure from fighting, or bloodshed, or destruction. As I said in an earlier book, a warrior is one who possesses high moral standards, and holds to high principles. He is willing to *live* by them, *stand* for them, *spend himself* in them, and if necessary *die* for them.

If we are utilizing the warrior's heart rightly, we will be energetic, self-sacrificing men, like our Lord. We will be alert, decisive, courageous, loyal, and persevering—all to the greater good of those near and dear to us. We will fight the good fight. And the world will be a better place for it.

One of the most humiliating things you can call a man is "coward." Maybe that's why many of us tend to lean toward the strong side and slip out of balance. Maybe that's why you seem, as a man, to stand aloof at times. Your warrior is a bit out of sync. Soldiering, after all, is connected with a lot of pain. And it hurts. You may have become a bit too accustomed to strapping on layers of protective insulation, hiding your tender heart under a half-inch of armor-plate. If you allow that to happen to you, again, your family will suffer.

Teddy Roosevelt captured some of the necessary balance for us:

A man's usefulness depends upon his living up to his ideals insofar as he can. It is hard to fail but it is worse never to have tried to succeed. All daring and courage, all iron endurance of misfortune, make for a finer, nobler type of manhood. Only those are fit to live who do not fear to die, and none are fit to die who have shrunk from the joy of life and the duty of life.[3]

The warrior in a man is a great asset. Still, generally speaking, many wish the warrior would disappear. This is the era of the "soft male." Fortunately, the warrior pillar in a man just can't be voted out. It is tenacious because, rightly understood, it is part of the divine design for masculinity. Wartime colors most of mankind's history, both good and bad.

It is a curious and irrepressible phenomenon indeed to see white-collared men slipping off into the woods on weekends to plaster each other with paint guns, develop survival skills, learn battle tactics, and generally play war games. It is the warrior in them. That's why Hollywood made the Rambos and the Schwarzeneggers. That's why they still produce films like *Braveheart* or *Rob Roy* or *Courage Under Fire*.

The warrior is here to stay. But hear me, friend…his energy needs careful channeling.

N E V E R   L E T   T H E
W A R R I O R   P I L L A R   L E A N

A warrior out of balance is a disastrous thing. He turns his strength in wrong directions. Women and children need to be protected *from* such a man.

I'll never forget a day I let my warrior pillar lean way out of balance. It fell so far that, apart from the grace of God that day, I might have lost my son. The pictures of those moments are still strong in my mind's eye. And the thought of them still hurts.

I grew up in a home where there were a couple of very basic and unalterable rules. Rule Number Two was simple and straightforward: "Never sass your Mom." When I did, Dad saw to it that I paid dearly. You simply did not mess with the woman he loved (even if she was "just my mom"). Years later, when I had my own family, that rule (and my misapplication of it) came home to haunt me on a Saturday morning. It was not a pretty sight.

I was doing something upstairs. My firstborn son and his mom were downstairs in the laundry room. They were engaged in one of "those" parent-teen encounters that are all too common. I could tell by the tones of their voices that a battle was shaping. Kent was just fourteen years old.

Do you remember being fourteen? I do. Worst year of my life! No longer a boy, but far from a man. Kind of a pubescent mutation from the land of the smoking lakes. Fourteen-year-olds live in a surreal world all their own. I realized later that Kent wasn't doing anything horrible. He was just being fourteen. But in the process he was getting a bit too close to his mom's face and space. What he really needed was a little mentoring from his dad. What he got was a warrior out of balance.

Hearing the turmoil, and remembering Rule Number Two, I bounded down the steps to intervene. The "great warrior" in me was going to defend his woman. I was going to become the man of the in-between and get between my wife and my son. When I did step in, it was too close and too forceful. Kent said something to me which I cannot recall now, but I let it set me off. Maybe it was his tone of voice. Or the young anger in his eyes. Or the developing independent spirit of a teenager. Maybe there was an element of disrespect in it.

Whatever it was, Rule Number One took over. There was only one rule in my home of origin that took precedence over "Don't sass your mom," and that was "Don't sass your dad!"

In that moment something took place that had never happened before, and has never happened since. It was absolutely horrible. Today we can joke about it, but every time we do, the pain of it all comes back to me. Today I can tease lightly about my response being an "involuntary reaction." But I know better. I know it was my own choosing. I allowed the warrior in me to cross the line.

My left arm (my strong side) flew up, and with the heel of my hand I struck my son in the sternum. Kent was standing next to the arm of the couch. The force and the surprise of the blow literally knocked him off his feet and he fell backward over the couch. I can still see my son, the shock of surprise and pain on his face, as he fell backward, out of control. Like a slow-motion, freeze-frame replay I can see every detail of the whole affair. It hurts me deeply to relive it. I hate it. I hate my sin. And the shame of my action. And my failure to father.

While Kent was still falling, as though in slow motion, I realized the horror of what I had done. In those split seconds, my mind went everywhere. Pain washed over me. And guilt. And fear. I wanted to reach out to my son. I wanted those actions back. I wanted desperately to get hold of them, recapture them, and stuff them in a bag to be burned. I wanted them not to have happened.

I had hurt my son. Oh, he would survive the physical encounter. He was a big strapping six-footer. But his heart had to be damaged. And it is out of the heart that life is lived. He was my son! Here was everything I loved. Everything I lived for. The young man who had made me a dad. The son I coached. The boy I loved more than is possible to imagine. The son I would die for. But I had ruined it all. I felt, in those split seconds, that I had destroyed the love of a lifetime.

Deep emotion washed over me. My face contorted. And not knowing what to do, I simply fell to my knees. He had fallen on the couch. I went all the way to the floor. It was fitting that I be beneath him. I felt, in those moments, that he was a far bigger man than I.

I heard my voice speaking. "Oh, Kent, can you possibly forgive me?"

They were words that I was not accustomed to saying. But they were the only words appropriate. I had done a horrible thing. I had hit a member of my family in anger.

I will be forever grateful for the strength in that young man. I am indebted to the character that God has instilled in him, and to his resilience. Kent stretched out those long arms of his. He opened them to me. I saw the traces of a smile on his lips, and I saw the life and the hope in his eyes when he said, "Yes, Dad, I forgive you."

Sometimes those are the most potent words a man can hear.

There, on the floor, with tears in my eyes, we embraced in the biggest, longest, closest bear hug of our lives. It was overwhelmingly emotional for me. The comfort and the strength of those moments will go with me to the grave. I remember it far more vividly than my son. To him it was but a momentary episode in a lifetime of adventure and growth. To me it was a lifetime in a single episode.

I do genuinely believe it was a turning point. A crossroads. I believe it shaped the years to come. In those moments with my son, I saw my incredible potential for disaster. And I saw the glorious realization of healed hearts. I had never seen so clearly my own angry failure. And I had seldom experienced such depth of joy. No words can describe the power of forgiveness.

Forgiveness. What power is in it!

Sometimes (often!) that's where we need to start, men. In our pilgrimage toward mature manhood and biblical headship, we often need a fresh start. That's what forgiveness is all about, a fresh start.

I expect that somewhere along the line, you, like me, have allowed one or more of the pillars in your heart to lean way out of balance. And others have paid a price for it. Everyone loses when the warrior in a man becomes a brute. And there is no solution like a biblical solution! Confession…repentance…and seeking forgiveness. It's the biblical path. A glorious journey. And the destination is out of this world. It's the ultimate R&R—reconciliation and restoration. Oh, the joy.

You see, this life is a pilgrimage. It's a process. Dad's learning, too. I don't know how many times I had to say to the kids, "Until you came along, I had never been a dad. So we're going to this school together."

We're walking this journey together. My kids don't want or need a perfect father. Neither do yours. But they do need a faithful one. A man big enough to confess his faults. A man big enough to speak heart to heart. A man big enough to ask forgiveness. A warrior strong enough to know when to call on the warrior, and wise enough to know when to let the warrior step aside and let another pillar take up the weight.

You see, my son didn't need the warrior that day. He just needed a friend and a mentor. A dad who had been fourteen once. A dad who remembered what it was like to begin to assert his independence from his mom.

If you and I can just be alert enough to our circumstances and the situations of those around us, we need only ask ourselves: "Which pillar is it that my family needs most right now?"

THE WARRIOR'S QUALITIES

Assuming, then, that by God's grace we've brought this pillar back into true balance, what are the warrior's positive qualities? How can the warrior in you help you in your personal, professional, and family lives?

The spirit of the warrior is an assertive, aggressive spirit. It must be disciplined to inject itself into situations only when necessary. The only way the warrior in the Christian man will know when aggressiveness is appropriate is through careful discipline of the soul in God's good Word. The only effective and discerning Christian warrior is a man of the Word. He will know when to act.

The heart of the warrior must be wedded to the vision of the king—a dream of stability and justice and order and security for those near and dear to him. Then the warrior's unconquerable spirit and incredible courage can contribute to a lifestyle of peace. General Norman Schwarzkopf said that in so many words in a letter to his children. He wrote it at midnight, just before the launching of the Gulf War offensive at 2:30 A.M. that morning.

> I hope you know how much I love you. The three of you have become the most important reason for my being on this earth....
> I could be rich and famous and have everything I desire, but

without you my life would be meaningless, my heart would be empty, and I would not want to live. The three of you are my immortality…. I am a father who knows his children love him and that makes me a very lucky man![4]

Characteristic of the true warrior is self-denial. He is not afraid of pain and death. He understands what is worth dying for, and willingly does so when necessary, as did the apostles of the first-century Church.

Yes, the warrior is a destroyer. The Christian warrior is out to destroy evil in all of its many forms—dishonesty, corruption, tyranny, injustice, pornography, child abuse, oppression, racism. Paul himself understood this foundational reality:

For though we live in the world, we do not wage war as the world does. The weapons we fight with are not the weapons of the world. On the contrary, they have divine power to demolish strongholds. We demolish arguments and every pretension that sets itself up against the knowledge of God, and we take captive every thought to make it obedient to Christ. (2 Corinthians 10:3-5, NIV)

Yes, the warrior is a protector. Men stand tallest when they are protecting and defending. And it is in the areas of the soul and the spirit that most of today's families need careful protection. Some anonymous warrior said it wisely and well: "Keep out of your child's life anything that will keep Christ out of his heart."

George Leonard said it well, too:

We need passion. We need challenge and risk. We need to be pushed to our limit. And I believe this is just what happens when we accept a warrior's code, when we try to live each moment, whether in education, job, marriage, child rearing, or recreation. The truth is that we don't have to go into combat to go to war. Life is fired at us like a bullet, and there is no escaping it short of death. All escape attempts—drugs, aimless travel, the distractions of the media, empty material pursuits—are sure to fail in the long run, as more and more of us are beginning to learn.[5]

God calls His men to *take on life*. To stand in the gap for their wives, for their children, and ultimately, for their nation.

Be a warrior. Yes! Just make sure you're a Tender Warrior.

*The present time is of the highest importance—
it is time to wake up to reality. Every day brings
God's salvation nearer.... The night is nearly
over, the day has almost dawned.... Let us arm
ourselves for the fight of the day!*
ROMANS 13:11-12, PHILLIPS

THE WARRIOR AT RISK

Sullivan Belleau was quite a man. A four-pillared man.

As with many of his friends, his life seemed to be falling into place rather nicely. He'd fallen in love with and married a beautiful woman. Sarah was the love of his life. He'd do anything for that woman. Their marriage was a union of best friends. Together they had a "litter" of boys that would make any dad proud. Sarah was the apple of his eye, and those little applets "hadn't fallen far from the tree," as people in the town would tell you.

Speaking of trees, Sullivan was very much aware of the need for healthy roots. He did not see himself as the center of his own universe. He knew life was larger than he. He knew where he had come from…and he had a dream for those who would come after him. He knew that he stood on the shoulders of previous generations, and that one day he would have to pass the baton to the next.

Sullivan's greatest joy was spending his time loving that woman and developing those boys. They were in the forefront of all his kingly dreams. He was a man of principle, and he longed to pass those principles to his sons. This was a family that had connected. They were friends. Sullivan's lifelong goal was simply to love Sarah and build a future for those little boys.

Ironically, that's what made him a warrior. He was willing to fight for those loves—his wife, his kids, and his principles. So when the call came, he signed up. His country was in trouble. When those principles, those loves, and those lives were threatened, Sullivan believed a man should stand up. When injustice was tearing people apart, a man had to get involved. When the lives and freedoms of others were being attacked, you could count on Sullivan Belleau to respond.

You see, Sullivan Belleau was a man who looked further to the future than the end of his own nose. He didn't live just for the weekends. He lived for family and principle. And he saw himself and his family as part of something larger than themselves.

So Sullivan Belleau became a soldier. The issues were foundational. The training was intense. So were the men. So was the heat of the summer sun that burned into the backs of their woolen uniform jackets. But it was worth it. Because the cause was larger than a man, larger than his family, larger than his life. The American Civil War was not child's play. Sullivan knew it would cost lives, more than likely his own among them. But there comes a time when a man sacrifices his own dreams for the sake of high principle.

So it was that a hot July day in 1861 found Sullivan Belleau, now a major in the Second Rhode Island Volunteers, writing home to his wife in Smithfield. He and his unit were part of the large Union force gathering just outside the nation's capitol. He wrote, laboring under the common premonition of a warrior, and with a great sense of duty. And he wrote determined to communicate his soul to the woman he loved.

Last words are lasting words. Major Belleau's letter of July 14 is a masterpiece of manliness. Read his words...and his heart. It is the heart of a *true* warrior:

Washington, DC
14 July 1861

Dear Sarah,

The indications are very strong that we shall move in a few days. Perhaps tomorrow. And lest I should not be able to write you again, I feel impelled to write a few lines that may fall under your eye when I am no more.

I have no misgivings about, or lack of confidence in, the cause in which I am engaged. And my courage does not halt or falter. I know how great a debt we owe to those who went before us through the blood and suffering of the Revolution. And I am willing, perfectly willing, to lay down all my joys in this life to help pay that debt.

Sarah, my love for you is deathless. It seems to bind me with mighty cables that nothing but Omnipotence can break. And yet my love of country comes over me like a strong wind and bears me irresistibly, with all those chains, to the battlefield.

The memory of all the blissful moments I have enjoyed with you comes crawling over me. And I feel most deeply grateful to God, and to you, that I have enjoyed them for so long. But how hard it is for me to give them up, and burn to ashes the hopes of future years when, God willing, we might still have lived and loved together and seen our boys grow up to honorable manhood around us.

If I do not return, my dear Sarah, never forget how much I loved you. Know that when my last breath escapes me on the battlefield, it will whisper your name. Forgive my many faults and the many pains I have caused you. How thoughtless, how foolish, I have sometimes been. But, Oh Sarah, if the dead can come back to this earth to flit unseen around those they love, I shall always be with you...in the brightest day...and in the darkest night...always...always! And when the soft breeze fans your cheek, it shall be my breath...or the cool air on your throbbing temple, it shall be my spirit passing by.

Sarah, do not mourn me dead. Think I am gone, and wait for me. For we shall meet again.[1]

One week after he wrote those magnificent words to the love of his life, Sullivan Belleau was killed at the First Battle of Bull Run. He was gone. But he died having left a legacy that lives. Now you and I stand on *his* shoulders. He lived hardly a century after the American Revolution. Now we live barely a century after his Civil War and ours. What will we do with that legacy?

How far from that tree will our generation fall? How far from the roots of truth, justice, freedom, duty, and honor will you fall? Hopefully we will not fall far from that same tree. But many men today have fallen—and far from that tree—only to rot on the ground of their own selfishness.

Sullivan Belleau's letter illustrates several key principles—biblical principles—which ought to reside in the heart of every warrior. You can call them what you will, but if they are not at home in your chest, then you are not a warrior of biblical stripe. Let's take them on, one by one.

1: THE WARRIOR IN A MAN IS UNDER AUTHORITY

A warrior without authority is an oxymoron. No, make that simply a moron. A warrior who is not under authority is not a warrior, he's a renegade. A pirate. A mercenary. Just another ruffian looking for a fight. The kind of man who abuses his wife, or his children, or other people at a whim.

We find such non-warriors masquerading all over the business world. Highly competitive but without principle or authority, they live by the unstated but very real motto, "I'll do anything to win—for me." They gobble up competing businesses, hire lawyers ("guns") to rifle through smaller companies, and take as many scalps as possible along the way. These impostor warriors fight—but only for themselves. Of course, they would never see it that way and would try to justify their mercenary lifestyles in order to live with themselves.

As with the king in a man, "the way up" for the warrior is "the way down." Getting under. Serving. Sacrificing. Jesus was the consummate warrior. He had a worthy cause—the glory of His father, the redemption of people, and the reclaiming of the kingdom from the usurper Satan. Jesus volunteered for the service. He reported for duty, took on the uniform of a human being, traveled to the battlefield of planet earth, and faced off with the forces of evil and their champion, Satan, The Adversary. As Paul described it, He...

> emptied Himself, taking the form of a bond-servant, and being made in the likeness of men. And being found in appearance as a man, He humbled Himself by becoming obedient to the point of death, even death on a cross. Therefore also God highly exalted Him, and bestowed on Him the name which is above every

name, that at the name of Jesus every knee should bow…to the glory of God the Father." (Philippians 2:7-11)

Because Jesus was no mercenary—no rebel—but humbly and dutifully sacrificed Himself, the Father awarded Him the highest of battlefield medals. He gave Him a name above every name.

If you are a man, you are a warrior under orders. In the military, we used to call them "general orders." Every soldier is under the same general orders. And a good soldier never forgets 'em.

Just for fun, the other day in one of our weekly elders' meetings, I passed a note to one of the guys (the agenda didn't require either of our attention at the moment—smile). Norm, in his seventies now, was a young tail gunner on a B-17 with numerous missions over Europe during World War II. I thought I'd see if this old soldier and retired dentist could still pull his general orders out of the hat. My note said, "Norm, please write out for me—if you can still remember it (ha!)—your first general order."

Without a second's hesitation, he began writing, then shoved the note over to me.

To walk my post in a military manner, keeping always on the alert, and observing everything that takes place within sight or hearing.

Seeing that I was impressed with his recall, he quickly jotted a fictitious "11th general order" and shoved that one at me, too. I almost laughed out loud. (We were beginning to be a disruptive influence in the elders' meeting.) This note said: "If it moves, salute it! If it doesn't, paint it!"

Like every good military order, your orders from the Father are equally explicit and direct. No ifs, ands, or buts about them. And like every good soldier you and I need to review those general orders regularly. What are some of your general orders, Christian man? A few of them jump to my mind right away:

- He gave us orders that we are to spend regular time with Him, so our relationship can grow deeper and stronger.

- He gave us orders that we are to love our wives at all costs, even the cost of our lives, being willing to give up some of our own hopes and dreams as necessary. When a man goes AWOL from his marriage, he has walked away from his most critical duty post. The consequences are incredibly stiff.
- He gave us orders to raise our children in such a way that they would know how to listen to their Lord and follow Him.
- He gave us orders to be involved in our local church, using our gifts and sharing our resources for the sake of His body. Your commitment to your local church is one of the most critical parts of your mission as a man.

Obedience to orders is something a warrior must learn first and foremost. If a soldier intends to be an effective warrior, he takes his orders very seriously. On the battlefield, anything less than blind obedience is the mark of a traitor. The heart of military training is the development of instinctive obedience. The point of every drill is instinctive obedience.

Listen to Colonel David Hackworth describe the making of a warrior:

What makes a marine? The challenge begins as anxious recruits arrive and receive the first command of the 11-week course: "Without pushing and shoving, get off the bus." Dressed in sweats or jeans, they hit the deck. They are not to use the word "I." Every time they open their mouths, the last word must be "sir."... The training is relentless, but constructive: 16 hours a day, seven days a week.... If a recruit at attention scratches an itch, a Drill Instructor shouts, "For what reason did you break the position of attention!" No excuse is acceptable. "I went there as an undisciplined pig," says [one 20-year-old]. "If you don't develop the right stuff in boot camp, you won't have it on the battlefield."[2]

The point is easily understood—follow orders. Do what you're told. Do it when you're told. Do it as you're told. It's a big job being a warrior in today's world. And tougher still than being a marine, is being a man at the head of a home. It's much tougher to be an excellent husband than to complete Marine boot camp. It's much tougher to successfully raise a family than to serve in the Green Berets.

Today I lost a friend who would know.

A   W A R R I O R ' S   H I G H E S T   H O N O R

I am writing these words on a Monday. I've just come from delivering the message at a funeral for an old friend, a member of our local church. Fittingly enough, Don's memorial service was on Veterans Day. The old soldier has fought his last battle. He enlisted during the Korean crisis and served with the U.S. Army Special Forces. "Airborne all the way," the old paratrooper's now made his last jump. Only this time, the jump was reversed! Not another static line jump from heaven to earth, but a spectacular leap from earth to heaven.

Don's service today was a fitting tribute to a great man. In the foyer just outside the auditorium, his four grown daughters had created a display that did him proud. There was his beret and pictures from his days in the military, along with training certificates and military awards. Alongside this was memorabilia from his twenty-one years with the U.S. Forest Service after his time in the military. Also represented was the small construction company Don founded when he retired from the Forest Service. And there were family pictures, too. Great shots of smiling, confident people. His wife, his daughters, and their children.

But one item stole the show. Don would likely tell you it was probably the highest award (other than Shirley's "yes!" to his marriage proposal) he had ever received. It was a poem written shortly after he died, by one of his daughters, now a mother herself. As people filed by the display, each stopped to read that centerpiece. Virtually every one of them, both men and women, struggled to hold back their tears. Many didn't succeed. I didn't. Here is what we read:

Dad, are you really gone?
> I'm certain I was there when you took your last breath.
> Yet it seems your life is still speaking so loud and clear.

Are you really gone?
I can see you in all my childhood days
Always taking care of us, letting our lives as children
Be as God intended: carefree, happy and adventurous, joyful.
Are you really gone?
I can see your smile and your fatherly wink
As I feel your familiar and vigorous hug.
I can see the joy in your face as your grandchildren embrace
You and you turn to me without hesitation
And say, "You're a good mother, I'm proud of you."
Are you really gone?
I can see you so clear, a man of God, a devoted father,
A loving husband, a church leader, a friend.
I can hear you say, "It's good to be alive,"
As you enjoy the simple pleasures in life.
Are you really gone?
I can see your Christian influence woven into the decisions
Of my life and it is only by your confident example that I
    can say,
You'll never really be gone from us.
And I can now hear our heavenly Father say to you,
"Welcome, good and faithful servant,
Enter into the joy I have prepared for you."

It doesn't get any better than that. No medal, ribbon, or citation even remotely compares to the deep, abiding love and respect of a daughter or son.

No, Don Vaughn's not really gone. He's only relocated to another and better world—the world for which he was created. And while he waits there for those he loves, he's handed them a baton of rich faith and heritage.

Don Vaughn stayed at his post. He loved his wife; mentored his daughters; and embraced his grandchildren. And the family stock is soaring. All because an old warrior took his orders seriously. He has left a legacy that would make any man proud. Right about now I expect he's saluting his Commander in Chief, the Lord of Hosts, and hearing, "Well done, good and faithful servant. Enter into your rest." ("Take five!" in military parlance.)

I want to hear those words one day. And you do, too. So we've got to take our orders seriously. We've got to live like men under orders. And we've got to stay at our posts.

2: THE WARRIOR IN A MAN REMAINS ON-CALL

One of the greatest tragedy's of David's life was the result of his sloughing off. If David had remained on-call, the tragic episode with Bathsheba would not have taken place. Instead of plunging his life and his kingdom into a terrible abyss, he would have been leading the charge against Rabbah. But David did not remain on-call. Misusing his kingly authority, he got away with being AWOL.

When he should have been at war with his troops, he took time off.

When he should have been leading, he was moping.

When he should have been focused, he was mentally lazy.

When he should have been in a disciplined mind-set, he was self-indulgent.

And *everyone* around him paid for it. He lost his self-respect. Bathsheba lost hers. Uriah lost his life. So did the little baby born of adultery. No one wins when a warrior sloughs off.

David could have taken a lesson from Uriah. Having sinned against the man and his wife, the king schemed to get Uriah home from the front so the soldier would be deceived into thinking the child was his. But Uriah was a warrior. He remained on-call. Listen to their conversation:

> Then David sent to Joab, saying, "Send me Uriah the Hittite." So Joab sent Uriah to David. When Uriah came to him, David asked concerning…the state of the war. Then David said to Uriah, "Go down to your house.…" But Uriah slept at the door of the king's house with all the servants of his lord, and did not go down to his house. Now when they told David…, David said to Uriah…, "Why did you not go down to your house?" (2 Samuel 11:6-10)

Now read Uriah's answer carefully. It is the noble answer of a noble man—and a warrior on-call.

And Uriah said to David, "The ark and Israel and Judah are staying in temporary shelters, and my lord Joab and the servants of my lord are camping in the open field. Shall I then go to my house to eat and to drink and to lie with my wife? By your life and the life of your soul, I will not do this thing." (2 Samuel 11:11)

Uriah remained on-call in spite of opportunities and high-placed encouragement to do otherwise. The man subjugated his own personal pleasures to the needs of the hour.

Fighting in the trenches—waging war—is not a nine-to-five job. The heart of a warrior is always at the ready. When the winds and fortunes of life shift and change, the warrior is ready to respond to the new circumstances. James, the half-brother of Jesus, had watched his Brother. He knew the way with warriors. He wrote to us: "Consider it all joy, my brethren, when you encounter various trials, knowing that the testing of your faith produces endurance. And let endurance have its perfect result, that you might be perfect and complete, lacking in nothing" (James 1:2–4).

My mind wanders to men I have known who have deserted their posts. Having ignored their general orders to husbands, having chosen not to keep their promises, having decided to indulge themselves, they left their wives. One impostor's name comes to mind; he left his wife and children on the very day his last child was born. Can you imagine! He is no man. He brings discredit to himself and to his gender. I have to confess, his name brings nothing but disgust to mind.

Oh, sure, "things were tough." Sure, he had "his side" to tell. Sure, there were obstacles to overcome. But he cut and ran. Like a coward on the battlefield of life, he just quit. Henley's little couplet could never apply to him:

In the fell clutch of circumstance,
I have not winced nor cried aloud;

Under the bludgeoning of chance
My head is bloody, but unbowed.

Friend, we've got to stay at it even when our noses are bloodied in
the battle. Warriors stay at it. This nation owes a significant portion of its
history (and its real estate) to a young buck who got his start as a powder monkey in the U.S. Navy. Promoted from powder monkey to mid-
shipman, young Sam Reid was given his first command, a small privateer, during the War of 1812. His ship was pursued by an entire British
squadron off New York. Through sheer energy, skill, and creativity (like
pumping water on his sails and by towing his vessel with rowers in the
ship's boats) he managed to avoid capture.

Shortly thereafter, in the Azores, his little privateer with seven guns
and ninety men faced off with the British squadron carrying 136 guns
and 2,000 men. The King's ships were relentless, throwing hundreds of
men and numerous boats at the young Reid. Ultimately the British succeeded in boarding his vessel. In the hand-to-hand combat that followed,
Reid dueled with the British commander and his crew succeeded in
repelling the boarders. The young commander then moved all his guns
to one side and cut new gun ports during the night. At dawn he succeeded in overwhelming one larger vessel with withering fire from his
repositioned guns. As *H.M.S. Plantagenet,* the huge seventy-four-gun
man-of-war, closed in on him, Reid simply scuttled his ship rather than
lose her to the much larger British force.

General Andrew Jackson later told young Captain Reid, "If there had
been no Battle of Fayal (as Reid's was named), there would have been no
Battle of New Orleans." Many believe Louisiana and the Northwest
Territories would be British today if Reid had not remained at his post
in what has been called one of the world's most decisive naval battles.

3: THE WARRIOR IN A MAN WILLINGLY SACRIFICES

It nearly goes without saying, doesn't it? Warriors suffer. Warriors are
wounded. Warriors die. So where did we ever get the idea that there is no
price to be paid?

We live in a day of self-preservation, self-concern, self-improvement, self-serving, self-concept, and self-interest. We have become our own focus. The highest value in our civilization has become "deciding for myself." We think our greatest investments must be in ourselves. Our lives seem to center around "my" pleasure, my desires, my enjoyment, my accomplishments, my achievements, my toys.

What are you spending your life on? Jesus gave clear instructions to his guys, "If anyone wishes to come after Me, let him deny himself, and take up his cross, and follow Me. For whoever wishes to save his life shall lose it; but whoever loses his life for My sake shall find it" (Matthew 16:24-25). Jesus has made it very uncomplicated and clear: Deny your self-isms, so you can spend yourself on following Him and serving others. Remember your general orders?

- We know we have been called to give ourselves away to spending time with and growing deeper in our relationship with the Lord.
- We know we have been called to willingly sacrifice for our wives, helping them to become all God designed them to be.
- We know we have been called to willingly sacrifice for our children, and the children of our society who are helpless to help themselves.
- We know we have been called to willingly sacrifice for our church, and for the lost in our communities.

It's really not all that complicated discovering what we ought to sacrifice for. The heart of the question at hand is, "Are you willing?"

Leith Anderson tells the story of missionaries in Zaire. Judy Anderson, whose husband is the West Africa Director of World Relief for NAE, grew up in Zaire as the daughter of missionaries. She remembers as a little girl attending a day-long rally celebrating the 100-year anniversary of the missionaries' arrival. After a full day of long speeches and music, an old man stepped to the front of the crowd and insisted on speaking. He indicated his death would not be long in coming and that he was the last one alive who could relate to them some very important information. He did not want to take it to his grave with him.

He explained that when Christian missionaries came a hundred years before, his people thought the missionaries were strange and their message unusual. The tribal leaders decided to test the missionaries by slowly poisoning them to death. Over a period of months and years, missionary children died one by one. Then the old man said, "It was as we watched how they died that we decided we wanted to live as Christians."

4: THE WARRIOR IN A MAN MUST SOMETIMES SAY AND DO THE HARD THING

While warriors are never brutes, neither do they shrink from battle. And sometimes that means the warrior in a man must say the hard thing. I read the other day of one crusty old saint who probably overdid it. Mark Galli described an episode in the life of St. Francis of Assisi. After describing Francis as "the saint who probably deserves the Nobel Peace Prize of all history," he goes on to say:

> You would think a life characterized by peace would make Francis a nice guy to be around. Not so. Just one example: Francis had a thing about money: his friars were not to touch it. And he did not mean "you-can-touch-money-but-just-don't-let-it-grip-your-heart" stuff.
>
> One day a worshiper at the Church of Saint Mary of the Portiuncula, Francis's headquarters, left a coin as an offering at the base of the sanctuary cross. This was a common offering to God in that day, but when one of Francis's friars saw the money—he tossed it over to a window sill.
>
> When Francis learned he had touched the money, he did not take the errant brother aside, explain his point of view, and then hug him so as to be sure there were no hard feelings. Instead, Francis rebuked and upbraided the brother. He then commanded him to lift the money from the windowsill with his lips, find a pile of ass's dung outside, and with his lips place the coin in the pile.[3]

Well, the old monk probably did overdo it, don't you think? This pastor doesn't much care to sign up for Francis's order. But I'll tell you what I do like: You knew where the man stood. It seems to me that Christians today act like they're not supposed to have any opinions. We have become so "inclusive" and "tolerant" in our attitudes, we can no longer muster the courage to say the hard things.

But sometimes it is true: Christians, if truly Christians, are not always "nice" or "agreeable" in the eyes of everyone. But they are appropriately honest. Truthful, not ugly. Firm, not antagonistic. Persistent, not discourteous. Sometimes being a Christian simply requires that one "say the hard thing." Jesus did it regularly. When your friend is about to step in front of a speeding car, you don't politely whisper a warning. You do what it takes to get the job done.

Sometimes the warrior in a Christian man just has to speak up. Like Pastor Joe Wright of Wichita, Kansas's Central Christian Church did. He delivered the invocation before the Kansas State legislature, and, as commentator Paul Harvey later noted, "he told God on them." By the time the good pastor had finished his prayer, no fewer than three members of the legislature began howling into their microphones. They thought Pastor Wright had been too "divisive" and "overbearing."

How bad could Joe Wright's prayer have been to generate such a pained and angry response? Personally, I think the warrior in Pastor Joe's chest had decided he'd been "nice" long enough. I think he said the hard thing. The legislators had been expecting some soft, bland, generic "inspiration." They wanted Pablum, and they got horseradish. They weren't expecting the reverend to call a spade a spade, and it upset their refined sensibilities. Here are the words that so shocked and offended them:

> Heavenly Father, we come before you today to ask Your forgiveness and to seek Your direction and guidance. We know your words, "Woe to those who call evil good," but that is exactly what we have done.
>
> We have lost our spiritual equilibrium and inverted our values. We confess that we have ridiculed the absolute truth of Your Word in the name of "moral pluralism."
>
> We have worshipped other gods and called it "multicultural-

ism." We have endorsed perversion and called it an "alternate lifestyle." We have exploited the poor and called it a "lottery." We have neglected the needy and called it "self-preservation." We have rewarded laziness and called it "welfare."

In the name of "choice," we have killed the unborn. In the name of "right to life," we have killed abortionists. We have neglected to discipline our children and called it "building esteem." We have abused power and called it "political savvy."

We've coveted our neighbor's possessions and called it "taxes." We've polluted the air with profanity and pornography and called it "freedom of expression." We've ridiculed the time-honored values of our forefathers and called it "enlightenment."

Search us, O God, and know our hearts today. Try us, and show us any wicked way in us. Cleanse us from every sin, and set us free. Guide and bless these men and women who have been sent here by the people of Kansas and who have been ordained by You to govern this great state. Grant them Your wisdom to rule, and may their decisions direct us to the center of Your will. I ask it in the name of Your Son, the living Savior, Jesus Christ. Amen.[4]

Three cheers for Pastor Joe! May his tribe increase. May Christian men become truth-tellers—even when the truth stings.

Does the warrior in you stand up when you should? Do you defend the truth in your personal conversations? With your children? With your neighbors? With your co-workers? Do people around you know where you stand? Don't get me wrong. I'm not asking anyone to be ugly, over-bearing, or arrogant. But I do think it more than reasonable that warriors wear their uniforms in public. I understand that it's easier to wear your "civvies" and remain anonymous, but that is not why your heavenly Commander stationed you on this planet. Walk your post. And say the hard thing when it's right and appropriate.

When you think about it, isn't that part of the quality that has indelibly imprinted the image of John Wayne across the American psyche? Yes, the "Duke" represented any number of flaws. Frankly, we've had more than enough of his go-it-alone brand of isolation, stoicism, and his implied disrespect for women (evidenced, among other ways, in his multiple marriages). But something must account for his ongoing hold on our imaginations. Why does his name come to mind when America thinks of its classic heroic figures?

As an actor, Wayne was no great shakes. One critic asked, "How could a hardworking but only moderately gifted actor playing predictable, monochromatic roles acquire the status of myth and come to embody 'America'?"

That same critic, Jackson Lears, answered his own question:

> Wayne's version of heroism tapped a rich vein in American cultural tradition. D. H. Lawrence made it famous…when he described Fenimore Cooper's *Deerslayer:* "A man who keeps his moral integrity hard and intact. An isolate, almost selfless, stoic, enduring man, who lives by death, by killing, but is pure white…. *He actually stands for something amid the mush of timidity and moral indifference.*[5]

It is that last sentence that I think today's Christian man needs to evaluate for personal application. The warrior in a man must contend for what he believes. A warrior must take a stand, say the hard thing, and not look back. It was in the tormented 1960s that Wayne made the statement that summed up his personal code both on and off the screen. "Perversion and corruption masquerade as ambiguity," said the Duke. "I don't trust ambiguity."

Say what you will about his other qualities, or lack of them, the man was a plain speaker.

Plain speaking was perhaps the most obvious quality of the prophets, warriors in the cultural wars of their day. For instance, after godless King Amaziah tried to kick Amos, God's spokesman, out of Israel, the old boy put it back to him straight:

> "I was neither a prophet nor a prophet's son, but I was a shepherd, and I also took care of sycamore-fig trees. But the LORD

took me from tending the flock and said to me, 'Go, prophesy to my people Israel.' Now then, hear the Word of the LORD." (Amos 7:14-16, NIV)

You can almost hear the old fig-picker's foghorn voice rising with a "NOW HEAR THIS!" Hear it, Amaziah, whether it pleases you or not. Hear it Israel, whether it ruffles your sensibilities or not.

Jesus Himself said the hard thing many a time. Jesus is the One who said, "Do not think I came to bring peace on the earth; I did not come to bring peace but a sword." Jesus was not about to toss "peace" around indiscriminately as though it were some kind of pixie-dust tranquillity. He knew better than anyone that ultimate peace would come only as the product of a war on evil. He knew it would come at great cost. And He was willing to pay it—a Warrior's death in the name of Truth.

The great English preacher, G. Campbell Morgan, caught the spirit of the warrior in Christ. Relating both to Jesus' words and those of His brother James (James 3:17), Dr. Morgan observed:

What is the way of peace? First pure. And what is purity of heart? It is the heart undivided in its allegiance to God. So this [is how the] Prince of Peace comes…. He comes to say, "I have brought a sword, and I have come to war against the things in your life that shut God out….

Jesus Christ does not come first with a song and a lullaby and a narcotic. He comes with a sword and flame and a fire;…you know that He will not make peace with the evil thing in your heart, in your mind, in your outlook, in your habits, and He will make no peace with it—for the sake of ultimate peace. Then do not be at war with Him, but end the war by letting Him win, even though it mean the breaking down of the idol, and the wounding of [your] spirit; for out of that wounding there will come peace, God's great peace, which is first pure.[6]

Yes, the warrior in a man is an appropriately plain speaker. Sometimes it is the "hard thing" that is just what your "rebellious" teenager needs. Read for personal application this story related to me by my brother-in-law, Rick Taylor:

Joey was a fourteen-year-old junior high student. At the time, I was doing community counseling and would occasionally be assigned a juvenile like Joey in an attempt to help the youngster avoid juvenile detention. At this particular counseling appointment, Joey was accompanied by his father. I attempted to ask Joey a number of questions. But his father kept interrupting me, attempting to answer for Joey—often before I could complete the question.

Twenty minutes into the appointment, Joey had still not uttered a word. His father's rambling had been filled with repeated statements about his love for his son, and his own frustration that Joey continued to defy him and deliberately disobey him.

Finally, I politely asked the father if I might meet with Joey alone for a few minutes. He agreed…reluctantly.

With his father gone, Joey initially continued his silence. He didn't respond to my questions. His head down, eyes to the floor, he simply sat there. I paused for several minutes, then decided to make a few statements rather than ask questions. I began by saying, "Joey, it seems that your dad loves you a great deal—" Before I could finish my sentence, Joey's head shot up. His eyes met mine. With his lips curled and scorn written across his every feature, Joey practically screamed, "No! No, he *doesn't* love me!"

Somewhat startled, I followed Joey's emphatic lead. "Why would you say that, Joey," I asked him, "when your father repeatedly affirmed his love for you?"

Joey's answer was much less scornful. He was hurting. He just blurted out, "If he loved me, he wouldn't let me stay out till two in the morning—and never ask me where I've been. He doesn't care! He doesn't love me. He only says that. If he loved me, he'd do something about it."

Reflecting on the incident later, Rick thought, *Joey should have been the counselor. He had it figured out long before the appointment. And he was right.*

A fourteen-year-old juvenile delinquent had hit the nail on the head. Sometimes the warrior in a man must prove himself by saying—and doing—the hard thing.

5: THE WARRIOR IN A MAN DEMONSTRATES A HEART OF MERCY

While the warrior in a man is prepared to walk his post, take his stand, and contend courageously and sacrificially, he must also know when to "call off the dogs." There is a time to press the battle, and there is a time to hold one's strength. There is a time for the warrior to sheath his sword, and show mercy.

David did it when he spared the life of the wooden-headed Nabal, and once again when he showed kindness to Saul's grandson Mephibosheth.

And isn't that what Jesus did during the greatest battle of His life? When He could have called legions of angels, He held His sword. When He could have wasted the lives of all associated with His death, He chose to grant mercy—even to the point of praying for their forgiveness. It had been the same earlier in the Garden of Gethsemane when He restored the servant's severed ear.

The wise warrior knows when mercy must be generously applied.

Denny Deveny, our Pastor of Counseling Ministries at Good Shepherd Church (and an especially close friend of mine), has developed an interest in learning more of his own heritage. In some of the family archives he came across a fascinating account of an ancestor, one Aaron Deveny, who fought in the American Revolution.

In a sworn affidavit dated October 20, 1834, the then eighty-seven-year-old man testified in conjunction with his soldier's pension. After the Battle of King's Mountain, he had been held prisoner by the British for a period of two weeks, and his fate was very tenuous. The affidavit describes his wife's pursuit of the prisoner's company.

Sarah Deveny managed to locate the ranking British officer and plead her husband's case. In the process, she ultimately "resorted to tears." The affidavit indicates that this last was "more than Colonel Ferguson could cope with." He agreed to parole Sarah's husband, commenting that he would "rather see twenty men die in battle than one woman languish in tears."[7] Perhaps the man had merely run out of patience, but I prefer to think he was one Redcoat officer carrying in his chest the warrior's heart of mercy.

The long shadows cast by the warrior pillar are a beautiful blend of strength, courage, reliability, sacrifice, mercy, and plain, truthful speaking.

Happy is the family—or nation—privileged to rest in that shade.

THE MENTOR
PILLAR

Lives of great men all remind us
We can make our lives sublime.
And, departing, leave behind us
Footprints on the sands of time.
HENRY WADSWORTH LONGFELLOW

Wisdom is a shelter
  as money is a shelter,
but the advantage of knowledge is this:
  that wisdom preserves the life of its
    possessor.
ECCLESIASTES 7:12, NIV

CHAPTER 10

LIFE COACHING

I remember the first time I heard my dad use the word.
It struck me as funny. And to a four- or five-year-old youngster, I guess it *was* funny. I started to giggle a little.

"Pop," he had said.

Dad had used the word to address his own dad, my grandpa. And there was something about the way he said it—such respect...tender-ness...honor...even deference—that I knew he was definitely not referring to my favorite soft drink. He was acknowledging something very deep inside him. He was bowing to his teacher.

I quit giggling. I was still a bit confused, but I understood something of the mystery instinctively, that this was somehow a term of highest esteem. Now, I knew soda pop. I loved it. Pepsi was my favorite. After all, Grandpa had taught me to love it. He always had some in his refrig-erator. And he would wink at me when we drank it together.

But something very large was beginning to dawn on my young mind. The most powerful man in the world to me, my dad, was bowing to another. As most little boys do, I thought my dad bowed to no one. But here, before my wondering eyes, my father was paying another man great respect. Many years later, when my grandpa was in the nursing home, with shrunken body and sunken eyes—requiring professional care—my dad would return regularly to his bedside and sit beside him. Just to be there. As though he had come to learn something.

Indeed, he had. He had learned a lifetime, at Pop's feet. Pop had been his life coach, his mentor, for all his days.

And that's why today I now call my dad "Pop." It is a title of great dimension. It is a term of endearment. It is a matter of deference. It means the world to me. When "Pop" crosses my lips, my head bows just

185

a little, my heart beats a nudge faster, and my soul quiets itself in his presence. He's my dad. He's my coach. He's my mentor. He's my life.

You hear the term "mentor" being tossed around quite a bit these days. But its roots come out of ancient Greece. *Mentor* was actually the name of the guardian of Telemachus, the son of Odysseus, who was away fighting in the Trojan War. It was Mentor who taught Telemachus the way life worked. It was Mentor who turned the boy Telemachus into a man. Howie Hendricks and his son Bill, in their book *As Iron Sharpens Iron,* base their foundational definition of the term "mentor" upon the story of Telemachus and Mentor:

> Based on this story, we now speak of a mentor as someone who functions to some extent as a father figure (in the best sense of the term), a man who fundamentally affects and influences the development of another, usually younger, man.... Mentors nurture our souls. They shape our character. They call us to be complete men, whole men, and, by the grace of God, holy men.[1]

Like you, I can look back through the chapters of my life and the list of men who most impacted me begins to form on memory's screen. As I sit here now in front of my computer screen, they loom up—lifelike—on the screen of my memory.

> My grandpa (who loved me);
> my dad (who cared for me);
> my sixth-grade teacher (Mr. Vandenbrink, my first male teacher, who introduced us to organized basketball and told us to quit laughing at Jimmy Hagemeier's jock just because we'd never seen one before);
> my pastor (who taught me the big picture);
> my high school basketball coach (the first adult male, besides my father, to really, truly believe in me);
> an artillery major (who also believed, deeply);
> a college president (who strengthened my soul with his honesty);
> a brigade commander (who "tender"-ized me);

a best friend (who stayed with me);
a seminary professor (who stretched me);
a fellow elder (who stood by me).

I can see their faces. I can hear their voices. I can visualize circumstances, and feel feelings. Strong emotions.

No two were alike. My grandpa was short. My dad was quiet. My teacher was thin. My pastor was heavy. My coach was fiery. The major was analytical. My college president was dignified. My brigade commander was regal. My seminary professor was a lion. My best friend was a visionary and a realist, all in one. My fellow elder was gentle.

And my relationship with each was quite different. Some were intense, others naturally more reserved. Some very intimate, others more task-oriented. Some were direct in their dispensing of information my way, others were amazingly subtle. Some hardly knew I was watching, others probably wondered if I would ever go away. The amount of time and personal exposure we had together varied enormously.

As I reflect on these things, I find myself asking, *What did these men have in common? No two personalities were alike. No two relationships were alike. What made these men my mentors?*

The answers come quickly. Knowledge. Drive. Purpose. Vision. Confidence. Experience. Wisdom. Strength. Character. These were straight-talking, straight-living men, unthreatened by those who opposed them. But one trait, I've come to realize, far outweighs all the others combined. Most importantly, they all had a relationship with me *at a point of need.*

In a word, they were heroes. My heroes. Up close and personal. Not at a distance. Not on a magazine cover or a television screen. But near me. Touchable. Heroes who knew me and cared for me. I agree with one writer who said, "Being cared about is something so desperately needed in this depersonalized world that people will crawl across a thousand miles of desert to get to it."

Bobb Biehl hit it on the head:

Defining mentoring is sort of tough, but describing it is pretty easy. It's like having an uncle that cares for you for a lifetime, and wants to see you do well. He's not your competitor; he's there to support you, not to compete with you or discourage you. He's not your critic as much as he is your cheerleader.[2]

"Mentor" is a good word. It's an even greater reality, and necessity. I don't think my grandpa had ever heard the word "mentor" during his lifetime. My own dad has heard it only in his later years. But both men fleshed out the word to the hilt. They knew life and they exuded life. Most importantly, they understood the first rule of mentoring: *Be there!* They knew in life what William Brownell said in words, "Many a son has lost his way among strangers because his father was too busy to get acquainted with him." My little grandpa and my quiet dad passed life-knowledge on..."that the generations to come might know" (Psalm 78:6).

We all need a mentor—or two or three. We all need a life coach. A wisdom teacher. There is a mentor in every man's heart. God put it there. Sometimes it's pretty rusty and musty, buried way down in there somewhere. It may require some resuscitation. And a lot of dusting off. But it's down there—somewhere near the center.

Sometimes it's a grandpa with his favorite whittlin' knife showing his little buddy how to carve his initials in a block of wood. Sometimes it's a daddy playin' catch with his son. Sometimes it's a daddy and his little princess talking about "why the girls down the street are acting weird." Sometimes it's a determined twosome on a Saturday morning in the garage, with dirty hands, oil-smeared faces, and laughter (it takes lots of laughter to mentor), tearing the daylights out of a lawnmower that refuses to run. Sometimes it's the father of the bride working through a young lady's last-minute jitters—and sternly tucking in his chin or chewin' his lip, in order to keep his own emotions in check.

And often, perhaps most often, there is no blood relationship. But there is a soul-coaching tie. It is friend to friend, mutually mentoring one another through life's realties.

Together. Always together. But especially at the point of need.

Wisdom. Always wisdom. Passing from one mind and heart to another.

Whatever the situation, it's the mentor in a man reaching out with the gift of the sage to teach life to those he loves most.

Men are (somehow) supposed to *know* about life. Men are supposed to teach life. There is a mentor in every man's heart.

> Listen, my sons, to a father's instruction.... When I was a boy in my father's house, still tender, and an only child of my mother, he taught me and said, "Lay hold of my words with all your heart; keep my commands and you will live." (Proverbs 4:1, 3-4, NIV)

The mentor function is modeled everywhere in Scripture. Mentoring is part and parcel of discipling. The heart of the mentor is a teaching heart. It is a coaching heart. The mentor knows, and he wants others to know. He is always discipling—first his wife and kids, then others. The mentor has a spiritual heart that tugs at the hearts of others. His heart makes you want to learn.

The mentor exudes, as Moore and Gillette say it (in referring to the archetype they label "the magician"), "the energy of initiation and transformation."

Men are supposed to know how life works. In an earlier book, I put it this way: A man is supposed to *know* things. Like how a car runs. Or the inner workings of a hair dryer. Or the capitol of Nepal. Or how many legs are on a spider. Or how many miles to the next rest stop. Or when the weather will turn. It's up to him to maintain a working knowledge of why electricity flows, dogs bark, birds migrate, hamsters die, trees lose their leaves, and dads lose their hair.

Why do family members ask the man of the house these things? Because men are supposed to know how things work. And what to do next. And where to go from wherever you are. Men are supposed to be able to teach life.

Secular writers Moore and Gillette elaborate:

> Whatever his title, his specialty is knowing something that others don't know.... He knows when to plant and when to harvest, or when the herds will arrive next spring. He can predict the weather.... He understands the hidden dynamics of the human psyche.... He is the one who can effectively bless or curse. He understands the

links between the unseen world of spirits—the Divine world—and the world of human beings and nature. It is to him that people go with their questions, problems, pains, and diseases of the body and the mind. He is confessor and priest. He is the one who can think through the issues that are not obvious to other people. He is a seer and a prophet in the sense of...seeing deeply.[3]

The mentor in a man teaches life. Sometimes mentoring is spiritual. Sometimes it is mechanical. Sometimes it is intellectual, recreational, or technical. But it is, at its heart, most consistently, personal and familial. And always transformational.

Mentoring is *in* life, *about* life, surrounded *by* life, and carries all the way *through* life. Mentoring never stops. I recall a pastor friend of mine who had spent a lifetime in the ministry. He had been a good pastor, standing beside his flock in all of life's circumstances. In his sixties he was stricken with a terminal disease. Of course, it was difficult news and hard to handle. But, uncharacteristically, my pastor friend was devastated. Surprisingly, it shook him to the core—just blew him away. He wasn't himself anymore. Beside himself, he became confused, fearful, even bitter at times. Sadly, he took on the manner of a pitiful victim.

Fortunately for him, and his flock, he had a mentor who never quit. His mother, still vibrantly alive in her eighties, seeing her once strong son in his emotionally distraught state, decided he needed a little more mentoring of the sort that only a parent can deliver. She sat beside his bed and in words both strong and personal, rooted for her son.

"Son," she said, "all your life I have watched you teaching people to live well. *Don't stop now*. Teach them how to die well."

And he did. All he'd needed was a little mentoring.

MENTORING BUILDS MEN WHO UNDERSTAND LIFE AND PASS IT ON

The greatest of men all seem to have had a significant mentor. Often, it is their dad. Two of the greatest men of our day, in my opinion, are Dr. James Dobson and Dr. Chuck Swindoll. Listen to Dr. Dobson tell us something about mentoring, at the funeral of James Dobson Sr.:

This man whose body lies before me was not only my father and my friend, but he was also the source of great inspiration for me.... When I was between ten and thirteen years of age, my dad and I would rise very early before the sun came up on a wintry morning. We would put on our hunting clothes and heavy boots...[and] we would await the arrival of the sun and the awakening of the animal world.... Something dramatic... occurred out there in the forest between my dad and me. An intense love and affection was generated on those mornings that set the tone for a lifetime of fellowship. There was a closeness and a oneness that made me want to be like that man...that made me choose his values as my values, his dreams as my dreams, his God as my God.[4]

That says it all. That is a clear definition of the term "mentor." No wonder our Weber family equivalent, "Pop," has such a reverent ring in my mind. "A righteous man who walks in his integrity—how blessed are his sons after him" (Proverbs 20:7).

Chuck Swindoll would likely say the same thing. He has a very similar story. In a book entitled *Make Up Your Mind...About the Issues of Life,* Chuck eulogizes his life mentor. I have never read a finer description of mentoring:

My dad died last night. He left like he had lived. Quietly. Graciously. With dignity. Without demands or harsh words or even a frown, he surrendered himself—a tired, frail, humble gentleman—into the waiting arms of his Savior....

As I stroked the hair from his forehead and kissed him good-bye, a hundred boyhood memories played through my head.

—When I learned to ride a bike, he was there.

—When I wrestled with the multiplication table, his quick wit erased the hassle.

—When I discovered the adventure of driving a car, he was near, encouraging me.

—When I got my first job (delivering newspapers), he

informed me how to increase my subscriptions and win the prize. It worked!

—When I mentioned a young woman I had fallen in love with, he pulled me aside and talked straight about being responsible for her welfare and happiness.

—When I did a hitch in the Marine Corps, the discipline I had learned from him made the transition easier.

From him I learned to seine for shrimp. How to catch flounder and trout and redfish. How to open oyster shells and fix crab gumbo...and chili...and popcorn...and make rafts out of old inner tubes and gunny sacks. I was continually amazed at his ability to do things like tie fragile mantles on the old Coleman lantern, keep a fire going in the rain, play the harmonica with his hands behind his back, and keep three strong-willed kids from tearing the house down.

Last night I realized I had him to thank for my deep love for America. And for knowing how to tenderly care for my wife. And for laughing at impossibilities. And for some habits I have picked up, like approaching people with a positive spirit rather than a negative one, staying with a task until it is finished, taking good care of my personal belongings, keeping my shoes shined, speaking up rather than mumbling, respecting authority, and standing alone (if necessary) in support of my personal convictions. For these things I am deeply indebted to the man who raised me.... Admittedly, much of my dad's instruction was indirect—by model rather than by explicit statement....

He leaves in his legacy a well-marked Bible I treasure, a series of feelings that I need to deepen my roots, and a thousand memories that comfort me as I replace denial with acceptance and praise.

I await heaven's gate opening in the not-too-distant future. So do other Christians, who anxiously await Christ's return. Most of them anticipate hearing the soft strum of a harp or the staccato blast of a trumpet.

Not me. I will hear the nostalgic whine of a harmonica...held in the hands of the man who died last night...*or did he?* The memories are as fresh as this morning's sunrise.[5]

"My son," wrote Solomon, "do not forget my teaching, but let your heart keep my commandments; for length of days and years of life, and peace they will add to you.... Write them on the tablet of your heart. So you will find favor and good repute in the sight of God and man" (Proverbs 3:1-4).

The words of wisdom and the life of a sage-like mentor far outlive our own threescore and ten. So much so that *"he being dead, still speaks."*

SOMETIMES MENTORING IS MERELY MODELING...OVER A LIFETIME

Bob Welch is a Christian writer living here in Oregon. Bob's family had a "Pop," too. Pop Youngberg was the family sage. Listen to Bob reflect on his mentor in an article entitled "If you could see us now, Pop Youngberg."

> Here I am, Pop, back in the same country cemetery outside Carlton, Oregon where we said good-bye to you 10 years ago.... I remember how strange it was that a man who was born in the days of horse and buggies was brought to rest in a baby-blue Cadillac.... You were a vanishing breed: A man who held one job his entire life—farmer. A man who was married to the same woman for 60 years. A man who died in the same house where he had been born 89 years earlier. A simple man who found meaning in tilling the earth below him, worshipping the God above him, and loving the family around him.... A man who remained faithful to his wife, taught his children right from wrong and kept his family together despite drought and Depression.... [A man] who got tears in his eyes when singing "Amazing Grace" at the tiny Baptist church he helped found...who made his grandchildren wind chimes...and helped other farmers bail their hay when a storm was coming...a man who insisted we all hold hands before a meal and, when he had

finished praying, would give the hands he was holding an encouraging squeeze....[6]

You can almost see the baton passing from generation to generation in that squeeze, can't you? And I'll bet you wish you were seated at that table. You wish you had been mentored. You wish you could *be* a mentor. And you can! It is never too late to begin. It is always too soon to quit. You don't have to speak a lot, or posture, or take over, or dominate, or take the special seat. But you do have to do at least two things: One, you do have to love those around you until they feel it. And two, you have to live out your own biblical values to the core. The chances are pretty good they will catch that kind of message. Loud and clear.

Listen again to Bob Welch describe the mentoring method of his life coach, Pop Youngberg:

> You never talked much about faith or values or character or any of that stuff. You just lived it. And I thank you for that.
>
> Every now and then, one of your great-grandsons, while playing baseball out back, will rip a line drive smack into the wind chime you made us. It'll jolt me, as if to say: *Don't forget. Don't forget.*
>
> I haven't, Pop. I can still hear your soft, farm-drawl voice. And I can still feel your callused hand squeeze mine after a mealtime prayer, as if passing on hope to a desperate generation.[7]

"The glory of sons is their fathers" (Proverbs 17:6).

Have you caught the picture? Mentoring is not primarily a program, though programs are okay. Mentoring is not enforcing the memorization of fifty verses of Scripture, though memorizing Scripture is good. (And mentoring is most certainly not obnoxiously jabbing strangers in hallways with inquisitional questions: "How many verses have you memorized today? How many books have you read in the last ten minutes?" etc.) Mentoring is not joining an organization, though organizations are fine. Mentoring is not necessarily formal and structured, though form and structure can certainly be profitable.

But mentoring, at its essence, does not belong to programs or regimens or organization. Mentoring belongs to *people*. People like you. Mentoring is living out your core values. Mentoring is "a long obedience in one direction." And rubbing shoulders along the way.

Mentoring is not for an hour on Tuesday.

It is daily.

It is moment by moment.

It is over a lifetime.

Howie and Bill Hendricks summarize the basics:

> Don't get hung up on whether the friendship that you and another man are building qualifies as "mentoring." Just pursue the relationship. Even those who run facilitated mentoring programs will tell you, a label means almost nothing. What matters is whether anything positive is rubbing off when one man deals with another.[8]

SOMETIMES MENTORING IS INSTINCTIVE COACHING

Sometimes mentoring takes place in a flash—for just a second or two. A spontaneous gesture at just the right moment. But always right in the center of life.

I'll never forget such a flash in my life. It was just a moment. But it has impacted me for over twenty years now. I think of that moment often, usually at least once a week. My mentor in that moment was a man I had not known previously. We had met that morning. We sat beside each other for a few minutes, and then we went our ways, never to cross paths again. But he had mentored me—in the heat of battle.

Yes, I had known the heat of battle before. As a GI in Vietnam, I had sweated through the heat of the Southeast Asian jungles. The heat of Southeast Asia was one thing. But this battle was something else. This was a new league!

I was a senior seminary student, working hard, busting my brains, minding my own business. Then, out of the blue, I got the call. When the nationally prominent pastor of a local church decided to take a week of vacation, his office contacted me and asked me to fill the pulpit.

Say what? Me? Oh, man. Oh, wow. Oh, criminy.

This was no "ordinary" pulpit—if there is such a thing. This was St. Peters and the Vatican all rolled into one as far as I was concerned—the mother of the denomination in which I had grown up. The mother of all churches. This was big. Heaps of people. Truckloads of pressure.

As I sat on the platform that morning and stared out at the huge crowd, some of whom were my professors, it was the closest thing to an out-of-body experience I had ever had. My *eyelids* were actually sweating. But when the worship pastor had reached the final verse of the hymn before I was to begin, something beautiful happened. Seated next to me was the silver-haired executive pastor of the church. A lifetime of experience had flowed beneath his ministerial bridge. He had seen it all—and done it. And he knew young men. Once upon a time, he'd even been one!

Apparently he knew my heart better than I knew it myself. He had obviously walked this way before. But this magnificent senior man, a true sage (now that I think about it), reached into his coat's inner breast pocket, pulled out a blank three-by-five card, and quickly scribbled something on it. He handed it to me less than thirty seconds before I stepped into what was, to me at least, The Largest Pulpit in the World.

I will never forget those scrawled words. I have the very card taped into the front of my Bible to this day. And I often think of his gesture when I am faced with a pressure-filled situation. There, in a script bearing the telltale marks of age, were these words:

"No mention of inadequacy...He is sufficient."

The words stunned me for a moment. And then I smiled. Of course! A wave of palpable relief coursed over me. I glanced at him. His eyes imparted confidence. His smile launched me.

That moment. That glance. That little word—just a phrase or two. It was a flash of mentoring, and it changed my morning. And my ministry. For a lifetime. Though I had never seen him before, and would never see him again, I had been mentored. Squarely. Now he's gone on ahead again. He rests in very green pastures. Someday in heaven, I will have occasion to thank Dr. John Siemens for his faithful mentoring of this young pastor. On a day. In a moment.

S O M E T I M E S   M E N T O R I N G   I S
S Y S T E M A T I C   T E A C H I N G

The invitation had come personally. It wasn't formal, but it was perfectly clear. My friend spoke nonchalantly. "Some of the guys are going to get together tonight. We're going to hang out, drink a little, and watch a couple of porno films. At eight o'clock. In the dispensary."

Well, there it was. Another crossroads. Another decision. Who was I going to follow?

We were in Vietnam. Back home, Sgt. Barry Sadler's popular song, "The Ballad of the Green Berets" was topping the charts. "Put silver wings on my son's chest. Make him one of America's best." You could hear it everywhere; it was sweeping the country. Only this Green Beret was out of the country, and no one was looking over my shoulder. None of the folks back home knew what I was doing or not doing. The social inhibitions in the States were nonexistent here. Out of the country, men regularly acted un-concerned, un-disciplined, un-married, and un-manly. After the porno films it was downtown to act out their sexual appetites with the prostitutes.

When I first heard Sgt. Sadler's ballad, I questioned whether he'd gotten it right. Were the elite Green Berets really America's best? Best killers? No doubt. Best *men?* I wasn't so sure, at least to my way of thinking (when I was thinking clearly). But, at the time, I was really wrestling inside. We had all experienced a certain amount of disorientation in the sixties. And though I continued to walk fairly straight behaviorally, I had abandoned the faith of my childhood. I didn't believe there was a God. I certainly didn't claim to follow Christ.

So why not? Why not hang out, get stoned, watch the flicks, and womanize a bit? No harm done. Some wild and crazy fun tonight, then a new day tomorrow. Back on the job, like always. And no one who mattered to me would ever know. If I happened to live through the year and made it home, life would be normal again. Or so I hoped.

I wrestled with that personal invitation most of the day. But when H-hour arrived, I couldn't do it. I couldn't go to the dispensary. I couldn't get plowed. I couldn't indulge in the films. And I couldn't run downtown. Why in the world not?

It was a simple reason, really.

I had been mentored. I knew my dad wouldn't do it.

And, somehow, without any dramatics, my mentor had placed a part of his own stout heart down inside my chest. I knew my dad would never do any such thing. It wasn't "a God thing." At that point in my life I didn't even believe in Him. I didn't care much about anything, really—other than my OER (officer efficiency report). And the womanizing? Hey, everybody was doing it. And, for cryin' out loud, no one—including my dad—would ever know!

But I couldn't do it. The life of my mentor was too deeply ingrained in my own soul. When push came to shove, I had to do what my mentor had taught me.

Twenty-three years later...

I had lived through that year. I had returned to the States, and to my family. Now, nearly a quarter of a century later, I sat across the table from my oldest son. We had gone to the restaurant together, just the two of us, to spend some time alone before he left the States to study in England at the Universities of Durham and Oxford. History was repeating itself, albeit in the somewhat more civil form of graduate studies as opposed to war. Still, this time it was *my* son who was going overseas. A generation had come to maturity. This generation was going overseas, too—to a noticeably more promiscuous European world. Far from anyone who mattered to him.

I looked into his eyes across that table and saw myself twenty-three years earlier. Oh, he knew what he *believed*. At twenty-four, he was a faithful man. Strong in character. Firm in conviction. But after all, he was a man. And I knew that, like me, he had red blood flowing in his veins.

So we talked. With characteristic male awkwardness (yes, it's okay—no one has it all together perfectly. You just learn by doing. Dive in with a pure heart), we opened up a bit about life. And faith. And red blood. And overseas. It was good. Then all too soon, the evening ended and he caught the plane. The conversation was history.

More time passed.

On my birthday almost two years later, I received a very special letter from my son. Among other things (very personal and rewarding things), he said this:

Somehow in God's good sovereignty I've managed to be placed in your care for my life's developmental portion, and I will never be the same for it.... You know what you said about Grandpa—how your love, fear, and respect for him while you were in Vietnam had saved you from making some poor choices? This has been completely transferable, 100 percent and then some.

The grace of God (though I've not always focused upon it) has saved me thus far from the same kind of sin, and I'm convinced much of the reason for it is you, my dad. I will always have a healthy fear of temptation, but I'm reasonably confident I'll not compromise sexually or morally...for I could not bear the thought (forever haunting) of your having reason to be less than pleased.

Perhaps that motivation is less than ideal (in terms of the "eyes of the Savior" upon us), but I am convinced that Christ gives us "little helps" to keep us focused on the goal. I thank God He has given you to me.... Thanks, Dad, for...loving me unconditionally, and instilling in me everything that matters. You're my champion, Dad!

Reading those words, I nearly exploded. You can imagine. There is no greater honor or joy than "to hear of [your] children walking in the truth." I'm sure I puffed up dangerously. Probably to the point of Lindy having to remind me that true "champions" (big as they may feel at the moment) still have to do the dishes! But it was a wonderful letter for this dad. It was a milestone in my life. I recall thinking, *Someday, maybe...just maybe...I'll get to wear the title "Pop."*

My mind drifted to that old Jewish talmudic proverb, *"A child tells in the street what his father says at home."*

Yes, mentoring spans the generations. Max Lerner said it very clearly: "The father-son relation is the basic link of continuity in life, carrying the male principle and the tradition of responsibility from one generation to the next."[9] Richard Strauss seconded that motion: "A boy particularly needs to know his dad. Dad represents the man he will become—the husband he will be to his wife, the father he will be to his children, the provider he will be for his family, the leader he will be in his church, and the witness he will be in the world.... He needs a dad he can be proud of."10

One of the men in our church caught that vision when he wrote the following:

> He climbed onto the seat and positioned his feet on the pedals, his hands on the handle bars. "Don't let go," he ordered. "I'll be right next to you," I assured him. "I won't let you fall...." I thought of the days ahead—of times when I would show my son balance, when I would run alongside him, when I would be there to hold him, and when I would have to let go again and again.11

Preston Gillham captured the big picture of mentoring:

> Boys become men by watching men, by standing close to men. Manhood is a ritual passed from generation to generation with precious few spoken instructions. Passing the torch of manhood is a fragile, tedious task. If the rite of passage is successfully completed, the boy-become-man is like an oak of hardwood character. His shade and influence will bless all those who are fortunate enough to lean on him and rest under his canopy.12

Mentoring is transgenerational. I have to chuckle every time I see its far-reaching fruit in our family. One of the boys will do something rather unusual in this culture—like the time one of them tipped a flight attendant *ten dollars* just for the gracious manner in which she put up with some particularly obnoxious passengers on his flight. The little group of flight attendants were still talking, well inside the terminal, about "that really nice blonde kid." And I had to smile, raise my eyes a bit toward heaven, and whisper under my breath, "Thanks, Grandpa. You'd have done that."

You see, that tender giving spirit, expressed in surprising little bursts of spontaneous generosity, is something that was in grandpa's baton which he passed from generation to generation in a God-designed mentoring process.

I remember him carrying that baton. For one small but consistent example, William Weber, who died more than a quarter century ago, always carried candy in his pockets to slip to children. He'd been an orphan, a street urchin, in the miserable tenements of lower Manhattan's East Side in the 1890s. And somewhere along the line he determined to have a giving spirit. He was willing, literally, to give you the shirt off his back. When Grandma noticed that some particular item hadn't been seen around the house for some time, she just assumed Grandpa had given it to someone who "needed it more than I did." That spirit was with him until he passed away. And the whole family knew it.

My dad is the same way. Giving flows in my veins, too. (It's still difficult for me to tip a waiter or waitress a mere fifteen percent.) And it's there in the next generation. One time I watched the eyes of the kid behind the counter at Taco Time bulge. My son had handed him a ten-dollar bill with the words, "This is for you for being such a helpful and positive person."

When we got to our table, I was half miffed with him. "What in the world are you doing, giving away ten-dollar bills! You'd think you had money or something!" But "my main man" mentored me when he responded, "Dad, we've been coming in here for months. And every time, that guy is the same way—cheerful, helpful, he really acts like he actually *wants* to serve you—and no one ever tips in a fast-food chain. So I decided to."

He was right. I smiled and thanked him for the lesson. And nodded heavenward—to my boy's great-grandpa. "Thanks, Pop."

There is a mentor in every man's heart. It's one of the pillars of masculinity. Keep it. Maintain it. See to it that the mentor pillar stands tall and straight. See that it never leans toward the know-it-all side nor the silent, passive side. See that it bears solid weight.

Without it, you'll never be a four-pillared man.

"Wisdom is supreme; therefore get wisdom.
Though it cost all you have, get understanding.
Esteem her, and she will exalt you;
embrace her, and she will honor you."
PROVERBS 4:7-8, NIV

All Scripture is God-breathed, and is useful for
teaching...and training in righteousness, so
that the man of God may be thoroughly
equipped for every good work.
2 TIMOTHY 3:16, NIV

THE MENTOR AT WORK

Ⓜy brother-in-law's official handle is Patrick Leroy Taylor. Rick, named after his father, Leroy, remembers his dad telling him a story that haunts the family to this day.

Rick's grandpa had taken little Leroy (Rick's dad) out into the woods. Evidently the man knew what was coming. But something in him held it in check, at least briefly. For whatever reason, he must have wanted to spend at least a few minutes of quality time with his son. Apparently he had planned something of an adventure, however brief, for his boy.

Out of his hip pocket trailed two pieces of an old rubber inner tube. In his hand was his ever-present pocket knife, the grip well worn with healthy use. Father and son were going into the woods to cut and craft a handsome weapon, a homemade slingshot. The leather pouch was in hand—probably the hide off an old baseball.

You can imagine the boy's intense excitement. Every step was a lesson learned. Locate just the right forked branch...cut it...eyeball it good...carve it...eyeball it again...shape the grooves just right to hold the rubber pieces...attach the rubber...stretch it...feel it...test it.

Such an adventure! Can't you see their eyes meeting? Little Leroy's were wide with anticipation. These were great moments!

But, curiously, something was missing. Where was the wink in dad's eye? And what was that faraway look that seemed to have replaced it?

Oh well, nothing could dampen Leroy's enthusiasm for that soon-to-be-taken first shot with his new weapon. Visions of great and future conquests filled his imagination. His dad showed him how to hold it and aim it. Its feel was just so—well, good! He could hardly wait to use the new masterpiece. It was a beauty. Then dad left the thrilled boy alone in the woods to practice with his new weapon. What an afternoon it was going to be! If he had only known how this day would live on in infamy.

When Leroy's dad walked out of those woods that day, he walked right out of the boy's life.

Forever.

As far as Rick knows, that little boy who would become Rick's dad would never see his father again—for the rest of his life. What a blow! What an ache! What a life-impacting, personality-affecting, future-shaping event! Young Leroy lost the only mentor he had ever known.

So much for mentoring. So much for that greatest of gifts—a childhood. Leroy's was over. So much for passing on what really matters to the next generation. Leroy's life would never be the same again. Because he was the oldest child, he took on several paper routes and sold magazines to help support the family. Because of all the responsibilities and pressures at home, he wasn't able to start first grade until he was nine years old.

Working and going to school became a way of life. No childhood. Only work and school. Without a father to mentor him. That was pretty much the only life Leroy knew in that small valley in Kentucky. By the time he turned eighteen, he was just two weeks into the ninth grade. And that's when the letter arrived from Uncle Sam. The war was on. His country needed him. So, after completing just two weeks of high school, Leroy joined the U.S. Navy.

And war, like fatherlessness, has a way of putting life on hold.

Fortunately, even world wars don't last forever. Leroy returned home, met and married his sweetheart, Pat. Not long after the war Pat gave birth to their son. Rick Taylor came into the world along with a whole lot of other baby boomers. When Rick was a youngster, about the same age Leroy had been when his dad walked out of those woods, Leroy accepted Christ as his Savior.

The man who had lost his mentor had found a Mentor. The Master Mentor had provided him with a Book. The Bible became his mentoring text. The forgiveness he received from his Lord became the center of a new and developing way of life. As an adult, Leroy began to devote himself to studying his Bible. The youngster with only two weeks of high school was now in a fast-paced graduate course of his own making. Rick vividly recalls the light shining out from under his dad's bedroom door until the wee hours of each Saturday night and Sunday morning. For nine years, until Rick turned eighteen and headed for college, he remembers that late-night light. For nearly a decade his dad served in the pastoral ministry, either part-time or full-time.

Rick reflects on those late-night hours, connecting his father's effort with the loss of his mentor: "My dad was studying the best he knew how, searching the Bible and reading from books he'd received from the Book of the Month Club. He was desperately trying to make up for what he had not received from his father—knowledge, and understanding, and wisdom."

I tell this story because a lot of men today are like Leroy; they've never had a mentor. Perhaps you're one of those men. And now you find yourself with the equivalent of "a mere couple of weeks" of background, having to take on the world and develop your own family. More than a few of my friends don't even know who their biological dad is.

But there is hope.

P A S S I N G   O N   T H E   S E C R E T S

Mentoring is "passing on the secrets of life." The only "secret" Leroy's father managed to pass on was how to cut up things. Like an inner tube, or a tree branch—or a little boy's life.

No one passed on the "secrets of life" to Leroy. So he was left to begin on his own, from scratch. Many men reading these lines are in similar straits. Without a father to pass down the information critical to life, where does a man turn to get started? Leroy had discovered the starter's blocks. He had the right idea—you've got to begin with the ultimate Mentor, the ultimate Father's perspective. You've got to begin with the Bible.

As Ray Steadman used to say, "When all else fails, read the instructions." Not an easy thing for a man to do. It's a well-known reality that when you get anything that is supposed to function, it usually comes with a book. From toasters to lawn mowers. From new telephones to new cars. But for most of us men, life's little instruction books usually remain securely enclosed in their plastic wrappers until defeat is undeniable. Then, and only then, do we rip open that plastic cover to get at the information we've needed all along.

We men are pretty much convinced we can make this thing called life work without help—of any kind. And sometimes, it seems, we're particularly suspicious of anything that comes from a book. Can anything "practical" come out of a book? (Why are we not surprised to learn that roughly 80 percent of all Christian books are purchased by women, not men?)

But if you're going to be the mentor God called you to be, you're going to have to start with a Book. Sometimes it's called the Book of Life, or the Book of books. You know it as the Bible. Mentoring begins with knowledge, knowledge of the Truth.

M E N T O R ?   W H O ,   M E ?

Just mention the word "mentor" and many men turn and run the other way. We don't feel qualified. And even if we were qualified, we find ourselves asking, "Who would want to learn from me?"

Don't let the word buffalo you. We're all mentoring in one way or another—unless we're the sole occupant of an otherwise deserted island. Most of my life I have been mentoring one step ahead of the hounds. I'm learning as I go.

Midcourse corrections are a fact of life. None of us knows it all. So it's best to never claim it or act like it. I've made mistakes. I've stuck my foot into it more than once. But in our little house we've all learned together that when we make mistakes we apologize to those we've hurt and ask forgiveness. My asking forgiveness from my wife and kids has been one of the greatest lessons I could ever give them. Like me, they need to learn humility and the seeking of forgiveness, because they aren't perfect, either. (Ah...life.)

So give yourself a little credit.

You're a man. God made you that way. You've experienced a lot of life—including some of it you probably wish you hadn't experienced. But do you know what? *That's* life, too. Don't waste any of it. And let's not doom the next generation to repeating it. If we can just take all that life experience—the good, the bad, and the ugly—evaluate it through the lenses of Scripture, and sort the positive from the negative, we've got precisely what EVERYONE wants to know so desperately: the very secrets of life.

Newspapers recently carried the story of a young high school girl from Fremont, California who did the impossible. Seventeen-year-old Karen Cheng scored perfect marks (1600) on the national SAT test, and perfect marks (8000) on the rigorous University of California acceptance index. No one before had ever achieved such a remarkable academic feat. This phenomenal girl, always a straight-A student in high school, thinks of herself as a typical teenager. Her teachers, recognizing her one-of-a-kind abilities, call her "Wonder Woman." Clearly, she will have her choice of America's most prestigious universities.

So, you ask, how in the world does *she* illustrate America's need for more mentoring—and especially from flawed, failing mentors like me and thee? As it happens, one newspaper account of the girl's genius included a question she had been asked by a reporter. It was the kind of question every human being should be able to answer. Certainly, one of the most intelligent teenagers in America ought to be able to offer some kind of response.

The question? "What is the meaning of life?"

Her response: "I have no idea. I would like to know myself."

Dr. James Dobson's analysis of the exchange with the reporter is insightful:

With no disrespect intended to this gifted girl, her inability to explain why she exists or the purpose of living is characteristic of her generation. Millions of young people who have grown up in the opulence of North America are equally confused about transcendent values. We have given them more material blessings than any comparable age group in history. They have had opportunities never dreamed of by their ancestors.... More money has been spent on their education, medical care, entertainment, and travel than any generation in history. Yet we have failed them in the most important of all parental responsibilities: we have not taught them who they are as children of God or what they have been placed here to do. The late philosopher and author Dr. Francis Schaeffer said it like this: "The damnation of this generation is that it doesn't know why it has meaning."[1]

The most basic questions of life are the ones we ought to pursue most vigorously. *Who am I? Why do I exist? What really matters in life? Is there a God? Is it possible to connect with Him? Is there life after death? How do I know?* Here is one of America's most capable young people who evidently never had the advantage of someone coming alongside her—a parent, a friend, a counselor, a Sunday school teacher—to help her understand the meaning of life. She doesn't need more head knowledge. She needs someone who has experienced some of the ups, downs, bumps and bruises of life to help put it all in perspective. She needs someone to talk to her about the most basic questions of all.

Some of you reading this have tried hard to do just that. You've stepped out of your comfort zone and given yourself to this effort at mentoring—only to be bitterly disappointed by the outcome. Those to whom you've tried to pass on the secrets of life have chosen not to follow.

That's a hard pill to swallow. But God didn't call you to force other people to follow the principles. He just wants you to pass them on. And as you do that, you just have to trust Him to keep working. Ultimately, those who have heard your words will be held responsible for embracing the secrets of life as their own and following them. Yes, a lot of batons are dropped in relay races. Just make sure that your hand-off has been solid and timely; running the next leg of the race is up to the one who receives that baton.

Maybe you already know these things, but you're saying inside, *Yeah, but that dropped baton still HURTS. What you say doesn't take the pain away.* No, it doesn't. It can't. Nothing can. But you do not have to bear or suffer from the guilt of *their* decisions.

To this point in life, I have not experienced great pain with the choices of any of my own sons. I have been a blessed man in that respect.

But as a pastor, I have poured my life into many people in the church who have walked away—from me, and the church, and the Lord—and abandoned the secrets of life passed on to them. The pain is very real. The hurt is deep. I've ached for them. I've prayed for them. More than a few times I've wept for them. I've endured the stabbing, lingering pain of disappointment. Every person who has ever attempted to mentor another has probably felt somewhere along the line what Paul called feeling like he had "poured himself out" in vain.

But the bottom line is: God is God. And God is faithful. And He reminds His men regularly that mentoring is part of being "about my Father's business." We need to entrust our pain and our ability to handle more pain, to our Father.

Frankly, learning to handle pain is a huge part of learning the "secrets of life." My dear brother-in-law and his wife, Rick and Judy Taylor, know about pain. Intense, indescribable pain. When their firstborn son was just five years old he died in a horrid drowning accident. Listen to Rick's words:

> Judy and I had poured our lives into bringing up Kyle to be the man God wanted him to be. Even at this early age of five years, we had devoted major portions of our lives into passing on the secrets of life to Kyle. When he died, it tore at our desire to go on as parents, as mentors to our growing family. What was the use? We felt betrayed by God...and like we had wasted five of the best years of our lives.
>
> Slowly...very slowly...but surely...and very surely...our faithful Mentor Father in heaven has helped me to see that I had three other children that needed a dad—a king, a warrior, a friend, and yes, a mentor. I would not trade the last seventeen years with Bryan, Eric, and Kelly for anything. Good investments usually have a way of eventually coming back and paying dividends. Sometimes it just takes awhile.

Rick's right. He knows. Sometimes it does take awhile. So you hang in there. You stay at it. You finish the course, and run right past your reluctance.

J O S H ,   T H E   R E L U C T A N T   M E N T O R

I'm thinking of one such reluctant would-be mentor. Josh was a senior guy who had lived a lot of life and was thinking about winding down a bit. Given his age, he had assumed any bigger promotions had passed him by. In fact, when he thought about it, he decided he probably wouldn't want the top job anymore, even if it were offered to him. But, sure enough, the day came when the man he had served under for several decades passed away. That left the company operations—affecting many, many people—without the man who had led them from their founding.

Wouldn't you know it, the job was offered to Josh. It really blew his mind. While he had to acknowledge the honor, the whole proposition probably caught him up short.

I expect he tossed and turned through a number of rough nights and days. Was he really up to this task? Did he have what it would take to be successful at this late stage in his life? The Chairman of the Board decided he did. The Chairman took him aside and was straightforward with Josh about his expectations for him. Read his words as though he were speaking them to you. (And by the way, He is.)

> "Be strong and courageous, for you will lead my people to possess all the land I swore to give their ancestors. Be strong and very courageous. Obey all the laws Moses gave you. Do not turn away from them, and you will be successful in everything you do. Study this Book of the Law continually. Meditate on it day and night so that you may be sure to obey all that is written in it. Only then will you succeed. I command you—be strong and courageous! Do not be afraid or discouraged. For the LORD your God is with you wherever you go." (Joshua 1:6-9, NLT)

A   M E N T O R   I S   A   S T U D E N T   O F   T H E   B O O K

It does take *strength* and *courage* to live this life, doesn't it? And the kind of strength and courage God was talking to Joshua about was an *inner* kind of power. It is a matter of character. Without knowing and living by the Book we never experience the kind of strength and courage God was talking about. It is the kind of potency that our hearts long for deep down inside.

So why is the Book so valuable, even essential, to our success? Listen to the words of one particularly strong and courageous brother:

> But evil men and impostors will proceed from bad to worse, deceiving and being deceived. You, however, continue in the things you have learned and become convinced of, knowing from whom you have learned them; and that from childhood you have known the sacred writings which are able to give you the wisdom that leads to salvation through faith which is in Christ Jesus. All Scripture is inspired by God and profitable for teaching, for reproof, for correction, for training in righteousness; that the man of God may be adequate, equipped for every good work. (2 Timothy 3:13-17)

There you have it! I don't know about you, but by the time I've been taught, reproved, corrected, and trained, I've pretty much been through the wringer. What else is there? What else could we possibly need? It's *all* there. God Himself says it's enough. Enough to make you adequate—no matter how inadequate you might feel. In fact, Paul is playing on words a bit here and he leaves us pretty much without excuse. The ultimate Mentor gave us the Bible, to paraphrase it a bit, "that the man of God (YOU) may be adequate—thoroughly, absolutely, completely adequate. And equipped—thoroughly, absolutely, completely equipped." For "any...and every...all possible...every potential" work or task that you could possibly face.

Friend, you can't get any more adequate than that! You can't get any more equipped than that! You could not possibly be any more ready than God is prepared to make you.

And, fellow mentor, try this one on for size as well: "And God is able to make all grace abound to you, so that in all things at all times, having all that you need, YOU will abound in every good work" (2 Corinthians 9:8, NIV).

Remember, God says we men are going to be exposed to a lot of deceit in this world—meaning we're going to be told many things that have the appearance of being right, or true, or good, but which are really rotten and will lead to our demise. How can we know the difference between right and wrong, truth and falsehood, good and bad? The Book. It's God's idea. And it's profitable for four essentials you will need if you are going to pass on "the secrets of life."

It is profitable for teaching.
It will show us the path of life, like a detailed road map full of things that are true—how life was designed by God to be lived. When I'm consulting a road atlas, I always like to have the updated, *this year's* edition. (That's how Rand-McNalley stays in business.) That way, I can be sure of having the latest information to help me on my journey. The Bible is always relevant to your life's circumstances. Its wisdom, applied by the Holy Spirit to the moment-by-moment events of your life, gives you firm principles to chart your course and light your way.

It is profitable for reproof.
It will *warn* us when we're veering off course as God designed life to be lived. It will place the traffic signs along your road, warning you of speed limits, approaching curves, and road hazards.

It is profitable for correction.
It will give us *emergency instructions* for how to get back on the road we've strayed from. It will show you how to get off high center and out of the rut. It will winch you back onto the route that will get you where you really want to go.

It is profitable for training in righteousness.
It will show you how to *stay on course,* the path of life God designed for us. It mentors us in a steady course on the secrets of living life as God intended. It's "the only way to go."

One more word here. Do you know what the most worthless thing in the world is? A map that never gets taken out of the glove compartment. A map is absolutely valueless for travel unless it is consulted. Folded up on the dashboard, it provides no guidance at all! So don't let someone else always read the map for you. Study your own map. Don't let the preachers be the only ones who get to study the map. Take the point, man. Pull the Book out. You be the tour director for your family. Don't trust your trip to someone else's memory. And don't be some kind of wuss, always rolling down the window and asking someone else for directions. Be a man. Read the map.

Like it or not, you *are* the man. Polish your mentoring pillar, my fellow pilgrim. You really don't have a choice.

As I write these words, a certain television commercial comes to mind. I'm remembering the face of Charles Barkley, smugly looking into the camera and saying, "I am not a role model." Sorry, Charlie. There are some things where you have no choice in the matter, as much as that may insult your large ego. And this, Sir Charles, is one of them.

One of Barkley's more potent hardwood opponents put it to him straight. Quoted in *Sports Illustrated*, Karl Malone did a little correcting of his own: "I disagree with what Charles says.... Charles, you can deny being a role model all you want. But I don't think it's your decision to make. We don't choose to be role models. We're chosen. Our only choice is whether to be a good model or a bad one."[2]

Thanks, Karl. The Mail Man delivers again.

Get out the Book. It'll make a good mentor out of you. And go to it as a servant. We can't be punching a clock, "putting in our time" between the book covers, simply getting it over with. We must go to it as a servant who honestly desires to know the designs and intentions of his Master. The Book is the fountainhead of your life and your mentoring.

A   M E N T O R   I S   A   S T U D E N T   O F   P E O P L E

Ever find yourself in a busy airport just people watching? As Yogi Berra is reputed to have said, "You can observe a lot just by watching!" Whether it's sitting in a shopping mall, visiting in people's homes, sitting in a duck blind, or eating at a table, you can "observe a lot just by watching." People all around us are living out the drama of life, are very much in the process of being...well, alive.

The Big Fisherman became a student of people. Peter switched from the wind and the waves of the sea to the men and women of his world.

He figured if you had to understand a fish to catch one, then you had better understand people if you were going to be any kind of a fisher of men. A mentor is a student of people. It was the old salt himself who said, "Husbands…, live with your wives in an understanding way, as with a weaker vessel, since she is a woman; and grant her honor as a fellow heir of the grace of life" (1 Peter 3:7).

The Book says study your wife. She is a woman. Learn how God designed them, how they are intended to function, what they need from a man, and what they can become when flourishing. Men often joke about this assignment: "Who can understand a woman?" God has answered the question loud and clear. *You can. You* can understand a woman. Husbands can understand wives if they will take the time and energy to focus on them as feminine persons who need their husband's honor. If a man is a poor student of his wife he cannot hope to help her reach her potential as a woman, a wife, or a mother. And if you stunt your wife's growth and potential—take a guess who else pays a price for that?

The ultimate Mentor and Bridegroom has made His bride the focus of His energy, "to make her holy, cleansing her…to present her to himself…radiant…without stain or wrinkle or any other blemish." And the Book adds, "In this same way, husbands [are obligated] to love their wives as their own bodies. He who loves his wife loves himself" (Ephesians 5:25-28, NIV).

Translated, that means there may be things I want—projects to work on, dreams to chase, promotions to pursue, big toys to play with—but I need to be ready and willing to set those aside if necessary in order to help my wife develop her God-given potential.

Sort of scary, isn't it? Mentoring our wives? But the Book says it's the way God intended. Walk in it.

Equally as challenging is becoming a student of children. It seems as though the children in every family have developed a "kids' conspiracy" —no two can be alike—just to keep us on the run. Becoming a student of your children is a demanding and *daily* task. We must work at understanding how they develop. We need to understand their unique personalities, their individual time of life, and how they view their world and their place in it. We need to know something about their hopes and dreams, their fears and passions, the things they enjoy and why. We need to relate to things that come easily for them. And the things that don't. The better students we are of our kids, the easier it will be to make decisions about how to relate to them, how to discipline them, how to encourage them, how to challenge them, and how to motivate them.

Listen to one father's experience with his daughter:

Just this week my daughter was extremely frustrated because she was having such a hard time in her high school AP Biology class. She had always loved biology, and excelled in it. Now she was struggling. I asked her how it was different than the other times she had taken biology. She explained that she just felt "dumb" because she was not able to comprehend the many new terms she was being given. She wasn't able to memorize them all.

I know there are some people who have photographic memories, but my daughter and I are not among them! She works best with analysis, logic, and rationale. But there was nothing to analyze here...only to memorize. She was feeling like she was "less than."

I really wanted her to understand that she was being precisely who God made her to be...an analyzer not a memorizer. She wanted to drop the course. But after our conversation, she decided to talk to her teacher and explain her frustration. He was very gracious and explained that there were only a few days left in the chemical memorization before they moved into other areas of exploration, experimentation, and analysis of data.

Spirits lifted. Engines revved. Mission accomplished. Whew!

Mentors are students of people, especially their own children.

A good mentoring dad knows, in the words of one wag, "what makes them tick, what tickles them, and what ticks them off." The Book is particularly poignant about the latter. It says, "Fathers, do not provoke your children to anger; but bring them up in the discipline and instruction of the Lord" (Ephesians 6:4).

Anger is an emotion given all of us by God. It is the God-given emotion that is intended to surface when we perceive an injustice taking place. We ought to get angry when we see it happening. Similarly, our children ought, and will, get angry when they perceive that we, as their dads, are not being fair and just with them. It's pretty simple, really: When we say we are going to do something with them, perhaps even saying it repeatedly, yet fail to follow through, they will get angry.

When we make them promises and don't keep them, they will get angry. When we are not being fair with one of their brothers or sisters— or mom—they will naturally get angry. When we don't spend the time and attention on them that they know in their hearts we ought to spend as their dad, they will get angry. When we are overly harsh with them, they will get angry. When we have only clichés for every situation, instead of hearts of compassion and concern for their lives, they will get angry. When we don't give them enough room to grow up, they will get angry. When we don't give them healthy boundaries for their growing up, they will get angry.

Speaking of boundaries, my old friend Steve Farrar says it pretty well: "Every child in America needs a strict moral relative—and that strict moral relative should be Dad." Steve points out that hundreds of thousands of kids in this country are wandering around the schools, streets, and malls desperately needing someone in their lives who loves them enough to say "no." Steve then characterizes the traits of a "strict" father:

- Strict fathers aren't mean to their kids.
- Strict fathers aren't aloof from their kids.
- Strict fathers aren't distant from their kids.
- Strict fathers aren't harsh with their kids.
- Strict fathers aren't verbally abusive with their kids.

But...

- Strict fathers love their kids.
- Strict fathers are affectionate with their kids.
- Strict fathers verbally praise their kids.
- Strict fathers emotionally support their kids.[3]

None of us is a perfect dad. If you've only just realized that fact, welcome to the club. Welcome to the fellowship of rusty knights. Yet in spite of our flaws and imperfections, Paul's words to fathers are clear as can be. Without a stutter, the good apostle says, "Fathers...do not provoke your children to anger" but *do* "bring them up in the discipline and instruction of the Lord."

Do "bring them up," he says. *Bringing* is one of those inflexible words. "Bringing" demands your presence. "Bringing" is not sending. "Bringing" is not delegating. "Bringing" means you will be with them. It's putting our hands around the bat along with theirs.

Discipline means training primarily by actions. *Instruction* means training primarily by words or precepts. Bringing them up in discipline and instruction is, simply put, "show and tell." You've got to be there to do it.

A mentor is a student of people, including those individuals at church, at work, at school, in the neighborhood, on the kids' soccer team, at the bank, and in the store.

A   M E N T O R   I S   A   S T U D E N T   O F   F A I L U R E

Does it surprise you that a mentor is a student of failure? Think about it. How many of the "secrets of life" have you learned through trial and error? Many, many.

There is plenty of failure in this very imperfect world—more than enough to go around. And more of it than we usually care to admit is our own. If we stop to think about it carefully, we would probably have to admit some of our greatest lessons learned were through the educational medium called "failure." There really is a School of Hard Knocks, and some of us have advanced degrees from that venerable institution.

But so often we men tend just to "keep score" with our experiences rather than seeing the opportunity and value of learning from them. When we have some exhilarating mountaintop experience we tend to rack it up to our sheer ability to climb the ladder of success. But when we stub our toes, our tendency is to pick ourselves up, dust ourselves off, and charge off toward the horizon of the next "success." But *all* of life—both success and failure—is for growth. Instead of seeing life as a series of successes or failures—points for or points against—we need to see life as a process...the process of living, learning, and growing. Then we can pass these learned "secrets" of life to others around us.

The older I get, the more I am realizing that hard times, frustrating times, times of embarrassment or failure, so-called, are *necessary*. Actually "essential"—like amino acids for the body.

I think one of the hardest things about being a mentor, a husband, a father is learning how to let those around us go through the hard, disappointing, frustrating, failing times of life. A general rule of thumb I have chosen to follow is pretty simple: Don't get involved to rescue unless the situation is life or health threatening—or it is too big and expensive a jump in the learning curve all at once.

Rick Taylor told me of one such learning opportunity for his son Bryan.

When Bryan was about ten years old, he had saved his money for over a year in order to buy a new bicycle. He had already learned at this point in life that he could buy something cheap—every few years—or he could buy quality just once. So he "delayed his gratification" in order to save enough to get the bike he really wanted. And it was a great choice, a quality bike earned by hard work and patience. But patience is one of those things you don't "learn" just once, check it off the list, and move on to the next lesson. There was more to be learned. Just around the corner. Actually, as it turned out, it was just around the curb.

The first week Bryan had the bike, through one of those childhood combinations of "accident" and carelessness, he collided with the curb and bent the front rim. The damage was serious enough to require replacing the rim before it could be ridden again. Quality bikes have quality rims. Quality rims cost money. And Bryan had spent all his on the bike. Lesson number two: Quality products require quality care.

It was hard for Bryan's mom and dad to know just what to do. It would be a relatively easy matter for them to replace the rim so Bryan could enjoy his hard-earned bike. But they chose the harder road, believing it to be the more valuable route in learning one of life's "secrets." Good choice. Today Bryan is a college senior, majoring in graphic design, and far beyond his years in terms of being a young man who "takes care of his stuff."

Bryan had been mentored by a dad who by his own testimony had learned "that facing and learning from disappointments and failures was absolutely necessary to growing into the person God designed" him to be.

Good or bad, fun or frustrating, all experiences are part of the process called life. It is not the experiences themselves that make us wise mentors, but it is the way we process and learn from them that shapes us. One "sage" said it well, "Experience is not what happens to a man; it is what a man does with what happens to him."

A healthy mentor studies all of life. And passes on its "secrets." Let's close out this mentoring chapter with the testimony of one little fella who couldn't say enough about his mentor:

> The dad in my life isn't really my dad, he's my Grandpa. But he's been like a dad to me since before I was born. Four months before I was born my real father left my mommy. My Grandpa drove 400 miles to come get my mommy and me. He took care of my mommy until I was born. When I came home from the hospital there was a cradle that Grandpa made just for me. Someday, my kids will sleep in the same cradle.
>
> When I was a baby I cried a lot at night. Grandpa would walk me around and around the kitchen table. He rocked me to sleep and he was my first baby sitter.
>
> Now I'm nine years old and Grandpa is my best buddy. We do lots of things together. We go to zoos, museums, and parks. We watch baseball games on TV and we have Chex Mix together—just the two of us.
>
> When I was four my Grandpa spent a whole summer building me a playhouse with a big sandbox underneath. He made me a tire swing and pushes me lots of times in it. He pushes me real high, way up over his head. Now he spends all his extra time building new rooms on our house so that Mommy and I will

have our own apartment. If we didn't live at Grandpa's house we would have to live in a little apartment in town and I couldn't have my dog, my two house cats, my barn cats, and my gerbils. My Grandpa doesn't like cats very much but he lets me keep two cats in the house and he buys lots of cat food and feeds the barn cats even when it's really cold out.

My Grandpa is really patient. When he is busy building things he always takes time to start a nail so that I can pound it in. After he's spent all day mowing our big lawn he is really tired but he will still hook my wagon up to the lawn mower and drive me all over the place.

My Grandpa loves Jesus and he wants me to learn about Him, too. Sometimes people on TV talk about kids from single parent families. I'm not one of them because I have three parents in my family. My Grandpa isn't my Father, but I wouldn't trade him for all the dads in the world.[4]

Little Jordan's essay was submitted in 1993 to the Minnesota Father of the Year contest. Clearly, one old mentor has still got what it takes to do the job.

So do you.

THE FRIEND
PILLAR

———

Man strives for glory, honor, fame...that all the world may know his name. He amasses wealth by brain and hand...and becomes a power in the land. But when he nears the end of life...and looks back over the years of strife...he finds that happiness depends on none of these...but love of friends.

AUTHOR UNKNOWN

I have you in my heart...I long for you all with all the affection of Christ Jesus. And this I pray, that your love may abound still more and more in real knowledge.

PAUL, TO THE PHILIPPIANS
PHILIPPIANS 1:7-9

CHAPTER 12

SOUL KNITTING

G lorious moments. Soul-expanding instants. Thin slices of eternity.

We've all had them. Moments in time which reach
beyond it. Moments so abnormally rich, so deeply personal, so emotionally potent, they almost seem to be out-of-body experiences. We wish
they would never end. Yet even when they have passed us by (as they
must), these sorts of moments demand reflection. Re-living. Re-tasting.
Again and again.

Max Lucado christens them "eternal instants" and—as you would
anticipate—describes them with beauty:

> An instant in time that had no time. A picture that froze in mid-
> frame, demanding to be savored. A minute that refused to die,
> after sixty seconds...a moment that reminds you of the treasures
> surrounding you. Your home. Your peace of mind. Your
> health...a moment that can bring a mist to the manliest of eyes
> and perspective to the darkest life.[1]

—At a wedding, eyes meet, music surges, time stops, spirits soar.
And everyone knows it...*connection!*

—At the birth of a child there are no words, only faces contorted with
emotion...*connection!*

—On a hillside at sunset, just the two of you, after years: "I love you,
honey"...*connection!*

—On a field, that little team of youngsters; they did it, the impossible dream; the trophy; all together...*connection!*

—At a funeral, a giant has fallen; a noble life story; an honored widow, grieving friends...*connection!*

—At the table the meal waits, steaming; Grandpa prays; the three-year-old "Amens," giggles with sparkling eyes...*connection!*

My eyes have "misted" through some rich, almost sacred moments. Magic moments. Eternal instants. Whence the magic? What's the common element? Have you noticed what most all such "eternal instants" seem to share?

People.

People together.

People together connecting.

Whether it's a marriage, a family, a team, or a group of friends, it is people...it is together...and it is connecting at an emotional, soulish level. G. K. Chesterton touched on life's bottom line when he said, "The only two things that can satisfy the soul are a person and a story; and even the story must be about a person."

People connecting. And you were made for it. Yes you, man. Right there, resident in your chest, there is...

...a King—to provide

...a Warrior—to protect

...a Mentor—to teach

and, don't ever forget it, a Friend—to *connect.*

But, for some internalized reason, we men find it difficult to accept that final pillar. Most of us are happy to step into the responsibilities of a king or a warrior. We might struggle with the "mentor" pillar, but deep down that makes sense, too. Men are supposed to know how things work, and that, too, represents strength, power, and authority. But "this friend thing"? We seem to hold back, reluctant to take the plunge. That last foundation post of manhood seems a little questionable. Are we reluctant because the Friend pillar is brushed with a touch of emotion? Is it because personal connection requires a measure of vulnerability? Why do we seem to resist and dislike getting in touch with our emotions—and perhaps even exposing them to others?

That tendency toward rock-ribbed, self-sufficient isolation is a killing disease among men. It's as common as prostate cancer and every bit as destructive to life.

You know what I hate more than anything else? *Alone.*

Separation. Isolation. Alone is hell. And I wasn't made for it. Neither were you. The Creator said it from the get-go: "It is not good for the man to be alone" (Genesis 2:18). And (as we've already noted), while the obvious and immediate context of that verse is marriage, I believe it is a foundational statement of comprehensive principle to be found *throughout* Scripture. Together is better. You were made as a friend, for a friend.

My favorite words in all the Bible appear in both the Old and New Testaments. And in each case they are spoken in incredibly significant settings by enormously significant Persons. In the Old Testament, they are the first words spoken to a desperate people by a loving God. In the New Testament, they are the last words spoken to a commissioned people by His Son. First, last, or in-between, those words have a way of making a connection, of marking a friendship that transcends both time and death:

"I will be with you."

When God, in a moment of overwhelming intimacy, introduced Himself by name to His despairing but chosen people, the Bible captures it in the vocabulary of friendship: *"I have come down to deliver...and to bring [you] up.... I will be with you"* (see Exodus 3:8-12). That sealed it. They had a Friend.

And when Jesus had finished His sacrificial work, just before He ascended to "prepare a place" for His people to join Him at the table forever, He commissioned His disciples in the vocabulary of friendship, saying, *"I am with you always, even to the end of the age"* (Matthew 28:20).

Those are words of connection. They are words of love, commitment, and promise. They are words which drive away all fear. They are words which overwhelm the heart, and fill it with courage. They are God's words to you and me.

Again, in a time of deep, life-shattering persecution and political turmoil, the writer of Hebrews penned a note to believers who were feeling tempted to cash in their faith:

God has said,
"Never will I leave you;
    never will I forsake you."
So we may say with confidence,
"The Lord is my helper; I will not be afraid.
    What can man do to me?"
                    (Hebrews 13:5-6, NIV)

At His heart, the very core of His eternal essence, our God is a Friend. And, man, He expects you to be, too. He made you in His image—for connection, for friendship.

When will we get over our reticence? When will we work past our illogical fear of emotion? When will we free ourselves up to be real friends? When will we men avail ourselves of the power that is available in vulnerability? When will we men be able to acknowledge the authenticity in emotion? Real men do.

If there is no soulish connection, then there is no reason for living. If the King provides but never connects, it's no good. If the Warrior protects but never connects, it's no good. If the Mentor teaches but never connects, it's no good. It is not good for man to be alone! It is the Friend in his chest that gives the King, the Warrior, and the Mentor a reason to exist. If one of the four pillars is to stand a little taller, a little straighter than the others, if one pillar must bear a little more of the weight of manhood than the others, it must be the Friend pillar.

Lee Iacocca, a CEO in American big business, learned at least the beginnings of connection in his own home of origin. He described it warmly.

Like many native Italians, my parents were very open with their feelings and their love—not only at home, but also in public. Most of my friends would never hug their fathers. I guess they were afraid of not appearing strong and independent. But I hugged and kissed my dad at every opportunity—nothing could have felt more natural.[2]

Kent Hughes would agree enthusiastically:

> Men are never manlier than when they are tender with their chil-
> dren—whether holding a baby in their arms, loving their grade-
> schooler, or hugging their teenager or adult children.... Today, as
> a grandfather of six, it is increasingly apparent that my most trea-
> sured possessions, next to life in Christ, are the members of my
> family.... Someday when all is gone, when I can no longer see or
> hear or talk—indeed when I may no longer know their names—
> the faces of my loved ones will be on my soul.[3]

I take great encouragement from Kent's words. He is absolutely
right. It was when I held my newborn son in my arms that I actually
began to get something of a grasp of true manliness. More about that in
a minute.

Dave Simmons, former NFL linebacker, takes it a step further, and
challenges us men to show our hearts outside the family:

> One thing I believe now more than ever before, because I've
> seen the absolute life-saving nature of it—real men need real
> men. And real men need open men. I wish there were more
> openness among men, that we could see the true tone of a man's
> heart.[4]

Remember the class of 1965, cited in Chapter One? Remember the
plummeting SAT scores? The soaring eating disorders? The 500 percent
increase in illegitimate births? Recall the 600 percent increase in juvenile
violent crime and the tripling of teenage suicide?

How do we account for this national disaster? What's wrong with our
country?

Bottom line—men are failing to connect!

The evidence is everywhere. Even the national media are beginning
to recognize that there is no substitute for a man in touch at home, for a
man who will allow the friend in his chest to connect with his family:

There are places in America where fathers—usually the best hope to socialize boys—are so rare that bedlam engulfs the [entire] community. Teachers, ministers, cops and other substitute authority figures fight losing battles in these places against gang members to present role models to preteen and teenage boys. The result is often an astonishing level of violence and incomprehensible incidents of brutality.[5]

So how are you doing, man? Are you breaking through those old emotional barriers? At the soul level? Can they *feel* your love? We must learn, as men, to connect. It's the key to effective masculinity.

DELIVERY!

When will we be free to experience all of the masculine life God gave to us? I remember when it began to dawn upon me. I recall when I began to see the pleasure and power of human connection in freely expressed heart and soul. It was at the birth of our youngest son.

Linda had been in labor through the evening. The doctor had induced her just after I got off work that day. Through the evening hours she worked. I sweated. We smiled at each other. I jumped, helpless of course, at every surge of pain she experienced. Then, just as we began to close in on the delivery, the hospital staff disappeared!

As it turns out, the nurses were needed more urgently across the hall where last-minute complications forced two other mothers to deliver by emergency Cesarean section. With all the nurses gone, it was just Lindy, me, our doctor—and one little person getting ready to see what the wider world was all about. There were some large moments coming.

Though we were delivering our third son, this would be my first "birth experience" as a father. I had not been permitted to attend the birth of our first two sons. They had been born in an earlier medical dispensation when fathers were considered unnecessary riffraff in the delivery room. (Am I still a little bitter? Yes. Those were irretrievable magic moments taken from me.) But, hey, this one was different. They let me in from the very beginning. I was scrubbed. Linda chuckled at my hospital garb—thought I looked like the jolly green giant.

I knew it would be magic. I knew it would be an Event. I already felt it was one of life's mountain-peak moments. But even so, I was not prepared for the sheer emotional power of that little slice of time.

The big moment had almost arrived. Smiling at the two of us, the doctor said, "Well, this will be fun. Just the three of us—and 'junior,' whoever he or she may be. I haven't done it unassisted this way since medical school." Then he added, with another smile, "Stu, you'll have to help me catch."

Say what? *Catch?* What is this? A sporting event? I didn't even bring my mitt.

Then he came. Our son. Gently. Naturally. Then with a rush he emerged from my wife's body. I was so proud of her! And *him.* It was a him! Dr. Upoff "caught" him and immediately handed him to me, cord and all. My son cried a little.

And I cried harder.

For the first time in my memory, I wept uncontrollably. Blessedly so.

Me? Crying in front of people? Stu Weber, the football captain. The Airborne Ranger. The Green Beret trooper. The man. Bawling like a kid? Oh, I had cried before, somewhere along the line. But when I did, it was alone, in the secrecy of my own closet, where I could feel like I was in control—even if I wasn't. But this time it was different. New. There was no shame, and there was lots of connection.

I have to admit the tears are drifting down my cheeks again as I write these words and relive the birth of my youngest son, Ryan. And I have to admit something else. *I'm enjoying it.* Emotions are such a great gift from God. And after a lifetime of stuffing them for athletic, military, and "manly" purposes, I love them these days. More than ever.

There in the delivery room, holding my son in my arms and crying so healthily, I felt initially awkward. But I didn't care. As I think back on it now, a picture comes to my mind: It's the picture of an old silver-haired slave, dancing awkwardly, and shouting through his smile, "I'm free. Thank God, *I'm free!*"

You see, I love my son. Oh...deeply, so very deeply. I know it. And he knows it. There is connection there, my friend. Connection! And there is nothing better in this life than that.

With my second son, Blake, it was very similar, though I wasn't quite as "free" at that point in my life. I was still bound up in some of those old "restraint chains" most of us have inherited from our fathers. The first time I saw my second-born was well after "the action." Things were wrapped up and tidied up. Then the "intruder" was allowed in by the "authorities." Linda and Blake were in their own room now. As I approached the bed, she held him up to me. It was, indeed, magic. I remember thinking, "a brother!" How great! A buddy, a companion, a soul-mate to run with. I held him to my chest. He is the middle son, still the center, the hub of so much family activity.

Were you present at the birth of your children? Do you recall the emotion that flowed through your whole being? Can you recall that sense of being overwhelmed? Find those feelings again, my friend. And don't keep them corked and bottled up on some dusty shelf inside your ribcage. Pass them around!

There is a friend in a man's heart. To connect. And when it does, the whole world is a better place in which to live. I saw it happen the other day before my own eyes.

T H E   S C R E A M

Linda and I were together at the Clackamas Town Center Mall. You know the kind of place. Huge. Indoors. Two stories high. Hundreds of shops. Crowds of people. It was a sale day; in my opinion, the absolute *worst* time to be in such a place. I think I would rather pay more and avoid the claustrophobia—or just go without! But I was there that day with the wife of my youth, edging through the thousands of bodies that packed the corridors and raised the decibel count to a level just below serious discomfort.

Suddenly, over all the other noise, we heard it.

A piercing, blood-curdling SCREAM cut through the air in that place. It stopped traffic. It practically stopped hearts. Every person in that huge public area literally winced at the terror in that little voice—the voice of a child in pain or terror. A little boy had been inadvertently separated from his parents. He was lost, utterly lost in the crowd, with no idea which way to turn. Alone, disoriented, and panic stricken, he *screamed* aloud.

If we had ears to hear, we would hear those screams all over America today. Kids are *screaming* because they're separated from their dads and moms.

When you read of another teen suicide, hear a SCREAM.

When you see on the news another gang-related murder, hear a SCREAM.

When you read of another drug death, hear a SCREAM.

There in that mall, however, we witnessed the solution to America's root problem: Restoration! While everyone in the mall that day heard the scream, two people heard it like no one else—the parents. The cry had come from downstairs and behind us. Near us on the second level, a mom and a dad responded immediately. The look on their faces told the whole story—eyes alarmed, but focused. *We've got to get to our child!* No embarrassment. No awkwardness. No nonchalant approach. They literally erupted off that second level, sprinted down the escalator and got to their child. Scooping him up, they held him close and tight.

Perhaps ten minutes later we beheld a beautiful scene. Our wanderings took us back around to the central mall area. There was the child and his parents. Time had passed. But they were still there, unable to move from the bench where they'd collapsed after their reunion. Still recovering from the shock of separation. Together again, holding one another, rocking the little one back and forth. He was still sobbing but had begun, gradually, to calm, to settle, to be at home again in his daddy's arms.

That little reunion scene reminded me of the restoration passage found in the Book of Malachi:

> "Behold, I am going to send you Elijah the prophet before the coming of the great and terrible day of the LORD. And he will restore the hearts of the fathers to their children, and the hearts of the children to their fathers, lest I come and smite the land with a curse." (Malachi 4:5-6)

We men need to get in touch with our emotions or we will never be able to connect with others, no matter how much we want to, or how hard we try.

Ever so gradually, I'm growing in this area. Good grief, it's about time! It's been a process of many years now. It began to pick up some serious momentum in the early eighties. It had been a long time since I had been in Vietnam, and I found myself thinking about it a lot more than previously. What began to happen to me then surprised me.

I'll never forget one day in particular...and one night a few years later.

T H E   W A L L

It was Veterans Day. At that time, I had not yet been to The Wall in Washington, D.C. But there was to be a public dedication in Portland of Oregon's Vietnam Memorial. I decided to go. Alone. I didn't want anyone I knew to be with me. I think I sensed I had some personal and private business to complete. But I wasn't prepared for what happened—and my response proved it.

Like many fall days in Western Oregon, it was a cloudy morning with a light rain falling. Not enough to really soak to the skin, but more than enough to be somewhat depressing on an already sobering day.

I was surprised at the size of the crowd gathered on that cold morning. Selecting a place away from the masses, I stood at the edge of the crowd, semi-alone, on a gently sloping grassy hill. Our nation's flag waved in the fall breeze, snapping slightly every now and then. The gentle rain dripped from the trees above me.

The black marble wall was mesmerizing. My eyes seemed fixed, nearly trance-like. Normally alert to my circumstances, I forgot entirely about the crowd. The dedication service itself held my attention. It was moving to me—I hadn't anticipated how moving it would be. My mind sorted back through some memories. I had my old, well-worn and somewhat-dirty Green Beret down inside my topcoat. When the speakers began their remarks, my hand almost involuntarily dropped inside my coat. I slipped it on my head. Emotions began to stir down inside.

And then the lone bugler played taps.

The melancholy notes of the bugle gripped me. I felt my stirring emotions welling up, taking on unfamiliar strength....

That's when I woke up. Evidently, the unfamiliar strength of my emotions was too much for me. So I did what I had always done when

I felt strong emotions. I *stifled* them. The old Stu took over, brought back my "control." I steeled myself against those emotions. I literally and consciously shoved them back down inside, and slammed a heavy lid on them. After all, I was a *man*.

As a child, I would have wept. And without shame. As a child, I would have experienced the health of my God-given emotions. But I had lost my childlike qualities. Or so I thought. Later, Jesus' words would come home to me: "Truly I say to you, unless you are [changed] and become like children, you shall not enter the kingdom of heaven. Whoever humbles himself as this child, he is the greatest in the kingdom of heaven" (Matthew 18:3-4).

After some reflection, I realized I needed to make some adjustments. This "stuffing it" was not real maturity. And it wasn't healthy either. Emotions are good for people. They are God-given. But I wasn't ready for all of that at the ceremony that day. I was a long way from thinking rightly. Pride would not allow me to display emotion. I would process that...for a long time. Years, actually.

Some years later I was lying in bed. Lindy was asleep beside me. I was reading a book entitled *We Were Soldiers Once...and Young.* It was written by Hal Moore and Joe Galloway, who had suffered through the wrenching battle in the Ia Drang Valley of Vietnam's Central Highlands in November 1965. Now, twenty years later, I read some words in that book which touched me. I identified with them. I lived them...and they triggered some of those same powerful memories.

My emotions stirred again. But this time, in the privacy of my own bedroom, I let them build.

And I wept.

I *chose* to weep. I *chose* to let the tears come. And they did. Like a river gathering momentum on the way to the sea, they flowed. It was unusual. Like what they call a thirty-year flood. I decided not to dam it up. My face contorted. I let the sobs come. My chest actually heaved, and it felt good. It *was* good!

Now think with me a minute. What I experienced was good, truly good. What I experienced was healthy. It was pure, rich emotion. It was not emotional*ism*. It was quite the opposite. It was *reason*. It was

deliberate. It was thoughtful. Yes, there was pain. But there was also pleasure. The healthy, rejuvenating kind of pleasure that belongs only to the
release of God-given emotion.

Why do we men fight our healthy emotions? Aren't strong, deep feelings good for us? Why should there be some nebulous sense of shame in
being moved by the memories of the past—or the hopes of the future?
Or by deep personal thoughts of a loved one, or a Loved One. Why
shouldn't we be moved by reflecting on the Savior's entering our world
and changing our destiny? What is the value in this so-called "mature
adult" exercise of pressing our tears and joys back into the silence of our
chests?

We need to experience the healthy, rejuvenating kind of pleasure that
belongs only to the release of God-given emotion. If we are ever going to
connect. If the Friend pillar is ever going to stand tall and straight, and
bear the weight of the world which God has given us to lead.

When I began to experience the freedom of owning my own heart
and its emotions, good things began to happen. Connections went
deeper.

I saw it happen in my own garage. And it happened to me. It was an
eternal instant of deep, personal connection. And a small civilization
endured by extending its soul into the next generation.

GARAGE   CONNECTION

One of my sons had been away for his freshman year in college. His first
year had gone much like mine more than two decades before. Halfway
across the continent—away from his home, his girl, his roots, and his
beloved mountains—it was a shock to his system. And, like his dad
before him, he had begun to feel like the only member of his class who
didn't have a rope around his future. He was so disoriented and confused
that he was no longer himself. No characteristic jokes, no more wry
smiles, no sparkle. The laughter had gone out of life. It had become a
months-long funk.

Home for a break, he was cleaning the garage with me. It was something to do. I watched him as we worked. My heart wanted his to be well.
Finally, not knowing what else to do, I broke the silence.

"Son, what's wrong? What's happening for you?"

His back toward me, he slowly put down the box he was lifting. He straightened up and faced me. We looked at each other for a moment, and his eyes glazed over. Eye to eye from across the garage, in tones fraught with disappointment and frustration, he said to me in obvious anguish, "Dad, I don't know."

Then he shouted it. "I DON'T KNOW! I don't know ANY-THING." He went on, "I go to school with classmates who are on some kind of track—at least they think they are. They've known since they were five years old they were going to be neurosurgeons, or artists, or microbiologists, or literature professors, or..." his voiced trailed off. He looked up again, through tear-filled eyes, to say, "And I don't even know what classes to take next term, let alone what my major should be—let alone what I'm supposed to become!"

My insides ached for him. With tears welling in my own eyes, I heard myself saying words completely void of any premeditation.

"Well, I don't know what you're supposed to do either, Son. But I do know this. As long as there is breath in my lungs, *I will be with you.*"

Those words. I realized as they crossed my lips, they were the very words of the Living One to His children. I started to move toward my son. He began to come toward me. There in the center of the garage, we met. My arms were held out to embrace him. His opened to me. We hugged like we had never hugged before. Our beards, unshaven that morning, locked together.

And then I felt his tears—my son's warm tears running down my neck. And mine began to run down his. In an eternal instant our two masculine hearts entwined themselves. We just stayed there in an embrace—two men, a father and a son...one heart.

In time, we straightened and looked at one another. His countenance had changed. His face shown. His eyes were filled with life again. Through the "mist" in both our eyes, he said, "Dad, I guess that's all I needed to know."

Yes. I guess it is.

It's enough to know...to love...to connect...to be together. It is the way of the Father, the Son, and the Spirit.

Connect, man. For God's sake. For your family's sake. For the sake of your own soul. Find a way. Find a place. Look for the opportunity. In a garage, or on the trail, or around a table, or at a holiday gathering. Take the initiative. Don't worry about feeling awkward, strange, or out of your element. Just step in like a man and get the job started.

It happened for my dad just a couple of years ago. It was the first time I ever saw a tear in my father's eye—and he was in his seventy-fifth year!

CHRISTMAS CONNECTION

It was Christmas, just two years ago now. "Pop's" family was gathered around him. His adult children had collected from around the country-side. One grandson was home from college in the Midwest. Another had flown in from the East Coast. A third, newly married, brought his bride and her parents. Sons, daughters, aunts, uncles, and grandchildren were all smiles. Cousins grinned and teased. It was an opportunity.

I read aloud from the Gospel of Luke, the story of the old patriarchal Simeon whose lifelong dream was realized as he held the infant Messiah in his arms. *"Now, Lord, Thou dost let Thy bond-servant depart in peace...for my eyes have seen Thy salvation, which Thou hast prepared in the presence of all peoples, a light of revelation to the Gentiles, and the glory of Thy people Israel"* (Luke 2:29-32).

It was a hushed moment as we imagined this magnificent and humble first-century saint holding high his own Savior and thanking his Lord for this unspeakable Gift...a Gift to all peoples and each family, across the many centuries.

We decided, spontaneously, to thank our Lord for His goodness to us—in this twentieth century. We asked each one in our family circle that night to describe, briefly and personally, our gratitude to God for allowing us to be born into this day and into this family, all in the context of enjoying the pleasure of God's perfect sovereign plan. We knew it had all the potential for becoming an eternal instant. It began simply and built (uncharacteristically for us Webers) emotional momentum quickly.

In an environment of praising their Lord, parents thanked children. Brothers expressed their love. Eyes welled up. Children thanked their parents for being both firm and loving. Tears flowed. Moms and dads, aunts and uncles, brothers and sisters, all visibly touched, dabbed at their eyes. And siblings thanked each other! For all kinds of things. Kleenex was passed. By the box. Two teenage girls, through increasing tears, thanked their older masculine cousins for showing them, in real life, what a man was supposed to be. They told the family that their dating standards were set wonderfully high by their own male family members. They knew there were men of godly character out there because they had observed their cousins' purity.

The Kleenex box ran out. "In-laws" expressed their deep gratefulness to each other for an overwhelming sense of acceptance and familial oneness and belonging. Another "Kleenex run" had to be made. There was, literally, not a dry eye in the place.

It was an especially potent moment when one of the older grandchildren spoke to his grandparents. This strapping two-hundred-twenty-pound, twenty-something grandson spoke for the whole family. He thanked his grandparents for setting the pace. He said he lived in a world of peers whose parents and grandparents are no longer married. He honored his senior grandparents for keeping their vows. He thanked them for their faithfulness to each other through the ups and downs of more than fifty years of marriage.

And in that moment, for the first time in my life, I saw a tear in my father's eye. His was not a generation to express emotion. But he felt it. And there, in the presence of his grateful and admiring family, he let them into the treasure chest of his emotions. This gentle but firm patriarch who was the earthly beginning point of the family assembled that night, became more than that. He became in that moment, however quietly, the capstone and completer of the family's emotional circle. It was full circle. It was transgenerational. It was...an eternal instant.

There is, my friend, somewhere down inside you, the power to connect. There is in every man's chest a friend, an emotionally connecting friend. Find yours. Unchain him. And find life on a richer level than you'd dreamed possible.

Thus says the LORD, your Creator…
And He who formed you…
"Do not fear, for I have redeemed you;
I have called you by name; you are Mine!
When you pass through the waters, I will be with you;
And through the rivers, they will not overflow you.
When you walk through the fire, you will not be scorched,
Nor will the flame burn you.
For I am the LORD your God,
The Holy One of Israel, your Savior."

ISAIAH 43:1–3

CHAPTER 13

A Man's Best Friend

W hat guy can forget his first fight?

Some of those childhood scuffles were real sweaty-palmed moments, weren't they? Oh sure, there was probably a minor tussle in the church nursery over a stuffed bunny or in preschool when some other kid wanted the same dump truck. But you couldn't really call that a "fight." Somewhere along the line, however, you were old enough to recognize that the Real Thing had arrived, and was in your face.

You were probably between seven and ten years old when it dawned on you that the guy talking trash and pushing on your chest meant business. Whoa! This was no recess squabble over the batting order; this was ugly. This was intense. This guy actually intended to *hurt* you.

What did you feel in that instant? Fear! Tension! Not to mention a little panic. You were probably sweating it on the inside while still attempting a little swagger on the outside.

When I was a youngster we lived in a fairly rough neighborhood for a while. It was "the wrong side of the tracks," as they say. I have memories of one unfortunate little kid getting a sharp stick stuck through a portion of his neck by some bully. On another occasion I recall a young ruffian howling with pain and rage when someone with a BB gun shot him in the forehead. The BB lodged just under his skin; it bled a little and we were all horrified—until we realized the physical damage to this young tough was only minor. Then, I must admit, it was all we could do to keep from laughing. And there was the time I got a target arrow stuck in my calf. Had my new Christmas roller-skates on and couldn't duck when that wild warrior "attacked." Come to think of it, that really was a rough little neck o' the woods. I wouldn't see that much combat again until I arrived in Vietnam. There were some tense moments.

LOOKIN' FOR A FRIEND...

But unless I miss my guess, during your first serious scuffle—when you were afraid to swallow and afraid to blink—that's about the time you started looking around you for a little moral support. In that moment, you were a fella who desperately needed a friend. Preferably a really BIG friend!

Rick Taylor and I got a kick out of his recalling his first schoolyard battle. Here's how he related it to me:

The summer just before I started into the fifth grade, our family moved to a new school district in St. Louis. As usual, I was the smallest kid in the class. At the very first recess, I mean *the very first,* I was surrounded by three bigger boys. I felt like a mouse at a convention of cats. They began pushing me around and calling me fifth-grade-type names—you know, the kind of names designed to establish the pecking order on the playground.

Now I may have been small, but I wasn't stupid.

So right after recess, after meekly surviving the first of what I anticipated to be several confrontations, I spotted an empty seat in the classroom and moved over there. I had noticed it was located right next to Mike, the biggest guy in the class. Mike was at least a full head taller than me. And I had observed that he was a pleasant enough guy—at least to his friends. I determined that was exactly what I was going to be in short order—Mike's friend. I began talking to him and extending myself to him. In a matter of just a few days we had more or less worked out an unspoken gentleman's agreement. I'd help Mike with the books, and he would be my friend on the playground.

Sure enough, a few days after our agreement was solidified, those same three jokers from day one spotted me and trotted on over. They came up from behind and pushed me to the ground before I even knew they were there. They started pointing and taunting and laughing. I felt like I was in a movie or some-thing—it seemed like some kind of weird, slow-motion, out-of-body experience for me.

And then—in a flash—the scene changed entirely.

Within a matter of moments, Mike was standing between me and them. I wasn't sure what was going to happen next; our agreement was untested on the battlefield end of things. But after what seemed like forever—just standing there—Mike broke the silence.

"You leave Rick alone. He's my *friend.* You mess with Rick, you mess with me!"

It really did look like a movie. Those three guys went white, like someone who had just seen a ghost. Sheepishly, they turned, broke into an awkward little trot, and then ran away. Mike turned back and reached down to pick me up. After that day, life was pretty good in the playground department.

Now, as you well know, all the same dangers and problems were still all around Rick on the playground. Nothing much had changed in the environment. But somehow life was a lot different now. Something had changed inside Rick. All because he had a friend. Rick walked taller, more confidently, and he enjoyed life a whole lot more, without nearly so much fear and insecurity. Mike, the Big Guy, now walked the play-ground with him. Rick had found a friend to help with his ten-year-old battles...a really big friend.

We all need that kind of a friend. A bigger, stronger friend who is utterly reliable in all that life's "playgrounds" throw at us.

Are you feeling like life's got you by the throat? Is your world too threatening to be comfortable? Does it feel like the daily grind is shoving you down and beating you up? Are you struggling at home? Or facing adversity at the office? Are there people out to get your job? Or people seeking to get ahead who are using you as their next steppingstone? If you're in a leadership role, have you heard the whine of snipers' bullets zinging by your ears?

Welcome to life on a broken world! The only way to get by or around that kind of pressure is to get *off* the world—which we're not ready to do just yet! What we need is a friend. A strong friend pillar can actually bear the weight of the whole building while we work on getting the other pillars under the load.

In this chapter, we're going to recognize that the friend pillar in a man's heart can never be in balance unless it takes its plumb from a friendship with the Living God. You will never be the friend (or the lover) you want to be, you will never connect completely with yourself and others, unless and until you connect with…

T H E   U L T I M A T E   F R I E N D

You see, there is help. You do have a friend. A very big and powerful Friend. An omni-competent Friend. God is there, on the battlefields of life with you. In this world we may be engulfed with pain, weighted with tension, and frustrated on every side. But the Bible says that God stoops to be involved in our world of pain. And His is a promise you can count on.

> Who can be compared with the LORD our God,
>   who is enthroned on high?
> Far below him are the heavens and the earth.
>   He stoops to look,
> and he lifts the poor from the dirt
>   and the needy from the garbage dump.
> He sets them among princes,
>   even the princes of his own people!
>   (Psalm 113:5-8, NLT)

Isn't that good? He reaches down, even if He has to reach into the dirt or a garbage dump. And He is more than capable of picking you up, dusting you off, and setting you on solid ground again. He said as much in His own words to His chosen people, reeling in confusion on the battlefields of their day: "I have come down to deliver…and to bring them up" (Exodus 3:8).

And the Living One says that promise is good to this day. "Surely I am with you always, to the very end of the age" (Matthew 28:20, NIV).

You can take it to the bank. The touch of our heavenly Friend can make all the difference in the world.

Life will always be full of pain. Jesus said you can count on that, too. It's the nature of things on this sin-stained planet. But His "I will be with you always" can open a lot of clenched fists, relieve a lot of heavy tension, and heal a lot of serious wounds. It can keep your four pillars stable and strong.

If you want to walk taller, and more confidently, then you need to put your confidence in the right place. You need to draw your confidence from the One who is a man's best Friend. To experience a personal friend-ship with Him, you need to understand a couple of simple, but profound realities.

1. God Wants a Relationship with You, and Seeks You Out Right Now

Do you believe that? Has that truth—the teeth-jarring, life-moving real-ity of it!—ever really penetrated the deep places of your soul? You may feel like you've blown it too badly, that no one (let alone God!) would want to be a friend to you. But He *does* want to. And hey, we've all blown it. But wonder of wonders, He continues to pursue us. He is a friend full of grace and truth.

For sinners like you and me, the truth is, we need His *grace*. We need his unmerited, unearned, undeserved, and almost unbelievable favor upon our lives.

I remember all too clearly catching a glimpse of that grace as a child. I can see myself right now, covered with shame, more or less hiding in the basement, waiting to face my dad. Not that I wanted to see him. No, I was *dreading* to see him. I had broken one of the cardinal rules in our family (no smoking!), and my mom had caught me in the act. Now I was going to have to stand before my dad as soon as he got home from work. I was not looking forward to it—at all!

I anticipated a whipping like none before. I just knew my dad was going to explode. I feared a year's worth of penance, grounding until the Second Coming, or some unimaginable fate. It was unbearable there, hiding in the darkness and gloom of the basement.

But I learned an unbelievable lesson that day. About my dad...and about grace.

When I finally stood before Dad, I was completely overwhelmed with his response. He didn't explode. He didn't shake me. He didn't whip me. He didn't yell at me. He just looked at me with great sadness in his eyes. To this day, I will never forget the pain I saw in those eyes—*pain that I, Stu Weber, had caused.* He didn't say anything for a long while. It was the longest silence of my life. My dad, the dad I loved more than any person on earth at that point in my life, couldn't speak to me. And then he broke the silence with words that I can never forget.

"Are you telling me, Son, that knowing how strongly I feel about these things you went ahead *and did them anyway?"*

Oh, wow! I could see I had hurt him at his center. I had bruised his heart. And it was killing me. I literally begged his forgiveness. I would have crawled on cut glass across the continent if it would have helped. But it wouldn't. Nor would anything else. The damage was done. I had blown it, and I had no way to erase the fact. I could not bridge that horrible gap. But my dad, the one offended, could and did.

Seeing my remorse, Dad broke the silence between us with these words:

"I forgive you, Son. Don't do it again."

We never spoke of the matter again. That was more than thirty years ago. Dad had actually forgotten all about it until I reminded him just the other day. He's seventy-five now, and he's still teaching me about grace.

It's the grace of God which gives us a relationship with the best Friend a man ever had. Unmerited favor. Enjoying what you do not deserve. A total gift. Love.

Brennan Manning came to the point where he couldn't live without it. He was a "bedraggled, beat-up and burnt out" old alcoholic. From his perspective, life was a pit. In fact, he was so low he had to stand on his tiptoes and lean his head way back just to begin to see the bottom of the pit. On top of all that he was a Catholic priest who was supposed to know better. Not a good thing! Can you imagine the discouragement (and the guilt) he experienced?

And then Brennan came to understand his Friend. The man walked right smack into an understanding of the grace of God in Jesus Christ. There in the miserable mud and humiliation of his self-indulgent "playground"—not liking himself one bit—he discovered an astounding thing.

He discovered that God really *liked* him.

He discovered, in his own words, that "the Scriptures insist on God's initiative in the work of salvation—that by grace we are saved, that the Tremendous Lover has taken to the chase...."[1]

Brennan, like you and me, just needed to know that God really loved him, that a man's best Friend accepted him just as he is—"bedraggled, beat-up, and burnt out." He realized he didn't have to get cleaned up in order to experience the grace of God. He learned that in the past, all his spiritual struggles had begun with himself rather than with God. He learned that a God-centered faith will change your life. He learned that God really loved him. No kidding. "God is not capricious; he knows no seasons of change. He has a single relentless stance toward us: he loves us."[2]

Brennan Manning's personal discovery of the grace of God changed his life. Listen to him describe the rejuvenating freedom and hope that a man experiences from his best Friend; what it's like when a man lets himself be gripped by the loving God who raises people from the garbage dump:

> The Good News means we can stop lying to ourselves. The sweet sound of amazing grace saves us from the necessity of self-deception. It keeps us from denying that though Christ was victorious, the battle with lust, greed, and pride still rages within us. As a sinner who has been redeemed, I can acknowledge that I am often unloving, irritable, angry, and resentful with those closest to me. When I go to church I can leave my white hat at home and admit I have failed. God not only loves me as I am, but also knows me as I am. Because of this I don't need to apply spiritual cosmetics to make myself presentable to him. I can accept ownership of my poverty and powerlessness and neediness.[3]

As I continued to read of this good man's growing love for his Lord and his developing maturity in Christ's grace, I had a good chuckle. Out loud. Because his words rang so true, and are so characteristic of so many men I know and love, I nearly died with identifying laughter:

> When I get honest, I admit I am a bundle of paradoxes. I believe and I doubt, I hope and get discouraged, I love and I hate, I feel bad about feeling good, feel guilty about not feeling guilty. I am trusting and suspicious, and I still play games. Aristotle said I am a rational animal; I say I am (a saint) with an incredible capacity for beer.[4]

It's so true, isn't it—we men do blow it. Badly. And Satan would love to keep us trussed up in the bonds of his accusations. But you can, as a man, learn to accept your powerlessness and neediness. You can accept it because God does, and He provides the antidote for it—the grace-full gift of His Son's death on your behalf. You can keep running back there. Back to Calvary, as they say. You can wrap up your failure and disappointment and sin, like a big awkward bundle in your arms, and hand it off to the One who lifts "the needy from the ash heap to make them sit with princes."

First, last, and in between, God wants a relationship with you. Yes, you! And Jesus Christ, through His death for us on the cross, opened the way. He bridged the gap that you and I never could have bridged in a million years of trying.

Are you troubled today? Weighed down? Just about done in from the pressure you are experiencing? A marriage? A job? A family conflict? Are you weary? Weary of waiting, weary of fighting, weary of walking, weary of running?

Jesus issues an invitation to weary people, to people tired of fighting: "Come to me, all you who are weary and burdened, and I will give you rest. Take my yoke upon you and learn from me, for I am gentle and humble in heart, and you will find rest for your souls" (Matthew 11:28, NIV).

Come to Him. Learn from Him. And accept His rest. In the process, you will learn something about His promises.

2. God Has Made You Some Promises, Granted You Some Guarantees
A promise can be a magnificent thing, depending on the trustworthiness

and ability of the one making the promise, and depending on the receptivity of the one receiving the promise. A promise is a personal guarantee that something is always true and can be counted upon *utterly*. The Bible is chock-full of promises, but as we wrap up our time together in this study of the "Four Pillars of a Man's Heart," I want to look at just two or three that are immediately relevant to most of the men I know.

Our Father, our Friend, has made us many promises. But there is one passage of the Bible that spells some promises that we might not think of right up front. In J. B. Phillip's classic paraphrase of Romans 8:18-26, Paul relates these words to us:

> In my opinion whatever we may have to go through now is less than nothing compared with the magnificent future God has planned for us. The whole creation is on tiptoe to see the wonderful sight of the sons of God coming into their own. The world of creation cannot as yet see reality, not because it chooses to be blind, but because in God's purpose it has been so limited— yet it has been given hope. And the hope is that in the end the whole of created life will be rescued from the tyranny of change and decay, and have its share in that magnificent liberty which can only belong to the children of God!
>
> It is plain to anyone with eyes to see that at the present time all created life groans in a sort of universal travail. And it is plain, too, that we who have a foretaste of the Spirit are in a state of painful tension, while we wait for that redemption of our bodies which will mean that at last we have realized our full sonship in him. We were saved by this hope, but in our moments of impatience let us remember that hope always means waiting for something we do not yet possess. But if we hope for something we cannot see, then we must settle down to wait for it in patience.
>
> The Spirit of God not only maintains this hope within us, but helps us in our present limitations.

There are at least three major promises here that we need to understand from our Father and Friend.

Promise #1: You will have trouble in this world.

First, God promises us that our journey through this world is going to see a lot of suffering, pain, misery, frustration, limitations, perplexities, and problems. "Whoopee!" you say. "Now isn't that an exciting promise? What kind of a guarantee is that?"

An honest one!

The greatest gift any friend can offer us is the truth. It isn't candy or pabulum or painkillers, it is *truth*. And, man, that promise about trouble in this life is truth! This world is a mess. And if you and I are looking for total satisfaction here, we're going to be disappointed, or worse. We need to understand this promise of the Father, and receive it, with all seriousness.

Oh, how much time we waste in life trying to get rid of the pain and suffering in our lives, and even in those around us. Some of us feel pain at the mere mention of words like "home" or "parents." Others of us are suffering right now because of some of the poor choices we've made in life. Some of us are in, or have been in, relationships that are confusing and agonizing. Some of us are totally undone inside because of the ways our children are responding, or not responding, to us. Some are trudging through years of a less than fulfilling marriage. All of these realities hurt. The pain at times can be beyond belief.

We may try to deny our pain...ignore our pain...put off our pain...but the pain in this world is in us and around us every day—whether we want it or not. But some of us feel that life is not worth living unless we can get rid of the pain. Our Friend knows we need to be reminded that such a thing will never happen. So He tells us straight. And He promises to use those difficult situations to make us better sons.

Think about it—you will likely have to admit it—the periods of greatest growth in your life probably involved some significant pain or helplessness. But lessons learned that way are life-changing, and rest-forming. Our Friend will see to it, if we will take on His yoke and learn.

Many years ago now, when Rick and I were busy in the early years of ministry and raising a family, he and his wife, Judy, learned a lesson that changed him, and all of us in the family, forever. In fact, out of it he wrote a book entitled *When Life Is Changed Forever...by the Death of*

Someone Near. It was an incredibly hard lesson, and it was some time in coming. But it will never be forgotten—by any of us in the family. Let Rick tell it:

Right after seminary my first ministry was in a small church in Florida. I went there to be an intern for the first year. But one week after I arrived the staff all left. So the second Sunday I was there, I was introduced as the interim pastor. I began working to make up for all the staff…about 80-100 hours a week. I was out 5, 6, even 7 nights a week.

Judy and I had three little guys already. I remember one evening in particular that I came home with only about 30 minutes to change clothes, eat and get to my next meeting. I ran in, changed and scarfed down some dinner. As I was rushing through the family room past the little family on the floor playing a game, I said, "Bye guys, I love you."

No one looked up, even Judy. But with heads down, they all in unison blandly said, "Bye Dad."

I was not even there. I was non-existent to my family. I was cut to the quick as I turned back and looked at my family on the floor, playing their game, not even realizing I was standing in the door watching them. Nor did they care. It killed me inside. This was not the way I wanted life to be for my family, or for me.

It was only a few months later that I left that ministry in favor of a Christian camping ministry…directing a junior camp. After a few increased responsibilities and a couple of promotions, guess who was working that same old 80-100 hours a week?…DayTimers don't lie.

My firstborn son, Kyle, kept asking me, "Dad, can we go camping?"

A reasonable request of the local camp director. My repeated response to his repeated request went something like, "One of these days soon we'll do that, Kyle."

But on April 7, 1979 my life was changed forever. I learned a really hard lesson a really hard way. On that day, while trying to save his youngest brother, Kyle drowned in a tragic accident. I never saw Kyle again. "One of these days" would never come. My spirit was crushed. Life is full of painful experiences that we either can't or don't count on.[5]

Rick would tell you that he and Judy had known perfectly well that there are no guarantees in this life. In fact, they knew that God had specifically said there would be trouble and pain. But, as they would also say, and as is true of most of us, they didn't really believe Him. At least not in their case. Troubles—deep, life-shattering troubles—were for other people. Rick and Judy were going to live the American dream, and enjoy their family. But it didn't work out that way. And their hearts just about sunk out of their chests. They were sick inside for a long, long time.

As the old song goes, "In times like this you need a Savior." And that takes us to a second promise which God gives us.

Promise #2: "I will be with you."
When Rick and Judy were battling through their pain at Kyle's loss, they had friends who came alongside and were there for them. But there was a promise of God that they needed even more. God never promises to take the pain away, but He does promise to go through it with us. They needed their *best* Friend close at hand. And He was there. Listen to Rick's heart:

> I don't remember when, but I finally spoke the words above my sobbing heart, "Kyle is dead. He is gone. I will never see my precious son grow up. I will never throw the football with him again...I will never again go for walks with him and hear him growing up as he talks with me. I will never see the man he would have become."

No, Rick never again got to walk with his son. But he did, very often, go on walks with his Friend. And the God who knows, like no other, what it is to lose a son, walked alongside Rick just like He had promised:

I've learned to stop fighting and resisting my heavenly Father. The pain is not evil and bad. It just hurts. There are worse things than hurting, like not growing.... When Kyle died, I prayed a great deal. But most of my prayers were venting my emotions and telling God how much I hurt. I spent little time asking God to help me know how to make my life work the way it should in the midst of my pain.

And when I did ask God for something, it was the wrong thing. I would ask God to take away my pain or to somehow bring Kyle back to us. Both requests were out of touch with real life.

But Rick's real-life Friend knew that, and continued to walk with him, letting him talk. Good friends often do that. Rick began to catch on:

Slowly I learned to pray that God would help me experience His joy in the midst of my pain. I began to pray that our family could trust God more. I asked for courage to endure the pain and not quit. I asked God to help us keep growing and maturing in our relationship with Him and with each other.

In his book Rick offers some sound advice to all of us who are trying to walk with God in the midst of pain, pressure, loss, and disappointment:

Instead of fighting the agony of your loss, ask for God's joy and confidence and perseverance and completeness in your relationship with Him. He's your Father [...and your Friend]. He knows what you need, and He wants to help you learn to live again. You need only ask. And then hang in there long enough to see Him come through for you.

God is there for you. He promised. So don't cut and run. Stay the course. And enjoy the finish.

251

And that thought brings us to another promise of God we all need to take hold of. A third promise that our Friend makes to us relates to our finishing the course to which He has called us. He guarantees us that what waits for us at the end of this journey with Him is more than worth it—no matter what! In fact, there is absolutely nothing at all to compare with it.

Promise #3: Following Him through life will be worth it.
He uses words like "glory" to describe what awaits us. He tells us that if we will accept the reality of this life's pains and limitations, not waste our lives trying to make it go away, trust Him to walk with us through it, and keep our eyes on the finish line and what awaits us there, we will experience *hope*...a confident expectation about where we're headed.

That translates into what the New Testament calls "perseverance." Perseverance is not just hanging on or "getting by" in life, it is *pressing ahead* to win at the finish line. God's Word encourages us to "strain ahead" so as to win. (See Philippians 3:12-14.)

Yes, He is a faithful Friend who will stand with you through the fiercest storm, the blackest night, and the deepest pain. He will never change. He will never walk away. He will never double-cross you. He will *always* be there for you. He is a Pillar you can lean on, a Pillar that will never shift or lean or crumble with the passing years.

In 2 Timothy 2:13, Paul reminds us that even "If we are faithless, He remains faithful; for He cannot deny Himself."

In other words, as Rick Taylor explains it, no matter what we do, our Friend is never going to say to us, "We are no longer friends. I've found someone else. I'm too busy." He *is* our Friend—no ifs, ands, or buts. Nothing we do is ever going to change that fact. Even when we act like spoiled brats, or fickle children who change "best friends" at the drop of a hat, He remains faithful.

Every pillar in the world may fall, but that one won't. Not in a millennium. Not for all eternity.

AFTERWORD

S ometimes as I lay in bed, my left arm wrapped around my wife, my heart wells up with gratitude for such a wonderful life companion. She is different from me in so many ways, but God in His infinite wisdom knew that it needed to be so.

I am struck with how she has stood by me and with me. And though she is an amazing person in her own right, she has been willing to place herself under my leadership and protection, seeking my advice, and counting me as her best friend. She could do and be so much on her own, but she has chosen to walk beside me.

And then I think about those three young men God placed in our lives. My sons. I am in awe that God made them to need me...to give leadership and provide for them, to protect their lives and their dreams, to coach them in the secrets of life, and to be there for them in the good times and hard times. They look to me to be the servant-king, tender warrior, wise mentor, and faithful friend God designed me to be.

Realizing that He has gifted me so, unworthy as I am, how could I be or do anything less?

As I reflect on the four pillars God has placed within me, I am gripped with the privilege and responsibility of playing such a part in the human drama. The role of a man. Of all the men I have known and admired most in life, it is the four-pillared men who have most impressed me—and most impacted their world.

These are not perfect men. They come from diverse backgrounds— from good homes, bad homes, no homes. They are men who had strong dads, weak dads, and no dads. Men who are rich and not so rich. Men who are famous in this world, and men known only to their small civilizations around them. But they are men who never stop growing. When one or more of the pillars begins to crack or lean out of balance, they turn to their Lord—the ultimate King, Warrior, Mentor, and Friend—to make them straight, strong, and true once again.

These men are not lone rangers. They realize the enormity and the impossibility of being a four-pillared man alone. They are rusty knights who need a round table of other rusty knights to share joys and challenges, fears and disappointments. They need men who will both call them to encourage them—and call them on the carpet. They choose to never be too busy—or too lazy—or too proud—to lock arms with men walking in the same direction.

These men are not cowards who give up and quit when the task seems overwhelming. They are not so concerned about their own personal rights, freedoms, and happiness that they sacrifice the sacred principles of manhood. They are men who have known failure, but not defeat; disappointment, but not despair. They are men who can see through these hard things in life because they have their compass set on the truth, not on the fancies of a fickle society. These are men who are willing to live—and if necessary, die—for principles far bigger and greater than they. They are men who are determined to live life to the fullest…by the Book.

The prayer of my heart is that you and I would be such men. Not perfect, but growing. Not going it alone, but in the company of brothers. Not shrinking from the enormity of the task, but placing our trust in the One who shaped those pillars—all four of them—as corner posts of our masculine heart. He is the very One who promised He would walk with us each step of the way.

My friend, you were made to be a King, Warrior, Mentor, and Friend.

So be it.

Amen. And amen.

A Woman
among the
Pillars

A Very Personal
Postscript for Wives

An excellent wife, who can find?
For her worth is far above jewels.
The heart of her husband trusts in her....
She does him good and not evil
All the days of her life.

PROVERBS 31:10-12

After spending thirteen chapters with the man in your life, something in me seemed to be saying my task wasn't quite finished. Here in the last few pages of this book, I want to take just a moment or two to share a bit of my heart with *you*—the most significant person in his life apart from the Lord Jesus Christ.

Your husband and I have considered at some length the "four pillars of masculinity": The King Pillar, the Warrior Pillar, the Mentor Pillar, and the Friend Pillar. It is my deep desire that men across this country will discover God's intentions for their lives, their marriages, and their homes. I've done my best to show them how the Ultimate Friend, Jesus Christ, can help them bring their lives into balance and stability—and into a strength colored all the way through with love.

We want men who are warriors, yes. But Tender Warriors.

And that's why I wanted these few moments with you.

As perhaps no one else on the face of the planet, you have the opportunity—and yes, the *power*—to either help those four pillars stand strong…or pull the whole structure down. You, too, are a pillar. A graceful, feminine pillar, perhaps, but one that brings incalculable strength and support into a man's life.

BESIDE EVERY GREAT MAN…

Perhaps you've heard a variation of the proverbial story of the city mayor and his wife.

Proud of their status in the community, they enjoyed a sense of "having arrived." After all, they'd grown up in the community, lived there all their lives, and now found themselves at the pinnacle of social recognition. On one occasion, while en route to a significant public function, Mayor-hubby pulled their late model luxury car into a local gas station to fill it up. Turns out the service station attendant had been an old high school classmate of the two of them.

Musing on their pilgrimage to the top, and feeling rather secure in his prowess, old Mayor-hubby turned to his wife with a smile. In the privacy behind the tinted windows of their car, he said, "Aren't you pleased, dear, that you married *me* as opposed to your old flame Jake there? Why, that poor guy is still pumpin' gas...and here you are in a beautiful evening gown on your way to the Mayor's Ball!"

Her response put the old boy in his place—and stated a reality all too often overlooked.

"Hubby, dear," she replied, "if I had married Jake, *he* would be the mayor today!"

Now, that little story could be quite misleading. It could be understood to imply that Jake was not "successful." But you know better than that. It is entirely possible that Jake is actually much more fulfilled and content than his stuffed-shirt counterpart. The trappings of what our society considers "success" are often just cheap imitations of the genuine article. In fact, many men in our culture push themselves toward "success" by pouring their time, energy, and lifeblood into their work—at the expense of their family and that which is true and lasting success. In God's economy, to fail at home is to have failed. Period. And no amount of "stuff," "status," or "stardom" can make up for it.

But I do think our little story can make the simple point of this chapter. Its undeniable premise is straightforward: *The power of a woman to make or break a man is enormous!*

Our contemporary culture has ridiculed the old line, "Behind every great man is a great woman." I'm sorry we have devalued such a potent reality. Now more than ever, we need to authentically acknowledge the biblical nobility of the "helpmate suitable." Yes, it should probably read, *"Beside* every great man is a great woman." Let's give her her due; she's more valuable than the greatest measurements of wealth. No one can deny that, and the Bible explicitly affirms it.

From whatever angle you choose to view it, the reality is undeniable. The influence of applied femininity is, by any measure, incredibly determinative. In every culture, in every age, the power is awesome.

And *dangerous.*

As with any significant reservoir of power it may be used for good or ill. Its impact may be constructive or destructive. Like a mighty river, it is a force that may turn the turbines and generate power that will light up a community, a home, and a man's whole life. But undisciplined and unchecked, it may devastate, demoralize, and utterly destroy.

Some women have no clue how much actual power they hold, and those are the women who destroy their husbands by default. Other women are acutely aware of their power and make a conscious decision to become high controllers. But still other women, keenly aware of the power God has invested in their femininity, make a deliberate choice to use that power only for good.

I am grateful that I know quite a few of this latter kind of woman. In fact, I approached a number of them in our church to ask for their help in developing this chapter, my wife among them. Others serve as influential leaders in our body. Much of this chapter is the fruit of their wisdom, and their careful, reasoned approach to life.

Wise are the women who pour out their great feminine ability to influence into positive, life-giving channels. May their sorority increase! The Bible tells the stories of many such women.

T H E W I S E W I F E O F A F O O L I S H M A N

Abigail of Carmel was under no illusions. She knew full well she lived with an impossible man. (I hesitate to use the term "jerk.") In reality, he was one of those "great impostors" I wrote about earlier in this book. He was a poor excuse for a man and brought nothing but discredit upon himself and his gender. The guy had an attitude, and loved nothing better than to flaunt his riches and his supposed power. He was selfish, arrogant, and small-minded. He reminds me of one of those lumbering dinosaurs with a thick hide and a brain the size of a medium walnut.

Abigail, caught in an unlikely and unhappy marriage, still worked in his behalf.

In a single sentence, the Bible describes the two of them insightfully. "The woman was intelligent and beautiful in appearance, but the man was harsh and evil in his dealings" (1 Samuel 25:3). The Living Bible describes him as "uncouth, churlish, stubborn, and ill-mannered."

Ah, how many gracious and noble women in history can identify with that unfortunate misery? I expect it is more than likely that folks who knew the couple also knew it was the woman who made the man. And when his despicable arrogance was about to cost him his life, it was Abigail who stepped in and saved his bacon.

The circumstances were extremely tense. Affronted and insulted by Abigail's husband, Nabal, David had literally strapped on his sword. And he had ordered his troop of four hundred grim-faced warriors to do the same. David had endured enough heartache and persecution at the hands of Saul; he'd had a bellyful of that kind of treatment, and he wasn't about to play games with a small-time, swaggering sheep-rancher. David intended to pay the man a visit—a very unfriendly visit. He was exercising what the military used to call "termination with extreme prejudice." David swore he would not leave even a single man standing! Old Nabal's days were numbered—and it was a very small, single digit number.

Abigail got wind of it. A bright and resourceful woman, she mounted up and rode into the mountains to head off David and his troops. I'd like you to note some of the qualities—which I have italicized—that she brought to that encounter. With *grace* and *diplomacy* she managed to turn the angry war party around. She had carried with her more than enough food to be *hospitable*—multiple loaves of bread and wine, five prepared sheep, plenty of roasted grain, and two hundred fig cakes! She *humbly* greeted David, even bowing before him. She *spoke plainly and transparently*, recognizing the facts for what they were.

She presented David and his men with gifts, honestly *asking his forgiveness* for intruding so boldly. And she *wisely dialogued* with David to the point that he understood it was not in his own best interests, nor the interests of the Lord he served, to carry out his destructive plans. In the process, she *acknowledged David's right to authority*, and humbly asked that he remember her when he came to full power.

Do you remember that dramatic picture coming out of the student uprising in China a number of years ago? It was an unforgettable snapshot of one young man in a white shirt, standing all alone, in front of a column of tanks. For that instant in time, he was barring that brutal repression with the force of his will and his own body.

That's what Abigail did. She stepped directly into the path of an armed force of four hundred angry men. All alone, armed only with her wits and the sheer power of her femininity, she stopped an army dead in its tracks.

A lesser man, of course, might have shoved her aside. But David was not a lesser man. He was absolutely struck with this lovely woman's *demeanor* and *insight*. In those few tense moments, she had won David's ear and his heart. Like Sarah before her, she had won the day by doing "what is right without being frightened by any fear" (1 Peter 3:6). Abigail had not only saved her husband's life, but David's honor. The future ruler knew full well that this noble woman had spared him untold grief and regret. She had kept him from acting rashly.

Abigail had done the seemingly impossible. She had turned the heart of a king! And she had served her difficult husband. Furthermore, she had done it by being honest and direct without being demanding. It wasn't an easy balance. (It never is.) But she pulled it off. And the king with all his war band turned in their tracks and went back the way they had come.

David himself recognized that it was *her careful behavior that had governed his actions* when he said to her, "Praise be to the LORD, the God of Israel, who has sent you today to meet me. May you be blessed for your good judgment and for keeping me from bloodshed this day and from avenging myself with my own hands" (1 Samuel 25:32-33, NIV).

David's "warrior pillar" had completely taken over. Abigail helped him remember he was also a king. She recognized what many of us men have had to recognize over the years. It is the gentle grace of femininity, wisely applied in our lives, that has held the "macho" in check and helped to keep the warrior pillar in balance and standing righteously!

" T H E   H E A R T   O F   H E R   H U S B A N D   T R U S T S   I N   H E R … "

Such capable feminine nobility is recognized and applauded over and over again in the Bible. The woman of the final proverb, for instance, had an accurate grasp of her God-given power and energy. And she used it rightly, benefiting her husband in every way.

Proverbs 31:23 is pretty pointed: "Her husband is known in the gates, when he sits among the elders of the land." Read your way through that entire chapter of Proverbs and you will have to admit that she was very much tied to her husband's success.

The heart of her husband trusts in her,
And he will have no lack of gain.
She does him good and not evil
All the days of her life.

(Proverbs 31:11-12)

Did you catch the force of that first line? *"The heart of her husband trusts in her."* That's the point! I believe this good woman recognized the power almighty God had invested in her femininity, and she applied it to winning her husband's trust. Her husband was then FREE to be and do what God intended for him.

By the way, it was not his being recognized in the gates that made him "successful." The biblical measure of success has nothing to do with wealth or status or impressive titles. But it has everything to do with being the man or woman of God's intentions. Together, this couple lived as God had intended from the beginning: male and female, completing and complementing one another, reflecting the image of God and living to His glory.

Like Abigail before her, it was this wise woman's attitudes and practices which made her such a paragon of womanhood. She had become what the New Testament calls one more "child of Sarah." The apostle Peter, that old Type A personality himself, penned these words by inspiration of the Holy Spirit:

> You wives, be submissive to your own husbands so that even if any of them are disobedient to the word, they may be won without a word by the behavior of their wives, as they observe your chaste and respectful behavior…the hidden person of the heart, with the imperishable quality of a gentle and quiet spirit, which is precious in the sight of God. For in this way in former times the holy women also, who hoped in God, used to adorn themselves, being submissive to their own husbands. Thus Sarah obeyed Abraham, calling him lord, and you have become her children if you do what is right without being frightened by any fear. (1 Peter 3:1-2, 4-6)

That is the kind of woman every man dreams to know, to love, and to marry. Here is a godly woman. Here is biblical femininity shining forth in all its splendor and glory. These words of Peter *mean* something; they are meant to be taken directly and seriously. They are not meant to be twisted, diluted, papered over, or explained away. They are meant to govern a woman's life.

A TWENTY-EIGHT-YEAR WAIT

As I write these words, I am sitting in an old log lodge high in the Colorado mountains. Linda and I are speaking at a couples' ski retreat. Last night at the evening meeting, a man and woman stood before the group and very movingly shared their testimony.

This "man's man" husband in his fifties lived a life typical of many so-called high achievers. He could tell stories of business conquests, athletic pursuits, expensive outdoor expeditions, pleasure-seeking, and alcoholism. His tearful wife, however, told of *twenty-eight years* of going to church alone while he competed in cycling events. She told of twenty-eight years (think of it!) of praying constantly that her husband might come to Christ. She described her frustration, disappointment, and even anger with God that He was not answering her prayers.

When it was his turn again, the man told us that it was one year ago—at this same ski retreat—that he had accepted Christ. My ol' buddy Clebe McClary had been the speaker that year, and when Clebe gave the invitation, this man had responded. He told us how he'd loved skiing so much that a year ago he would have accepted an invitation to go skiing from the devil himself. And here, while skiing of all things, and after TWENTY-EIGHT YEARS of faithful feminine living and praying on his wife's part, he bowed his knee to Jesus Christ.

As his wife wept before us, he described the total and complete changes in lifestyle that the last year had brought. His grown children are astounded. ("Dad's talking the talk and walking the walk!") It was 1 Peter 3, "won...by the behavior of his wife," right before our eyes, in the flesh. We all wept with them. If you had been there, you would have, too!

I thought again of those verses in Proverbs 31: "The heart of her husband *trusts* in her." The husband in that passage *trusted* his lady with his heart, with his insides, with his very life. He felt safe with her. She was a confidante and friend. She would never misuse what she knew about him. He could be real with her, knowing she would never betray him or cut him down behind his back. Years ago, I recall a nationally prominent Christian leader stating his gratitude to his wife who, as he frankly admitted, "could *ruin* me in a heartbeat if she told all she knew." The life and career of many a man and many a leader rests in his wife's hands.

B R I N G I N G   A   M A N ' S   S T R E N G T H   I N T O   B A L A N C E

We've all heard of the "fragile male ego." Such a curious phenomenon! We guys can be a lot like the old prickly pear—tough and sometimes bristly on the outside, while tender on the inside. But we don't always know how to bring our strength into balance. It's not easy for us to deal with our insides, where real life is lived. One man I know, who owns and operates a hugely successful multi-million dollar company, said to me recently, "How come I can, without fear, tackle any obstacle, work any negotiation, conquer any problem, and close any million-dollar business deal—and still cower before that little five-foot brunette wife of mine!"

We men quickly understand the task side of life. We can deal with the strong side. But we don't often know quite what to do with the relational side, the tender side, the real side of life. So we bluster—when in reality, we're dying inside. It takes a 1 Peter 3 wife to help us relax enough to get real.

It is only when we feel respected and admired that we are able to be transparent.

It is only when we feel safe that we can be open.

It is only when we know that our lady will do us good and not harm that we can trust her with our wounded insides, the real us.

A wise woman learns how to deal with that fragile male ego. She knows about the power of her femininity, and she will not abuse it any more than a biblical husband will abuse his masculine headship. This Proverbs 31 woman was a lady who knew how to care for such fragile realities. Her husband could open up to her because he knew she would always act in his best interest, every single day of her life. On her "good days" she acted rightly toward him. On her "bad days" she acted rightly toward him.

One of the women I asked to help with this chapter is an extremely gifted woman with multiple skills. She also happens to possess a very strong personality. In fact, her personality is much stronger than her husband's. But because she has recognized how God intends her to steward her femininity in regard to her husband, she has chosen never to allow her strength to dominate his more passive temperament. It is a reality and a struggle she must deal with every day of her life.

The key for a woman is *keeping her focus.* What are her feminine priorities? If her husband isn't her primary focus, right after her heart for God, then she won't act in her husband's interests. In actuality, however, many wives place their husband's needs way down the list. A woman works with long lists—her work, her children, her house, her friends, her hobbies, and so on. And if her husband is not at the top of that list, there is little hope his heart will learn to trust in her.

Keeping that balance is the hard part for most women. One of the mature women I asked to help me with this chapter put it this way:

> This is [notice the present tense; it never goes away] a constant struggle for me. When our kids were little, I was of necessity preoccupied with their needs. Now my kids are older, and I have a lot of "stuff" that takes up my time. Keeping my husband's needs paramount in my focus is tough for me.

It is commonly acknowledged that one of a man's deepest needs is the need for respect, particularly from his own wife. A man appreciates being loved. But what he really wants, down deep at his core, is respect. And he will do almost anything in order to be respected by his wife.

HOW TO SUPPORT THE "KING PILLAR"

Abigail helped David's king pillar to stand strong—eventually bearing the weight of a nation. The king in a man is a provider. He is to provide in several key areas: physically, emotionally, and spiritually.

Physical provision may mean his starting at the "bottom" with a minimum-wage job. It may mean his taking a second job. And it may mean he has to work hours that are undesirable. How does your attitude as a wife impact any or all of these factors? If you believe in him, if you are grateful for the courage it takes for him to accept a minimum-wage position, it'll help him climb that mountain. If, however, you belittle his efforts, making him feel small in his own eyes, you will both lose.

If you have an attitude that says "I will follow you anywhere, anytime," it will go a long way in helping him feel successful. As a man he will tend to measure his success in terms of income, but his wife needs to measure his success in terms of his faithful family connection and leadership. If she continually affirms him in this way, it is possible that after ten, fifteen, or twenty years, he may *begin* to believe it. Kenny Rogers's country song captures the heart of a lot of men when he sings, "She believes in me. I don't know what she sees in me, but she believes in me."

Choose to believe, woman of God. Choose to accept and affirm.

Physical provision may mean giving up some hobbies or fun activities in order to keep things afloat for a time. A woman who complains about not having enough money for this or that is telling her husband he is not a good provider. A wise woman is resourceful. She makes a game out of saving money on groceries by buying sale items only, or maximizing use of coupons, or…whatever! I can remember a time in our marriage when Linda and I subsisted on smelt (tiny migrating fish) friends caught out of the river, and ten-cent packages of freezer-burned peas. It isn't something I'd care to do again, but hey, we survived! And Linda's skill in stretching our meager resources enabled us to endure that season of life. There was stress, yes, but we also had some fun—and learned to lean on one another as never before.

A wise woman is perfectly capable of shopping for clothes or household items at sales only or even by shopping in secondhand stores. I've seen some attractive wardrobes come out of those places by selective shopping on a creative woman's part. Garage sales are not beneath a wise woman. She constantly compares notes with other savvy shoppers.

Emotional provision is another matter…and it is not easy for most men. A wife may have to make provision for some of her own emotional needs in order for the home to be even-keeled. She does not expect her husband to meet all her emotional needs. Most of us men need some time and practice to learn to flex our emotional muscles. A wise woman is patient. She seeks encouragement from other women. She deliberately chooses to stay away from women who criticize their husbands, for she knows that such a critical and comparative environment will poison the well and create only discontent. A godly woman will find a sister who truly loves her husband, and she will choose to run with such a contented friend and let it rub off on her. She will find an older woman who is happy in her marriage to encourage her.

I have a friend whose marriage today is a happy and fulfilling one. It was not always so. She wasted far too many years trying to "fix" her man—improve him, change him. The technique *never* worked, but she kept trying! Eventually she gave up and began simply to pray—with the right heart attitude. Like Ruth Graham, Billy's wife, this woman learned that "It's my job to love Billy. It's God's job to change him." Listen to her words:

Have I always felt so positive about my husband? Absolutely not! I remember times early in our marriage when we were having conflict and there were things I didn't like about him. I thought that meant I married the wrong person! It even crossed my mind that maybe I should get this marriage annulled!

I remember him spending a lot of his free time with his friends out golfing, etc. I wondered why and he told me it was because his friends *accepted* him—and I didn't!

I remember days when he would be depressed and drawn inward, and I didn't have a clue what was going on for him. One day, I finally got so frustrated I went into the bedroom and shouted, "Would you just get up and *do* something!"

I used to be very dependent upon my husband for my happiness and security. I always thought of him as the Rock of Gibraltar, never having his own insecurities, fears, or problems. I was too busy focusing on my own, and expected him to take care of me like I was used to being cared for growing up.

One wonders, "What changed?" Did hubby get his act together? Did he all of a sudden wake up a new man, dedicated to being the best husband in the world?

Hardly!

I know this woman well. And have admired her for many years. She's paid her dues and earned the right to speak with authority. I asked her to account for the change in her marriage. She listed several keys, and some of my other "wise women consultants" added a few of their own:

"Read, learn, apply, and grow."

She read every book about marriage and men she could get her hands on. In fact, she read so many that at one point her husband actually said, "Why don't you stop reading all those 'how-to' books and just start *doing* some of 'em."

Well, she did. She started doing. But she didn't stop reading because—for the first time—she was really beginning to understand her man. She'd had no idea what the basic needs of a man were. To feel adequate. To feel sufficient. To sense the respect and admiration of his wife. She began to zero in on his strengths and minimize her preoccupation with his weaknesses. She became his greatest fan. And over the years she has thoroughly enjoyed being his cheerleader in the game of life.

"Love unconditionally."

About twelve years into their marriage he asked her, "Why are things better between us? What's changed?"

Listen to her answer: "I knew what was different. I told him I had finally decided to quit trying to change him." She had chosen to accept his weaknesses. She began to realize she was not perfect either (!) and that in the balance his faults were really no worse than hers. She began to let her husband know he was not only "okay," she liked him *just like he was*, even if he never changed! She began to realize that remaining in a state of disappointment was never going to help either of them.

"Listen intently."

How many times does a husband venture to say something, verbally or nonverbally, only to find his wife hasn't really tuned in to what he was trying to express? For a man to open his soul, his wife must listen—really listen—for the little clues to his heart. She must ask more sincere questions and deliver fewer statements. She must begin to genuinely appreciate the differences between men and women.

"Don't expect him to meet all your emotional needs."
We've heard that before! But oh, what a potent truth. So many women I have seen in my years of ministry long for their marriages to improve, and feel intensely frustrated when they don't sense that same longing in their husband. They assume he doesn't care as much as they do. They therefore presume "the problem" is his. So they naturally begin to feel the need for intensive marriage counseling. The tendency is to badger the husband long enough to "get him into counseling." Yet very often a better approach is to go ahead and get into counseling individually. Listen to this mature woman's own words:

> I have personally benefited from individual counseling. God has brought healing into my life over the last several years. I discovered I was a very dependent and somewhat insecure person who hadn't really grasped who I was in Christ. I had to do some hard work and come to the place where I didn't depend upon my husband (or his approval) to fix everything—especially me! Lean on your Lord. Don't suffocate your man.

"Understand the power you have."
This is really the basic point of this entire chapter. When a woman gets a grip on just how powerful God has made her to be in serving her marriage, she understands she can "make it or break it." A woman can so *easily* crush a man's spirit. With a look. With a word. With a shrug of indifference. And when she does, it only serves to seed and feed a growing anger in him. On the other hand, a woman is equally capable of causing her husband's spirit to soar. I have to admit that one of the saddest things I see in ministry is a woman who belittles her husband. Even if he has indeed failed in some way, his wife's disparaging words compound the

disaster exponentially. Her cynicism is utterly emasculating, and many times, incredibly subtle. Like a fine, thin blade it slices deep, penetrating to the very core of his masculine soul.

On the other hand, a woman who understands her power, and uses it rightly, can make him feel like an absolute world beater.

"See your husband as God's gift to you."
As a matter of biblical fact, he is! No matter how you started your marriage, or how many mistakes you've made along the way, the sovereign God is not surprised. Nor is He overcome. Whatever your past, if you have a husband today then God has a plan for your relationship! Beginning right now! Marriage is the greatest human development program on the face of the earth. Cultivate it and keep it.

"Appreciate the little things he does, as well as the 'big' things."
Do you notice when he pitches in at home? Do you express your gratitude for his taking out the garbage, running the vacuum, picking up the dishes, or reading to the kids? Do you appreciate the fact that he comes home every night on time, works every day, fixes the car, stands up for truth, or escorts you places? Say it! More importantly, *mean* it.

"Give him some space."
Men and women respond differently to life. Stress encroaches in different ways. Women tend to need to be close when faced with tough issues. Men tend to need space. When a man is genuinely seeking to be a provider, he works hard at it. He arrives early to scheme and plan. He spends himself at the task. He stays late to mentor a beleaguered co-worker. He befriends his colleagues. Often, he needs a window of alone time when he comes through the front door—at the very moment when his wife wants to talk about her day! Yes, he needs to give a little, too; but wisdom recognizes his need for a few minutes to regroup.

In fact, your man needs more space than a few moments here and there to "collect" himself. Men are simply built to need some personal space apart from their mates from time to time. Linda really gripped my heart when, recognizing this need for "alone time," she created a room in our home that's just mine—a place for me to retreat, fortress up a bit, and read, reflect, listen to a little music, and dream. I love her all the more for her insights into her man.

"Physically appreciate him."

No one has a perfect body. Find his strong traits and build him up for them. Even if he is overweight, or underweight, or balding, or too hairy, think back to what drew you to him initially and dwell on it. Allow yourself to be attracted to his body. Make his sexual fulfillment a priority. Initiate affection. Be the first to hug—and open your arms to him often.

"Follow his leadership."

"Submit to your husband as to the Lord."

Says easy. Does hard.

But those words are not my words, they are *God's* words. And they mean something. Try it. Stay at it. According to God's Word it will actually pay dividends...to both of you...your marriage...and the kingdom of God.

"See your marriage as a journey, not a destination."

Because that is precisely what it is. In fact, marriage is not just your average journey. It's more like climbing a mountain. Together. Early on, down in the foothills among the wildflowers, you start out side by side and hand in hand. But then the way becomes steep and barren. The flowers are far behind. There are a thousand obstacles on your trail. There are rocks to move. And some huge boulders you can't move without help. (Get that help!) Sometimes a season of bad weather comes along, and both of you become weary and exhausted. As you cross one ridge after another, however, the horizon begins to open up a little. Whole new vistas come into your view. Occasionally, you come to the kind of plateau where you can stop and rest; bask in the sun, and enjoy the view. Breathe in the fresh air.

Unfortunately, too many climbers let their weariness get to their minds. They quit climbing. They become overwhelmed with the chill in the air or the grain of sand in their shoe. Complaining sets in, and they don't like climbing anymore. So they head back down the mountain. Believing they would enjoy climbing better with another partner, they start the trail all over roped to someone else—only to find the very same obstacles along the way! The rocks and boulders and bad weather still affect the climb. And now they not only have the obstacles to negotiate, they have to carry the weight of their regrets.

But those who stick with the climb, hanging onto the hand of that original partner—these are the ones who move higher. Sometimes one has to carry the other, but their commitment to reach the summit keeps them moving. Together. Yes, the sand still irritates. The cuts and scrapes still sting. But they've come a long way, and they're not about to throw away the investment they've made thus far. Start over? Not a chance! They keep climbing. And one day, on up ahead, they will reach the top. And there, in one another's arms, they'll celebrate the climb, sing to the world, and drink in the elixir of a climb well done.

The view from the top will be full and panoramic. And hand in hand, they'll look back down the long trail they've ascended. From the top, it doesn't look so very far at all. The perspective will be altogether different. And those obstacles that seemed so overwhelming upon an earlier day will have diminished to insignificance.

Stay on the journey. You'll love the views ahead. The climb, like all of life on a sin-stained planet, is hard, but God is good. And one day He will actually reward you for climbing well enough to reflect in your marriage His love for His own Bride.

STUDY GUIDE

QUESTIONS FOR GROUP DISCUSSION

CHAPTER 1

1. What are some of the "crossroads" you have faced in your own life?

2. How would you answer these variations of the questions Stu asked himself when he stood at a critical crossroads? "What difference would it make if I were to die today?" "What difference would it make if I were to live for some years longer?" "What do I believe really matters in this thing called 'life'?"

3. What are a few of the decisions or choices you have made that you believe have changed the direction of your life?

4. Stu declares, "But when I decided to follow Christ without reservation, I became a man." What evidence do you think he might cite to "prove" the truth of that statement? Is his conviction true of your life, too? Explain why or why not.

5. How does William Bennett's statement, "Courage does not follow the rutted pathways" apply to us as Christian men?

6. How does this statement impact you? "[America is] destroying herself today because her men, standing at a crossroads without a map in their hands and only a broken compass in their hearts, are choosing their own way."

7. What decisions, if any, do you need to make right now if you are going to fully follow your Ultimate Authority?

CHAPTER 2

1. What thoughts go through your mind and heart when you hear the challenge, "Play the man!"?

2. What are some of the issues we wrestle with today when asked the question, "What is a man?"

3. How can men and women be fundamentally different yet at the same time be "equal"?

4. Why is it so strategic for Satan to attack "gender differences"? In what ways has this strategy succeeded in America?

5. How has "gender confusion" affected *your* life in this society?

6. Relate how you, or someone you know, made a strategic choice to "Play the man!" What impact did this choice have?

7. What is one specific thing you would be willing to ask others to pray for that would help you "play the man" God intends you to be?

CHAPTER 3

1. In what ways is it true that "A king who is not a servant is merely a tyrant"? Any examples?

2. In what ways is it true that "A warrior who is not tender is only a brute"? Any examples?

3. In what ways is it true that "A mentor who is not wise is just a know-it-all"? Any examples?

4. In what ways is it true that "A friend who is not faithful is at best an acquaintance, or worse, a betrayer"? Any examples?

5. Explain how it feels to have to shoulder the "weight of responsibility" to be a king, warrior, mentor, and friend.

6. Consider and respond to the implications of these words, "But wait...there is good news! Manliness on-course and in hot pursuit of God's intentions for masculinity enjoys an incredible power for health and healing." How does this contrast with "masculinity off-course"?

7. What is one thing you'd like to ask God to help you with in light of this chapter?

CHAPTER 4

1. What does this mean: "Leadership is everything, whether it's Hitler's Germany, Kennedy's America, Khomeini's Iran, Arthur's Camelot—or your own home. As the leaders go, so go the people. Camelot is the responsibility of the king"?

2. In what sense is it true that we as men in general are "still strutting about, demanding submission. We're still playing by the outdated rules of self-assertion, self-promotion, self-absorption, and self-elevation, which *never were* appropriate in God's kingdom"?

3. In what ways is it true that, "Someone is always in charge"?

4. Compare and contrast the concepts of "headship," "leadership," and "authority." In what ways are these all required of a king?

5. Why do we as humans struggle with the reality of authority?

6. In what ways are the concepts of headship and leadership misunderstood in our "domination-sensitive" culture?

7. Explain how a spirit of meekness is an essential leadership quality.

8. If the King of our universe were standing before you right now and demanded a status report of your heart, what report would you give?

C H A P T E R   5

1. What are some ways you have observed that a man can become an impostor of the "servant-king" role God intends for His men?

2. What does he mean when David Popenoe concludes, "The United States...may be the first society in history in which children are distinctly worse off than adults"?

3. Respond to this claim, "When the king is in his castle...his wife is energized, his children are purposeful, and the relationships within the family become the springboard from which the challenges of life are successfully met." Do you agree? Disagree? Please explain.

4. In what ways, and why, are some men abusive of their power as "king"?

5. In what ways, and why, do some men "abdicate" their power as "king"?

6. In which areas do you struggle as a "king"?

7. What is one step you can take that will be a benefit to those under your care? (Consider Larry's course of action in the story which concluded this chapter.)

C H A P T E R   6

1. Do you know a man who inspires you with a sense of, "We're going somewhere, and where we are going is good"? Describe him. What makes him an effective leader?

2. Take a moment to write down, and then share, some of the questions you need to ask and have answered regarding the future of those you care for.

3. What are some of the "potential dangers" you might have to face in the next ten years?

4. What are some of the things that those under your care need to have you provide for them now and in the future?

5. What is the next time-of-life change on the horizon for you? How might this affect those under your care? How can you best prepare for the change?

6. For what area of your life would you especially appreciate having others pray for you?

C H A P T E R   7

1. Read Psalm 23 and replace the words "The LORD" with "My dad." Does the psalm fit your dad? If so, in what ways? In what ways does it not fit you dad? How might your life have been different if your dad had been more like the Shepherd?

2. What are some of the physical, emotional, and spiritual needs of your wife? Your children? Others under your care? How can you help meet those needs?

3. What are some of the rules around your home that are "clear and consistent"? What are some that are most likely "unclear and/or inconsistent"? Are there rules—either posted or unspoken—that only make sense to, and benefit, you? Please explain.

4. What is one way you might honor your wife this week? What about each of your children? What about an employee or fellow worker?

5. Why is it so crucial for us as men not to abandon those under our care?

C H A P T E R   8

1. How would you respond to this assertion: "That old warrior in each of us [men] sometimes gets twisted around a bit, doesn't it?"

2. Why do so many in our culture cry out against the warrior pillar in a man's heart?

3. What are some of the lions out there from which those under our care need our protection?

4. When a warrior acts like a brute, how does that impact his wife? His children? His community? His church?

5. When a warrior acts like a coward, how does that impact his wife? His children? His community? His church?

6. In what way is it true that, "The heart of the warrior must be wedded to the vision of the king—a dream of stability and justice and order and security for those near and dear to him"? Any examples?

7. What things must a warrior have and/or do to keep the warrior pillar from leaning to the right or to the left? Which one of those things would you be willing to ask someone else to pray about for you and to hold you accountable?

C H A P T E R   9

1. Why do you think this chapter is titled "A Warrior at Risk"?

2. What happens when a warrior stops putting himself under the orders of the Authority? How are you doing at following each of the four "general orders" spelled out in this chapter? (Take time with this one!)

3. What are some situations in a man's life requiring that, as a warrior, he must remain on-call?

4. What are some of the sacrifices as a warrior that you have made for your wife? Your children? Your church? Are there some you should be making?

5. What are some appropriate ways and situations in which men need to wear their warrior "uniforms" in public? What are some inappropriate ways this can be done?

6. How have you exhibited a heart of mercy to your wife? Each of your children? Someone at church? Someone in the community? Is there an area where you should be showing mercy?

7. If after you die your loved ones were to describe the "warrior" in you, what are some of the words you would want them to use?

C H A P T E R   1 0

1. Did your dad, or another father figure, coach you in the living of life? If so, can you recall something he passed on to you? If not, how does that affect you today?

2. Are there others who have mentored you, in large or small ways? Name them, and the one thing for which you most remember each of them.

3. What does it take to be a coach in anything, including life?

4. List those people who are, or might be, looking to you to share with them about the "secrets of life."

5. Can you think of one person who could use a note or word of encouragement from you? Will you write a note or pick up the phone today?

6. What are the life skills that you feel best prepared to pass on to others right now?

7. What are those life skills that you would still like a mentor to help you with? Is there someone you could approach regarding this? Make this a matter of regular prayer.

CHAPTER 11

1. What are some of the reasons most men experience feelings of inadequacy as mentors?

2. Have you ever come alongside and invested in someone's life? What were your joys? Your disappointments?

3. Read Joshua 1:6-9. Which of the words of encouragement described in the passage do you need most as a mentor?

4. Are you a student of the Book? Why or why not? If you aren't, what will it take to help you become one? What needs to be your first or next step toward becoming a better, more diligent student of the Book?

5. What are the things you would want your wife to know if she had to live without you? What do you want your children to learn from you before they leave home as adults?

6. What makes your wife and each of your children unique individuals? How can knowing these things help you as a mentor?

7. What are some of your "failures" that could, if shared, help you pass on some critical secrets of life to someone else?

CHAPTER 12

1. Why is it so hard for so many of us men to recognize, admit, and share our feelings?

2. Can you describe a particularly powerful moment when you "connected" with another person?

3. When was your last emotional connection with your wife? What choices do you need to make that would help you to emotionally connect with your wife more often and in more profound ways?

4. Name each of your children, and describe how connected you are with each of them. What frustrations, if any, do you experience when attempting to connect with any of your children? What course of action might you take that could help?

5. Do you have a friend you can connect with? If so, what makes it possible to connect with him? If not, what would it take in a friend to be able to connect with him? Where might you find such a friend?

6. What can you do as a husband and dad to help the other members of your family to connect with one another?

7. What is one thing you want to trust God to be changing in your life right now?

CHAPTER 13

1. Do you ever recall a time in your life when someone—a friend, parent, or sibling—stood up for you or with you to help you face something or someone in life? Describe that occasion and explain how that person's help and presence made you feel.

2. What are some of your "adult" skirmishes that would be easier if you had a "big friend" to go through them with you?

3. Jesus is a Friend. What words would you use to describe your relationship, or lack of relationship, with Jesus Christ?

4. Have you experienced the grace of God in your life? If so, can you describe one or two specific ways?

5. Three promises from our heavenly Friend are mentioned in this chapter: 1) You will have troubles in this world; 2) Christ will be with you always; and 3) following Christ during your lifetime will be worthwhile. Can you think of a particular situation in your life when you experienced the truth of all three promises?

6. How can your friendship with Jesus affect your other relationships?

7. How can you grow closer in your friendship with Jesus?

C L O S I N G   Q U E S T I O N S

1. What are the three most significant principles you are taking away from this book?

2. What is the next step you plan to take in your masculine journey of growth?

3. Who is one person with whom you will share your plan for growth, and who will hold you accountable for your progress?

For conference or speaking information, contact Stu Weber at:

Stu Weber
2229 N.E. Burnside, #212
Gresham, Oregon 97030

NOTES

CHAPTER ONE

1. Author's note: I've described that critical time in more detail in an earlier book, *Tender Warrior* (Sisters, Ore.: Multnomah Books, 1993), 16.

2. Robert Frost, "The Road Not Taken," quoted in William J. Bennett, *The Book of Virtues* (New York: Simon & Schuster, 1993), 523.

3. Ibid.

4. Scott Minerbrook, "Lives Without Fathers," *U.S. News & World Report,* 27 February 1995, 50.

5. Nancy R. Gibbs, "Father," *Time,* 28 June 1993, 55.

6. David Blankenhorn, *Fatherlessness in America* (New York: Basic Books, 1995), 1-2, 13.

CHAPTER TWO

1. J. B. Lightfoot, trans. and ed., *The Apostolic Fathers* (Grand Rapids, Mich.: Baker Books, 1971), 112.

2. Charles Colson, "The Thomas Hearings and the New Gender Wars," *Christianity Today,* 25 November 1991, 72.

3. Ibid.

4. Richard Halverson, *Somewhere in Eternity* (Portland, Ore.: Multnomah Press, 1980), 84.

5. James Dobson, *Focus on the Family Newsletter,* September 1991.

6. J. Grant Howard, unpublished class notes, Western Seminary.

CHAPTER THREE

1. Robert Moore and Douglas Gillette, *King, Warrior, Magician, Lover* (San Francisco: Harper San Francisco, 1990), 9.

CHAPTER FOUR

1. Mohandas Gandhi, quoted in Stu Weber, *Along the Road to Manhood* (Sisters, Ore.: Multnomah Books, 1995), 21.

2. Anne Quindlen, *The Making of a Father,* quoted in *Along the Road to Manhood,* 31.

3. Dennis Foley, *Special Men* (New York: Ivy Books, imprint of Ballantine Books, 1994), 45.

4. Wayne Grudem, "The Myth of Mutual Submission," *CBMW News* 1, no. 4 (October 1996): 1.

5. John Piper, "Mature Masculinity," *People of Destiny* 13, no. 2 (March/April 1996): 3-6.

6. W. Phillip Keller, *A Gardener Looks at the Fruits of the Spirit* (Waco: Word Publishing, 1979) quoted in *Servant Life* 3, no. 1 (July/August 1996): 1.

7. C. S. Lewis, *The Inspirational Writings of C. S. Lewis* (New York: Inspirational Press, 1991), 400.

8. Moore and Gillette, *King, Warrior, Magician, Lover,* 62.

9. Richard Byrd, quoted in Weber, *Along the Road to Manhood,* 38.

CHAPTER FIVE

1. David Popenoe, *Life Without Father* (New York: The Free Press, 1996), 2.

2. C. S. Lewis, *God in the Dock,* quoted in Stu Weber, *Tender Warrior,* 95.

3. Jo Ann Larsen, quoted in Jack Canfield and Mark Victor Hansen, eds., *Chicken Soup for the Soul* (Deerfield Beach, Fla.: Health Communications, Inc., 1993), 43-45.

CHAPTER EIGHT

1. Dave Barry, "Guys aren't stupid; they just *act* that way," Knight-Ridder newspapers, date unknown.

2. C. S. Lewis, *English Literature in the Sixteenth Century,* quoted in Weber, *Along the Road to Manhood,* 74.

3. Teddy Roosevelt, quoted in Weber, *Along the Road to Manhood,* 65.

4. Norman Schwarzkopf, *It Doesn't Take a Hero* (New York: Bantam Books, 1992), 412.

5. George Leonard, "The Warrior," *Esquire,* July 1996, 64, 66.

CHAPTER NINE

1. Sullivan Belleau, quoted in Phil Coulter, *A Touch of Tranquillity* (London: Shanachie Records Corp., 1992). "Dear Sarah," PBS TV documentary on the American Civil War.

2. David Hackworth, foreword to *Special Men*, by Dennis Foley (New York: Ivy Books, imprint of Ballantine Books, 1994).

3. Mark Galli, "Saint Nasty," *Christianity Today*, 17 June 1996, 25.

4. Paul Harvey, "Message of Truth Too Much," source unknown.

5. Jackson Lears, "Screw Ambiguity," *The New Republic*, 22 April 1996, 38.

6. G. Campbell Morgan, quoted in *The Westminster Pulpit* 5 (Westwood, N.J.: Fleming H. Revell), 17.

7. Unpublished Deveny family archives.

CHAPTER TEN

1. Howard Hendricks and William Hendricks, *As Iron Sharpens Iron* (Chicago: Moody Press, 1995), 18.

2. Bobb Biehl, quoted in *As Iron Sharpens Iron*, 165.

3. Moore and Gillette, *King, Warrior, Magician, Lover*, 99.

4. James Dobson, *Straight Talk* (Dallas, Tex.: Word, 1991), 40.

5. Charles Swindoll, *Make Up Your Mind...About the Issues of Life* (Portland, Ore.: Multnomah Press, 1981), 90-91.

6. Bob Welch, "Reaping What We've Sown," *Focus on the Family*, July 1996, 2-3.

7. Ibid.

8. Hendricks and Hendricks, *As Iron Sharpens Iron*, 101.

9. Max Lerner, *The Unfinished Country*, quoted in Weber *Along the Road to Manhood*, 9.

10. Ibid., 112.

11. Ibid., 123.

12. Preston Gillham, quoted in Weber, *Tender Warrior*, 139.

CHAPTER ELEVEN

1. James Dobson, *Focus on the Family Newsletter*, May 1996.

2. Karl Malone, "One Role Model to Another," *Sports Illustrated,* 14 June 1993, 84.

3. Steve Farrar, *Pastor to Pastor* 23, June 1996, 1.

4. "Grandpa and Me," *Today's Father* 2, no. 1, 4.

C H A P T E R   T W E L V E

1. Max Lucado, *God Came Near* (Portland, Ore.: Multnomah Press, 1987), 92.

2. Lee Iacocca, quoted in Weber, *Along the Road to Manhood,* 155.

3. R. Kent Hughes, *Disciplines of a Godly Man* (Wheaton, Ill.: Crossway Books, 1991), 53.

4. Dave Simmons, quoted in Weber, *Along the Road to Manhood,* 161.

5. "Honor Thy Children," *U.S. News & World Report,* 27 February 1995, 42.

C H A P T E R   T H I R T E E N

1. Brennan Manning, *Ragamuffin Gospel* (Portland, Ore.: Multnomah Press, 1990), 15.

2. Ibid., 18.

3. Ibid., 21.

4. Ibid.

5. Rick Taylor, *When Life Is Changed Forever by the Death of Someone Near* (Eugene, Ore.: Harvest House, 1992).

For conference or speaking information, contact Stu Weber at:

Stu Weber
2229 N.E. Burnside, #212
Gresham, Oregon 97030